Mega-Universities and Knowledge Media

Technology Strategies for Higher Education

John S Daniel

KOGAN PAGE

To my Father and Mother,
educators both.

First published in 1996
Reprinted (twice) 1997
First paperback edition published in 1998

Kogan Page Limited
120 Pentonville Road
London N1 9JN

© John S Daniel, 1996

British Library Cataloguing in Publication Data

A CIP record for this book is available from the British Library.

ISBN 0 7494 2634 9

Typeset by Kogan Page
Printed and bound in Great Britain by Biddles Ltd, Guildford and King's Lynn

Contents

List of Figures and Tables

Figures

Tables

Series Editor's Foreword

In his book *Mega-Universities and Knowledge Media: Technology Strategies for Higher Education*, Sir John Daniel reviews the challenge that the combination of computers, communications technology and the cognitive sciences – the 'knowledge media' – poses to the renewal of both conventional and distance teaching universities. He does so from the vantage points of his unique position as Vice-Chancellor of the Open University, his previous experience as a university president in Canada, and his unrivalled knowledge of the world's eleven mega-universities.

He sets out the competitive agenda for all universities in terms of *cost leadership* and *differentiation* and asks what the knowledge media can contribute. Most importantly, he does not stop at analysis. The final chapter describes, in practical terms, how those charged with guiding the destinies of higher education can implement viable technology strategies.

Fred Lockwood
Institute of Educational Technology
Open University

Foreword

Russell Edgerton
President, American Association for Higher Education

All of us who reflect on the state and direction of higher education have been scrambling to understand the Second Coming (or third or fourth) of information technology. Something in our gut tells us that this time it's really going to make a difference. Hardly a day goes by without coming across new evidence of the persuasive effects of the information revolution. But most of us feel like we were driving along in a foreign country, wondering what the road signs mean, without a map that shows where we are and where we might be going. This insightful book provides exactly the map we need – and more.

One reason I find this book so valuable is the unique vantage point from which the author views the scene. Sir John Daniel wrote this manuscript on the run, while serving as Vice-Chancellor of the British Open University. This is not another academic treatise about the role of technology, abstracted from the Realpolitik of the higher education industry. But neither is it the view of someone so immersed in the daily life of an institution that the forest is lost from sight. Sir John is rather like a general who has struggled onto some high ground and now, from these heights, can finally see the whole terrain. It's a commanding view, but also a realistic one.

What he sees, of course, is partly filtered through his own experience. Sir John brings to this assignment, not only years of direct engagement with the immediate issues at hand, but the enlarged perspective of a dedicated and humanistic educator who truly thinks globally while acting locally. I write this Foreword having just returned from a conference where faculties from America's established, campus-based universities were denouncing distance learning as a threat to quality and to their own jobs. Picking up Sir John's book, I came across his gentle reminder that 'Most people in the world have yet to make a telephone call'.

The point I want to make is that throughout the book the analysis is informed by Sir John's awareness of a larger horizon: the vast and changing education and training needs of people throughout the world. The context he would have us bear in mind is a world in which more and more people need access to continuous learning throughout their working lives – a world in which the costs of campus-based models of higher education will always be outside the reach of literally millions of people. This certainly does put our own debates into perspective.

Another reason for my enthusiasm is that this book explores and brings together portions of territory that are usually covered separately and in isolation from one another. Writing and conferencing about the role of technology in higher education tends to focus either on the instruction of residential and commuting students (on-campus instruction) or on 'distance learning'. Meanwhile, as we persist in this dichotomous thinking, the Internet and the World Wide Web are rapidly erasing the boundaries that make these distinctions meaningful.

This book explores the situations faced by traditional 'campus' universities (a phrase that should make more than a few of my colleagues sit up straight in their chairs) and by distance learning institutions as they confront the challenges and the opportunities presented by the new 'knowledge media'. In Sir John's view, each type of institution has inherent advantages and disadvantages; each type has much to learn from the other.

Finally, this book contains more than just of map of the territory. It also includes a rich discussion of strategy, of how to lead one's institution across the terrain. Sir John turns out to be one of those highly intellectual sort of generals who is fascinated by the art of leadership. And what he sees going on 'out there', if not a battle, is a decidedly aggressive competition among educational institutions driven by ambitions to acquire students, funds, and prestige at the expense of other institutions.

Drawing on Michael Porter's framework for analyzing the dynamics of competitive advantage in organizations, the book builds toward a final discussion of strategies that leaders might consider. Sir John makes a compelling argument that every institution needs to have a technology strategy. He discusses what kind of choices go into a sound strategy, such as whether to compete on the basis of costs, the distinctiveness of instructional approach, or both. He offers shrewd advice about choosing particular technologies that give value to students, and ends by sharing some of the concrete planning that has been done along these lines at his own institution.

What you have here, in sum, is a rare combination of scholarly analysis, statesmanship, and political savvy – all brought to bear on the most important and confusing issue that higher education faces today. This is a book that truly does illuminate the pathways that lie ahead.

Acknowledgements

This book grew out of study for a degree that took me 25 years to complete – but this is the era of lifelong learning! I am grateful to Concordia University for re-admitting me, in 1994, to the MA programme in Educational Technology that I began when it was still Sir George Williams University in 1971. Through those early courses, and an internship which took me to the infant UK Open University in 1972, I was seduced by the excitement of distance learning and reoriented my career. From metallurgy I moved into educational technology and thence to a variety of academic leadership roles in both distance-teaching and campus-centred universities. Completing the programme in the 1990s has given me a chance to reflect on the challenges that all universities now face and the achievements of a quarter of a century of distance education. I thank Concordia's educational technology group, in particular Gary Boyd, Dennis Dicks and David Mitchell, for evoking and developing my interest in new approaches to higher education and the work of the late Gordon Pask.

The Open University kindly granted me a month's leave at the conclusion of my studies. I spent it in Montreal where I enjoyed the warm hospitality of Pat and Ted Roman and shared with them the anguish and excitement of Quebec's 1995 referendum campaign.

Past and present heads of the mega-universities and their staff have shown a lively interest in the book. I am indebted to them and to Keith Harry and Thaiquan Lieu of the International Centre for Distance Learning for information on these remarkable institutions. Without the ICDL's database and documentary resources it would have been very difficult to review the mega-universities as a group.

Colleagues in North America have been just as helpful. In recent years I have had the honour of serving as a trustee of the Carnegie Foundation for the Advancement of Teaching during the presidency of one of America's great educators, the late Ernie Boyer. Sharing with my fellow trustees his insights into the issues facing the academy was an inestimable privilege. I am indebted to Russ Edgerton of the American Association of Higher Education, whose work I have come to admire through those Carnegie meetings, for writing a foreword to the book. Visits to institutions have also been very enriching. I thank particularly Tony Morgan of the University of Utah, Jim Mingle of the State Higher Education Executive Officers, and Michael Moore of Pennsylvania State University for talking to me about the role of technology in US universities. In Canada I am especially grateful for discussions with Tony Bates, who first established the use of media in distance education as a field of research. From Ontario, where I spent six memorable years, Marian Croft kindly provided regular electronic updates on how universities were coping with the vicissitudes of public funding. From British Columbia my former boss and mentor, Sam Smith, sent helpful comments.

Open University colleagues have helped me in many ways. In my office Sheila Watts, Stephanie Cheshire and Liz Halls made it possible to find time to write a book while leading a large and wonderfully stimulating institution. Diana Laurillard, Marc Eisenstadt, Paul Bowen, Joe Clinch, Ann Floyd, Dick Housden, Richard Lewis, Jim Burrows, Alan Yates, Jeremy Chapple, Richard Austin, Tim O'Shea, Steve Chicken, David Hawkridge, Bob McCormick, John Naughton, Robin Mason, Paul Bacsich, Tony Kaye, David Asch, Greville Rumble, Blaine Price, Simon Buckingham-Chum, John Linney, Michelle Selinger, Alan Woodley, Fred Lockwood, Gill Kirkup, Josie Taylor, Tom Vincent, David Sewart, Geoff Peters, Bob Masterton, Martin Watkinson and many others helped me understand, through their own work, how technology might be used to academic advantage. Kitty Chisholm's insightful critique of successive drafts encouraged me to maintain a broad perspective and pulled me up on some important details. I thank them all.

When the urge to become a student again came to me in 1994, my wife Kristin suggested that I complete the studies in educational technology I had abandoned many years earlier. I thank her for that inspiration. Our marriage has taken us to seven universities in five jurisdictions. For her love and support throughout that fulfilling academic odyssey I am deeply grateful.

Finally, producing a book is a very practical challenge. I could not have done it in the time available without the dedicated help of my son Julian. He can make computers sing and dance and makes desktop publishing look so easy. I also thank Apple UK for the loan of the Powerbook which has become a central element of my personal technology strategy.

Glossary of Acronyms

AI	Artificial Intelligence
AU	Anadolu University
BBC	British Broadcasting Corporation
CATV	Community Antenna Television
CD-ROM	Compact Disk–Read Only Memory
CETV	China Educational Television Station
CIRCE	Corporate and Individual Records for Customers and Enquirers (UKOU)
CITE	Centre for Information Technology in Education (UKOU)
CNAA	Council for National Academic Awards
CNED	Centre National d'Enseignement à Distance
CTVU	China Television University system
CCRTVU	China Central Broadcasting and TV University
DIANDA	Chinese acronym for CTVU
DTU	Distance Teaching University
FUI	Free University of Iran
GAEL	Logistics information system (CNED)
HE	Higher Education
ICCE	International Council for Correspondence Education
ICDE	International Council for Distance Education
ICDL	International Centre for Distance Learning
IGNOU	Indira Gandhi National Open University
INSTILL	Integrating New Systems and Technologies into Lifelong Learning
ISDN	Integrated Services Digital Network
KACU	Korea Air and Correspondence University
KNOU	Korea National Open University
NIME	National Institute for Multimedia Education
OECD	Organization for Economic Cooperation and Development
OEF	Open Education Faculty (AU)
OPENET	Open Educational Network (IGNOU)
PC	Personal computer
PLUM	Programme on the Learner Use of Media (UKOU)
PNU	Payame Noor University (Iran)
PRINCE	Information systems development methodology (UK)
SACHED	South African Council for Higher Education Development
SAIDE	South African Institute for Distance Education
STOU	Sukhothai Thammathirat Open University
TVU	Television University (China)
UK	United Kingdom
UKOU	United Kingdom Open University
UNED	Universidad Nacional de Educación a Distancia
UNESCO	United Nations Educational, Scientific and Cultural Organization
UNISA	University of South Africa
USA	United States of America
UT	Universitas Terbuka
VAN	Value-Added Network
VCR	Video cassette recorder
YÖK	Higher Education Council (Turkey)

Introduction

'The objects of the University shall be the advancement and dissemination of learning and knowledge by teaching and research, by a diversity of means such as broadcasting and *technological devices appropriate to higher education*, by correspondence tuition, residential courses and seminars and in other relevant ways and shall be to provide education of university and professional standards for its students, and to promote the educational well-being of the community generally.'

(Article 3 of the Royal Charter of the UK Open University, 1969)

Higher education is in crisis in much of the world. What is the nature of the crisis and how can we resolve it? In Chinese lettering the ideogram for crisis is made by combining the signs for *danger* and *opportunity*. This book develops that paradox. Universities combine perceived weakness with potential strength. They often fail to live up to the hopes of the communities that support them. But those same communities look to their universities for help and leadership in the knowledge revolution that is changing the world.

I start from three beliefs. First, I hold that the academic mode of thinking, which I contrast with the ideological mode of thinking, is among the most precious assets of humankind. The world should treasure the continuity of its universities, which have trained students as academic thinkers since the foundation of the University of Bologna in 1088.

My second belief is that universities are alert to the need for renewal. They are aware of the criticisms frequently levelled at them: higher education does not accommodate the volume and variety of student demand; universities do not give value for money; teaching methods are inflexible; the quality of higher education is haphazard; and the sense of academic community is disappearing.

My third tenet is that technology, which has already made a dramatic impact in most areas of human endeavour, is a key to the renewal of higher education. The purpose of this book is to suggest how universities can best use technology, by which I mean both systems and devices, to promote the academic ideal in a new millennium.

Chapter 1 recalls the essential idea of the university and looks at the crises that universities face in different parts of the world. To respond to the

1

expectations of the people they serve universities must renew both their missions and their methods. Chapter 2 surveys the issues facing campus universities and suggests that the core function of undergraduate teaching is being threatened by the increasing variety of peripheral functions that universities perform. Can technology-based teaching redress the balance? Chapter 3 examines a remarkable group of universities that have risen to the challenges of cost and accessibility by using technology in its widest sense. These 11 mega-universities teach at a distance and serve nearly three million students. I identify their common features and review the challenges they now face. The Appendix gives profiles of each institution.

The mega-universities base their success on distance education. Many campus universities are now adopting and adapting distance education for some of their activities. Chapter 4 outlines the essentials of distance education by looking at its history and the technologies through which it has evolved. The two traditions of distance education, remote-classroom teaching and correspondence study, have different pedagogies and cost structures. However, a new generation of technology, the knowledge media, that results from the convergence of computing, telecommunications and the cognitive sciences, is bringing these two traditions of distance education together. The book's central question is how the knowledge media can contribute to the renewal of universities, particularly through the further development of distance education.

The aim of university renewal must be to provide greater value to people at a time when learning is a lifelong pursuit. Chapter 5 therefore applies Michael Porter's analysis of competitive advantage to universities. Focusing on a university's value chain helps identify those activities where new uses of technology can allow the institution to serve people better. However, technology cannot inspire the renewal of universities unless the various stakeholders of the academy, especially students, are willing to acquire and use it. Chapter 6 reviews Geoffrey Moore's writings on the technology adoption life-cycle in order to determine what will lead university students to embrace new study methods and equipment. A key requirement is that they promote academic learning. I draw on Diana Laurillard's reflections on university teaching to identify the qualities that this implies.

Chapter 7 also looks at current experience with the knowledge media and Marc Eisenstadt's ambitious claim that these technologies change qualitatively the relationship between people and knowledge. Do current and potential uses of the knowledge media meet the criteria for successful use of technology? The answer seems to be affirmative. However, effective use of the knowledge media will require a collective effort. The final chapter suggests how institutions should build technology into their planning for a successful future. It provides a framework for developing a technology strategy in a campus university and reports how a mega-university is now harnessing technology for academic advantage.

Chapter 1

University Renewal for a New Millennium

Where are those new universities?

In the last seven days, somewhere in the world, a new university campus should have opened its gates to students. Next week, in a different location, another new university ought to begin operations.

At the end of the millennium in which the idea of the university has blossomed, population growth is outpacing the world's capacity to give people access to universities. A sizeable new university would now be needed every week merely to sustain current participation rates in higher education. New institutions are not being created at this frequency. A crisis of access lies ahead.

There are similar problems at other levels of learning. Demand for all education and training has grown steadily in most parts of the world in recent decades and is likely to remain buoyant in the future (Coombs, 1985). The earth's population will climb until well into the 21st century. Individuals and governments are pitching ever higher their ambitions for educational attainment and the acquisition of skills. In the industrialized world there is increasing demand for post-secondary education and training. In the developing world, where the great majority of children are being born, countries are still struggling to achieve universal primary schooling and wider access to secondary education.

Growth in the demand for education gathered speed in the 1950s and 1960s. In those days governments usually had the financial means to help satisfy this demand with public funds. In most countries, however, 'education managers and their systems were caught in a squeeze between rising unit costs and resisting budget ceilings' by the early 1970s (Coombs, 1985: 136). The increasing severity of this squeeze has led governments to ask consumers to bear a greater proportion of the costs of education and training at all levels, and particularly in higher education. This trend has inevitably drawn attention to those costs.

Until very recently face-to-face instruction has accounted for an overwhelming proportion of all formal education and training. The unit costs of face-to-face teaching are relatively inelastic and insensitive to volume. To reduce these costs significantly requires alternative instructional methods. In the course of the 20th century most fields of endeavour have seen dramatic technological developments that have transformed their cost structures. However, there are few instances where alternative approaches to education and training have reduced costs enough to have had a noticeable impact on national education budgets.

This is a challenge for humankind in the 21st century. A scarcity of physical resources may limit the quality of the material environment in which many people live. However, the world's educators should aim to ensure that all people can develop their potential in the essentially unlimited domain of human skill and intellect.

Education for all: an imperative for world security

Providing education and training for the burgeoning population of the developing world is not only a challenge for the countries concerned. The security of humankind may well depend on it. Already 50% of the world's population is less than 20 years old. In developing countries the proportion is much higher, rising to 70% in Palestine and 80% in South Africa. Without vigorous action many of these young people will grow up to be unemployed, unconnected and unstable. Mass training for work and employability is required. Even more vital is the need for individuals to acquire the frameworks of ethics and values that allow them to become self-regulating. Modern communications make it increasingly difficult to impose such frameworks by authority. Education and training are a primary route to responsible citizenship.

Meeting this challenge will require more cost-effective methods of education and training. It is particularly important that higher education addresses this issue. In most countries governments are concentrating scarce public resources on making systems of primary and secondary education and youth training universal and effective. This is an appropriate policy because educated and competent people are the essential foundation for democratic societies and market economies (World Bank, 1988). Recent studies (*The Economist*, 1996a) show that it is more effective to give young people basic education and skills for employment than to offer them remedial training when they are older and unemployed. The personal autonomy that people acquire through a sound basic education benefits the wider collectivity as well as themselves. Higher education also creates benefits for both the individual student and the community – but the balance of advantage lies further towards the individual.

There are three additional reasons why universities should take a larger share of the responsibility for developing more cost-effective educational methods than schools. First, the socialization that is a central function of the education of children will always require extensive face-to-face and personal contact with teachers and other adults. Second, a steadily increasing proportion of university students are working adults who do not find regular attendance on campus a convenient way to learn. Third, people who are already literate and numerate may gain more from learning media and technologies. The challenges of university renewal in an era of lifelong learning and new technology are the focus of this book.

Comfort of continuity; challenge of change

The oldest university in continuous existence, the University of Bologna in Italy, was founded in 1088 at the beginning of a new millennium. Throughout the millennium universities prospered and multiplied. They have appeared to be models of constancy. A generation ago Clark Kerr's Carnegie Commission (1968) wrote, in an oft-quoted aphorism:

> 'Taking, as a starting point, 1530, when the Lutheran Church was founded, some 66 institutions that existed then still exist today in the Western world in recognizable forms: the Catholic Church, the Lutheran Church, the parliaments of Iceland and the Isle of Man, and 62 universities... They have experienced wars, revolutions, depressions, and industrial transformations, and have come out less changed than almost any other segment of their societies.'

Could it be, that as a new millennium begins, universities will have to contemplate substantial change? They have, of course, been prime contributors to most of the scientific, technological and social changes of the last thousand years. But have they lost the capacity to change themselves? Zemsky and Massy (1995) frame the question as follows:

'There is a growing sense that colleges and universities have become too set in their ways to change – the last holdouts against the restructuring that is recasting the American enterprise. What banks, retailers, manufacturers of every description, insurance companies, hospitals and governments have undertaken has somehow remained beyond the reach and will of higher education. Though their faculties are the principal inventors of the new digital technologies, colleges and universities remain persistently averse to letting information technology change how they deliver instruction or provide basic administrative services. In an age of downsizing, they are becoming more labour-intensive and more resistant to being judged either by their customers or in terms of their educational efficiency.'

The principal challenge to the flexibility of universities is the changing nature of the student body. The term 'lifelong learning' is now part of the vocabulary of the industrialized world. It describes the need for people to continue their education and training throughout life because they will face multiple careers in changing economies and enjoy longer lives in evolving societies. The word 'learner' now designates a role, not a person. Whereas the economic benefits of training the unemployed are distressingly slender, once people are in work, on-the-job training brings clear improvements in productivity and wages (*The Economist*, 1996a). Furthermore, there is evidence that children work harder in school when their parents are also students.

Most universities have reacted to the era of lifelong learning by adding new programmes and services for the increasing numbers of older people who seek to combine employment with part-time study. Special arrangements have been developed for these students but the core activity of the university, teaching to full-time, young undergraduates, often goes on much as before.

It was predictable that the spreading culture of lifelong learning would eventually change the attitudes of young people to their initial post-compulsory education. Academic programmes designed to launch graduates into lifetime careers are unlikely to be the best preparation for lives of multiple careers and regular job changes. Moreover, if work and study are to be combined throughout life, why not combine them from the start by finding a job and taking a degree part-time? In much of Europe, for example, where finding work now seems more of a challenge than getting a degree – and where employers appear to value work experience as much as a degree – the combination of work and study is a sensible option for young people.

Such changes in behaviour pose a challenge to universities. Even where universities have programmes and structures in place for older part-time students, these arrangements are often seen as peripheral. To allow such students to define the mainstream function of the institution is a difficult psychological adjustment.

Higher education is beginning to change in response to these challenges. A new type of university that has emerged in last quarter century holds lessons for the renewal of all universities. It is the distance teaching university. Some of these new universities, several hardly a decade old, are already very large. The 11 mega-universities, described in Chapter 3 and the Appendix, each enrol over 100,000 students.

These mega-universities provide a powerful response to the crises of access and cost. Each accounts for a substantial proportion of the university students in its country and teaches them at a fraction of the cost of the other universities. Their success in responding to the challenge of flexibility is mixed. By delivering their courses nationally (often internationally) to students in their homes, these institutions allow students to choose where and when they study. However, the cost structures of these universities, which we examine in Chapter 4, sometimes limit the curricular choice available to students.

Collectively these mega-universities have led the renewal of forms of education, correspondence tuition and off-campus lecturing, which had low status only a generation ago. The reputation of the mega-universities varies between countries and none can yet take the credibility of their distance education methods for granted. This makes the mega-universities especially relevant to two current issues in higher education: the debate about quality and the potential of technology.

Universities and quality

The reputation that the public accords to a particular university combines various factors. First, in most countries, there is a strong correlation between the reputation of an institution and its age. Second, people tend to equate quality with exclusivity of access. Third, universities with lavish resources are assumed to be better. Fourth, educational systems with small classes and plenty of human interaction are well regarded.

These traditional elements of reputation challenge any attempt to renew universities. Institutions can do nothing about their age, except wait for time to pass. However, even young institutions will already have developed strengths which contribute to their public image. Change can be risky.

Newish universities that have been unusually successful (eg, Waterloo in Canada; Warwick in the UK) may find change particularly difficult. Gaining a reputation as a good university is, rightly, a slow process. Fortunately, losing a reputation takes time too, so institutions should not be overly cautious about the risks of innovation on this count.

Exclusivity, the second popular yardstick of quality, must be challenged head on. Increasing the volume of access to universities is driving the renewal of higher education in the developing world. Increasing the variety of access is still important in the industrialized countries. It is an imperative of academic renewal that more should not mean worse. This is where technology can help, for in most aspects of life people now assume that more and better technology means higher quality.

Better technology usually means greater cost-effectiveness as well. This must be a central purpose of academic renewal for the 21st century. It is the most difficult challenge of renewal for universities to accept, for two main reasons. First, there has indeed been a good correlation between available resources and the rankings of universities in quality assessment exercises. For example, a report by the UK's Higher Education Funding Council for England (HEFCE, 1995: 34) on its first round of quality assessments of teaching, showed that, with one notable exception, the number of excellent ratings that a university received broadly matched the funds available to it. The exception was the Open University. Public expenditure per full-time-equivalent student at this institution is about the lowest in the UK system, yet it was one of only 13 of the 70 universities offering a comprehensive curriculum to receive excellent ratings in more than half the subjects assessed. The significance of this exception is that the Open University has developed a technology-based teaching system.

The second factor that makes academics reluctant to give priority to cost-effectiveness is the monumental function of universities. The noble ideals of the academy have always attracted the support of the wealthy: kings, queens, bishops, merchants and industrialists, who wanted their memories to live on in the names of campus buildings and professorial titles. In medieval times Europe built cathedrals, to the greater glory of God, whose dimensions and splendour went far beyond the simple requirements of worship. In the last century, most especially in America, the wealthy have built and equipped university campuses far beyond the basic needs of teaching and research. Who can blame university staff for enjoying the civilized environments of these well-endowed seats of learning and for being reluctant to exchange them for organizations that are less extravagantly over-engineered?

Although some of the mega-universities also offer pleasant working conditions to their staff, they pose a stark challenge to the popular quality criteria of age, exclusivity and wealth. These young institutions were set up with the express purpose of breaking the perceived link between quality of education and exclusivity of access. Their enrolments are huge – the 11 mega-universities have nearly three million students between them.

The fourth common yardstick of quality is the intensity of contact between teachers and students. Although some of the mega-universities give closer personal tutorial attention to students than is available on campus (Rickwood, 1993: 13), the sheer size of the mega-universities, as well as the term 'distance learning', make it hard to communicate that reality. Students on campus may fear that their interaction with staff would be the first casualty of the development of technology-based teaching.

Technology and the agenda for renewal

The agenda for university renewal challenges popular concepts of academic quality. This is one reason for exploring carefully the contribution that technology can make to the implementation of that agenda. We define technology as the application of scientific and other organized knowledge to practical tasks by organizations consisting of people and machines (Open University, 1978). The significant elements of this definition are:

- its recognition that there is more to technology than applied science. Non-scientific knowledge (design, managerial, craft, tacit) is involved;
- the explicit assertion that technology is about practical tasks (as compared to science, which is mainly about understanding);
- technology always involves people (social systems) as well as hardware.

This definition attaches as much importance to the softer aspects of technology (rules, systems and approaches to problems) as to the burgeoning array of hardware and software that the term more commonly evokes.

Both facets of technology have transformed many aspects of life in the 20th century. This book asks whether they can renew universities in the 21st century. Universities are often at the leading edge in the use of technology for research. Indeed, many of the technologies now ubiquitous in everyday life grew out of work in university laboratories. Academics have been much slower, however, to develop technology within the teaching function of their own universities. The overhead projector is still somewhat threatening.

Some argue that it is now imperative for academics to embrace change because the latest manifestations of technology actually alter the relationship between people and knowledge. Eisenstadt (1995) coined the term 'knowledge media' to describe the convergence of computing, telecommunications and the cognitive sciences. Others speak of a 'third generation' of distance learning technology that is distinguished by a much greater capacity for rich and rapid interaction between members of a learning community.

How and where can technology help university renewal? This book focuses on the teaching function because that foundation underpins the two other elements of the university's mission: service and research. The central goal of universities is to train people in the academic mode of thinking. The academic mode of thinking, which we contrast to the ideological mode of thinking, is a glory of human development and perhaps Europe's most precious gift to the world. The relationships that universities create between knowledge, communities and credentials are grounded in it.

Yet criticizing universities is today a popular pastime in many countries. The precise strictures vary in content and force from one country to another but five accusations have wide currency:

- national university systems are not accommodating the volume and variety of student demand;
- higher education is too costly and does not deliver graduates with the skills employers value;
- teaching methods are too inflexible to answer the needs of a diversifying student body;
- the quality of higher education is not assured;
- the sense of the university as an academic community is being eroded.

Can new technologies – and new uses of old technologies – help to resolve the crisis of higher education? Will they help universities deliver the radical and continuing improvements in cost-effectiveness and value for money that are needed? Will they enable institutions to answer questions about quality with more confidence? Can they help to re-create the spirit of community within the academy?

The following chapters address these questions. The next chapter looks at the challenges facing campus-based universities and examines the potential impact of technology there. It concludes that the key imperatives are to enhance teaching effectiveness and learning productivity. Chapter 3 then examines a very different set of institutions, namely the large distance-teaching universities. In the countries where they have been established these institutions have greatly increased the capacity of higher education while reducing its costs. However, they too face questions about educational effectiveness and academic community.

These reviews reveal that universities at different ends of the institutional spectrum have some similar expectations of the role of technology in the renewal of the academy. These expectations centre round the approaches to teaching and learning that have come to be known as distance education. Chapter 4 describes the essentials of distance education and provides the framework through which we examine the contribution of technology to academic renewal in subsequent chapters.

There are many questions to be answered. Will students want to buy the new technologies and use them for study? Will the knowledge media, this third generation of distance-teaching technology, make learning more efficient? Can campus universities use teaching technology cost-effectively on a small scale? Will the mega-universities retain their cost advantage as they migrate from well-tried systems to new approaches? Will universities of all types exploit the great potential for collaboration between them in the development of technology-based teaching? What will be the effect of the huge cost differentials between institutions in different countries as higher education becomes a global business? Will the notion of an academic community be strengthened or weakened as its geographical base erodes?

Summary

One new university per week is required to keep pace with world population growth but the resources necessary are not available. Higher education must develop more cost-effective methods so that public resources can be focused on schools and youth training. The example of the large distance-teaching universities shows that with new approaches wider access and lower costs can go together. Popular perceptions of university quality are a barrier to change that can be surmounted. The appropriate use of technology adds quality in other areas of endeavour and can help universities overcome the criticisms levelled at them.

Chapter 2

Challenges on Campus

A world of contrasts and similarities

Turkey's Anadolu University has an enrolment of over 500,000 in its distance education programmes. They represent the majority of all Turkey's university students. Such a pattern is still unusual. For most students in most countries, university study means attending courses on a campus. Developing countries that do not have enough campus universities to cope with present and future demand may look to distance education to provide much of the new capacity. However, they would also like to maximize the benefits of their investment in the bricks and mortar of their existing campuses.

In the industrialized world, by contrast, capacity is no longer the key issue. North America, in particular, is already richly endowed with college and university campuses. There and in parts of Europe supply and demand for higher education are roughly in balance, at least for young school-leavers seeking opportunities for full-time study. (Although in the US states of California, Florida and Texas enrolments look set to grow for the foreseeable future.) The imperative for government policy-makers is to make the existing networks of institutions more efficient, more effective and, above all, less costly to the public purse. For the majority of universities, those that are not comfortably ensconced at the top of the pecking order for student applications, the imperative is to compete successfully for new students and to retain those already enrolled. This may mean offering new programmes or more flexible modes of study. Even in jurisdictions where the demand for full-time study is no longer growing there may still be increasing interest from people wanting to study part time if it can be made convenient for them.

Notwithstanding this basic difference in the balance of supply and demand between developing and industrialized countries, universities face common difficulties in most parts of the world. However, the mood of crisis that seems to afflict higher education nearly everywhere may supply the incentives for change.

Universities and governments

Underlying trends in the relationships between governments and higher education in different countries are strikingly similar (Neave & van Vught, 1991). The issues facing the academy are becoming global as previously distinct traditions converge. As Berg (1993) has remarked:

> 'Looking closer at the individual national systems, we find that there is a clear trend in favour of the decentralisation of decision-making in countries which traditionally had a centralised system, while the Anglo-Saxon system is moving in the opposite direction.'

Reviewing trends in the Canadian provinces, for example, George and McAllister (1995) reported that governments were pressuring universities to become more cost-effective and more accountable. In some provinces (Alberta, Ontario) one lever used to make universities more cost-effective has been significant cuts in their support from public funds. There is also a trend in Canada for governments to co-locate, in one department, the civil servants dealing with universities and those concerned with other post-secondary provision and employment training. This has the advantage of placing policy-making for the academic enterprise in a broader social context but it may lessen the opportunities for universities to influence government decision-making through special pleading.

For the United States McGuinness (1995) stressed the role of the fiscal crisis that began in 1990 in setting the scene for the decade. He identified seven trends that are now shaping the relationship between higher education and governments in the USA:

- increasing demand for all dimensions of the higher education mission (teaching, research and service) will out-strip available resources;

- the USA may retreat from its commitment to universal access to higher education. There is now tension between the commitment to access for all citizens as a public good and the view that higher education is primarily a private good;
- political leaders are taking more aggressive action on issues of quality, although the meaning of 'quality' is unclear. Often the question of whether higher education is 'doing things right' gets mixed up with the question of whether it is 'doing the right things';
- federal policy and fiscal constraints are shifting more of the costs of higher education to undergraduates: 'public policy is encouraging parents and students to shift the cost of higher education to the next generation';
- tensions are mounting between major public research universities, that are increasingly international in focus, and state governments that want to use these institutions for more local purposes;
- technology, distance learning and global networks for scholars and students are transforming institutional practices in ways that may make current institutional structures and government policies obsolete;
- state structures of university governance may hinder institutions in responding to changing conditions.

The United Kingdom is an example of the recent centralization of a higher education system. Its Higher Education Act of 1992 gave university status to a large group of polytechnics and colleges and placed all higher education within a common public funding framework. Most of the issues identified by McGuinness for the USA also apply to the UK. In particular, the tension between demand and resource became a contentious issue in 1995 when the government reduced funding to universities after a period of brisk enrolment growth. Since British universities have not charged tuition fees to full-time undergraduate students from the UK and Europe for many years – and the government opposes the introduction of such fees – institutions catering primarily for full-time students have little flexibility to respond to their straitened circumstances.

Elsewhere in Europe, as Berg (1993) noted, there has been some decentralization of previously national university systems of the 'Napoleonic' type. Here again, however, governments are finding they can no longer afford the growing expense of university systems that have traditionally been free – or charged only nominal fees – to qualified school-leavers. France was just one European country to experience student unrest in the mid-1990s as its government tried to cut public expenditure on universities.

The difficulties that afflict universities in the industrialized world are also found in developing countries. The challenge facing them, however, is of an entirely different magnitude. At present, their total university capacity is small in relation to population so participation rates are low. Furthermore, the condition of university buildings, equipment and libraries is usually poor and sometimes actually deteriorating. It is, of course, in these countries that new university campuses should be opening weekly to serve growing populations. Even if building were taking place at this rate, which it is not, the participation rate in higher education would merely remain constant. Most countries would actually like to increase it towards western levels but simply do not have the resources required to do so if it means building more campuses.

Commenting on the scene in Africa in a proposal to create an African Virtual University, the World Bank (1996) notes:

> 'Unfortunately tertiary institutions in their present form – overwhelmed with problems related to access, finance, quality, internal and external efficiency – are not up to the challenge. Enrolment levels are shockingly low. Limited space and declining budgetary levels prevent universities from servicing the growing demand for education. As a result, universities in sub-Saharan Africa (SSA) suffer from low numbers of trained faculty, virtually non-existent levels of research, poor quality educational materials (eg African libraries have suffered immensely as collections have become out of date and laboratory equipment is old, in disrepair and out of date), and outmoded programs.... It is thus highly questionable whether tertiary institutions can afford to continue to develop under this traditional model of higher education, particularly if the countries of SSA wish to expand – more than marginally – access to higher education while maintaining quality.'

Challenges and opportunities

In summary, the current model of the campus university faces a number of challenges and opportunities, including the following:

- The costs of this form of higher education are too high for the majority of those around the world who will aspire to university training in the future.
- Even if the financial resources were available it would not be feasible, because of the shortage of trained academic staff, to create university campuses fast enough to meet potential demand in the developing countries.
- In order to remain employable, people will become lifelong learners. The mature and part-time students who are already a majority in some national university systems are often not well served by campus instruction.

- The growth of lifelong learning is having an impact on initial higher education. Growing numbers of young students, who wish to combine work and study, are looking for more flexible ways of obtaining a degree.
- An increasing proportion of the world's population will live in very large cities. Travelling within them will become slower but telecommunications networks will improve steadily.
- People will adopt customer attitudes and expect their education and training to be personalized. Most campuses become more impersonal as they expand student numbers.
- The wide distribution and diffusion of responsibility within the contemporary university makes it difficult for institutions to guarantee quality, coherence and consistency, especially in a period of expansion.
- The essence of higher education is connecting people into learning communities. New technologies, notably the Internet and the World Wide Web, may provide superior ways of creating academic communities. Some claim, even more ambitiously, that the knowledge media created by the convergence of computing, telecommunications and the cognitive sciences change fundamentally the relationship between people and knowledge.

The undernourished core

Listing challenges and opportunities is easy. But how can universities rise to the challenges and seize the opportunities? What are the obstacles to change? What must universities do to compete successfully without abandoning their academic values? Can technology help?

In a perceptive analysis, Zemsky and Massy (1995) have given some answers to these questions. They looked at the core production processes that define and constrain the delivery of teaching and research. Campus universities owe their current predicament to a perspective on production processes that dates back to the 19th century English economist John Stuart Mill. According to Mill there is limited possibility of substitution between inputs and outputs. Wool and mutton are the classic example of a Millian production process. The average amounts of wool and mutton yielded by a flock of sheep of a given size are essentially fixed. If the farmer produces more wool by increasing the size of the flock, the amount of mutton also increases. Total outputs can be increased but the proportions stay the same.

In Zemsky and Massy's analogy the university's core academic faculty is the flock of sheep. Teaching and research correspond to the outputs of wool and mutton. This means that the university cannot respond to a new teaching opportunity without also increasing its capacity for research, whether needed or not. There are three further and related problems. First, the academic tradition values faculty for who they are rather than what they produce. Second, this perception of the faculty resists substitution of capital for labour with the result that technological change produces add-on improvements rather than lower costs. Third, for all these reasons, there is little interest in finding out what things cost.

These authors worry that such Millian assumptions about production will harm the core functions of campus universities:

> 'What has changed is not just the public's mood, but its willingness to support institutions that allocate goods rather than serve customers and that value producers more than products.' (Zemsky & Massy, 1995: 49)

They also argue that there is growing tension on campuses between the academic and administrative core, funded largely by undergraduate tuition and public funds, and a growing outer skin of new institutes and centres. This outer skin is less bound by Millian production, following rather the tradition of another 19th century economist, R W Shephard, who allowed free substitution between inputs and outputs. The Shephardian outer skin of the university tends to draw faculty away from the central function of undergraduate teaching but resents being taxed to keep the core of the institution going. This led Stanford University president Donald Kennedy to remark, in the midst of US higher education's first billion-dollar campaign: 'How can we look so rich and feel so poor?'

The analogy can be extended by considering the growth of a living cell. The cell depends for its energy on the nutrients absorbed through its outer surface. As the cell grows the area of this outer surface increases as the square of the cell radius. However, the volume of the interior of the cell, which consumes the nutrients, increases in proportion to the cube of the radius. This influences the size to which the cell can grow.

In a university the relationship between the academic and administrative core and the outer skin of research institutes and centres is complex. The activities of the outer skin undoubtedly bring resources into the university. However, it is the inner core which ultimately sustains the outer skin, most importantly by underpinning its legitimacy and standing in the scholarly community. Zemsky and Massy urge universities to define more carefully the transactions between inner core and outer skin, making subsidies more explicit and putting 'cost accounting on a more Shephardian basis' (eg, distinguishing between the costs of teaching and research). They conclude that the elements of the university making up the outer skin:

'will have to decide to what extent they could succeed detached from the academy – as stand-alone research institutes, service bureaux, or consulting groups. We believe that in the end, the benefits of being part of a college or university will be judged as more than worth the price of continued or even increased subsidies for the core functions that themselves are more efficiently organized and more effectively monitored.'

In some universities the department of continuing education may provide an important link between the inner core and outer skin. As a dean of one such department put it, 'we are operating at the margin of the university but not from a marginal perspective'. The experience of such units in conducting the teaching function of the university in a real marketplace, and often using a variety of technologies to do it, is an asset in undertaking the renewal of the academic core.

We shall see in Chapter 4 that distance education systems are closer to Shephardian than Millian concepts of production. However, recent discussion of their production processes within a Fordist framework, which has given rise to a diverting, if sometimes impenetrable literature, suggests that they too could have difficulty adapting to a changing world.

An example: the University of Utah

To understand the effect of these trends and challenges on campus it is helpful to set them in the context of a real university. The University of Utah is an example of a well-managed American research university that, while not at the top of the national league tables, ranks in the top 50 universities on the basis of its intake of national merit scholars and its externally funded research. Although the economy of Utah is buoyant, the University feels itself under some financial pressure. However, it has not experienced the large budget cuts imposed on public institutions in states such as California.

In 1994–95 the University of Utah enrolled 25,645 students (20,787 undergraduate; 4,858 graduate) and awarded 4,656 degrees (3,354 bachelor; 1,302 graduate). Its annual revenues were $839 million (University of Utah, 1995a). This does not, of course, imply an expenditure of $33,000 on each student, for this research university is a good illustration of an institution that has to balance the needs of its administrative and academic core with those of a large outer skin of ancillary operations. If we assume that the revenues supporting the core are broadly equal to the sum of tuition fees ($65m) and state appropriations ($158m) then the core represents barely more than a quarter of the turnover of the University. Indeed, the core attracts less revenue than the university hospital ($253m) which is the largest single component of the institution's outer skin.

What are the challenges facing such an institution? In 1994 the president of the University of Utah, Arthur K Smith, identified six strategic issues (University of Utah, 1994). Three of them focus on the health of the institutional core: the quality of undergraduate education; outreach programmes; and enrolment planning. The three others, although they might be considered, in terms of the Zemsky and Massy analysis, to be more closely related to the outer skin, also hold the key to some undergraduate and graduate programmes: the future of the academic health science centre; the university's research mission; and a long-range capital development plan.

For our purposes the three strategic issues most directly related to the institutional core are of most interest. How is the University addressing these issues? Assuming that these are reasonable and appropriate responses to current challenges, how can technology help in their implementation?

The quality of undergraduate education in America's large research universities has been a focus of criticism in the nation's press. Part of the University of Utah's response has been to increase the level of preparation required of entering freshmen and transfer students and to improve support and training for teaching available to faculty and graduate teaching assistants. More fundamentally, President Smith urged his colleagues to consider four principles:

- The undergraduate experience must be conceived as the totality of experiences students have at the University. Enhancing that experience therefore requires integrated and coordinated effort across the institution.
- An urban, public research university must be realistic about the diverse nature of its clientele and offer quality experiences to meet the fullest possible range of legitimate needs.
- High quality and motivated faculty are at the core of any concept of the undergraduate experience. The University must recognize and value the various and important roles played by regular full-time faculty, part-time adjunct faculty, graduate students, and others.
- The University's plans for the undergraduate experience must play to its strengths as an urban research university. These include strong discipline-based departments, an array of problem-oriented interdisciplinary programmes, and ample opportunities for the application of concepts and theory as part of the learning process.

The interest in outreach programmes at the University of Utah increased sharply in 1996 because of the personal engagement of Utah governor Mike Leavitt in promoting the concept of a Western Virtual University (now called the Western Governors University) linking all the states in the American West (Western Governors Association, 1996). In his charge to the University in 1994, President Smith had focused his comments on formal planning for the establishment of a number of branch campuses and had noted:

'Substantial discussions and analyses have now taken place with respect to branch campus planning and other forms of outreach such as distance education and technology delivered education... Faculty who have an interest in this arena, whether it be to develop courses for delivery through interactive television, to ensure the integrity of programmes and courses as we embark gingerly on the electronic highway, or whatever, are strongly urged to become involved.' (University of Utah, 1994: 3)

Two years later much attention was focused on the proposal for the Western Governors University and its implications for the University of Utah. Many universities around the world are also having to react to proposals from government or industry to transform higher education through the use of new technology. Previously, such proposals might have called for the creation of a new and distinct institution, as happened with the distance teaching mega-universities we shall examine in the next chapter. Today the more usual aim is to link existing institutions together electronically into a new and more loosely bound type of mega-university. The Western Governors University, for example, is intended to allow students to interact with all the participating universities in the western states as if they were a single institution. The proposal for an African Virtual University starts from a similar concept.

Views at the University of Utah were fairly typical of the attitudes that such schemes evoke in campus universities. On the one hand people felt that the proposal for the Western Governors University contained a number of naive assumptions. On the other hand, in the event that the concept did develop, they wanted to be in at the beginning to help mould it. A specific response of the University has been to launch a scenario planning exercise (of the type developed by the Shell Oil Company) on how changes in technology might affect the current structure and cost patterns of the University of Utah (Morgan, 1996).

The issue of enrolment planning at the University of Utah is a good example of the competitive environment that now obtains in higher education in some industrialized countries. In 1993–94 the University's enrolment grew but still fell 6% short of the target set by the state government for funding, leaving a revenue shortfall of some $7m over two years. A number of actions were taken to address the issue, some of which imply, directly or indirectly, new uses of technology (University of Utah, 1995b):

- Improve understanding of enrolment factors and develop long-run goals for enrolment.
- Attempt to increase enrolment by action on four fronts:

  (a) Improve student access by adding course sections to remove bottle-necks and by doing more off-campus teaching.
  (b) Improve student recruitment and support programmes by granting additional tuition waivers and reviewing recruitment processes, advising and orientation.
  (c) Reduce bureaucratic impediments by improving the telephone registration system and planning for registration via the World Wide Web.
  (d) Improve retention through better integration of students into the University with special programmes for first-year students and transfer students.
- Impose expenditure ceilings.

This summary of strategic thinking at the University of Utah is a good example of how a long-established and well run university is reacting to the challenge of change. One element of frustration is that government policies sometimes run counter to wider trends and desirable innovations. For example, governments that have assigned roles, missions and territories in a tidy manner to the institutions in their jurisdictions will find distance education disturbs that neatness. In Utah the government controls the University of Utah's pricing policy by setting its fees (which go into the state treasury). This removes an important planning lever from the hands of the University, for the government's pricing policy will inevitably reflect the needs of the state budget and the overall needs of its higher education system rather than the efficiency requirements of one institution.

Another challenge for the University of Utah is to derive maximum advantage from its previous investments while responding positively to those urging it to migrate to a new technology of teaching. In the USA this became a national issue in 1994 when Vice-President Gore announced the administration's intention of connecting the classrooms, libraries and hospitals of America to a national information infrastructure.

Visions of the technological future

In the longer term it seems likely that the development of such national information infrastructures – which will quickly become international information infrastructures – will require a fundamental rethinking of many of the assumptions on which universities rest. These range from approaches to developing intellectual content and curricula, through delivery mechanisms and organizational structures, to policies on funding and governance.

James Mingle, of the State Higher Education Executive Officers, has provided an excellent summary of the issues (Mingle, 1995). Although focused on the USA his analysis is also relevant to systems elsewhere.

Mingle begins with four scenarios of imaginary individuals likely to be served by universities using the new information infrastructures. The variety apparent in their ages, locations, family circumstances and employment leads him to identify some common elements of higher education in the future.

First, the delivery of education will be *unbounded* by existing campuses because it will be available anywhere and anytime. The distinction between on-campus instruction and distance education will blur because students will use the same devices (eg, computer conferencing) wherever they are.

Second, both curriculum and delivery mode will put academic content in *real-world contexts,* notably the home and the workplace. Learning, working, family and social life will converge in an era of lifelong learning.

Third, courses will become more *affordable* to students, largely because opportunities will be easier to access and more directly targeted on individual needs. Mingle suggests that governments should not expect technology to reduce higher education budgets but, rather, that it will allow them to avoid extra costs. In other words, taxpayers will get more effective and convenient services for the same level of investment.

Fourth, technology will create a market for higher education that will give students much greater *choice*. They will be able to decide where to study and to mix and match courses by picking and choosing between providers. This will increase pressures for governments to spend the public funds available for higher education by supporting students rather than institutions.

Fifth, and inherent in the coming emphasis on affordability and student choice, the effectiveness of technological delivery systems will be measured by criteria that *centre on the learner*. Did the course address the learner's needs? Was it enjoyable to study? Were the promised outcomes achieved?

Sixth, Mingle draws attention to a common concern about the educational experience sketched out in the previous paragraphs. Will it be too fragmented? Will it ignore the transmission of values? In short, will it preclude the *civilizing function* that has historically been associated with universities?

From vision to reality

The technologies that inspire such visions of a new academy are becoming more common. Some students are enthusiastic about using them. Like the University of Utah, institutions understand that their decisions about technology will influence their future competitiveness. Stories in the mass media sometimes suggest that the ingredients of a bright new educational future based on technology are all to hand and just waiting to be blended for mass consumption. This is not yet true anywhere. In developing countries it is far from true. In Turkey, for example, only 7% of the half million students of Anadolu University have computers at home (Bir, 1996). Even in the industrialized countries the conditions for the mass delivery of education through technology are as yet unrealized. What are those conditions?

Mingle (1995: 10) suggests seven prerequisites.

1. *Ubiquitous systems.* If creating the information superhighway means having a computer with a broad-band link in every home then no country is close to completing its construction. Even workplaces and campuses do not all provide convenient access to such facilities. However, narrow-band telephone links are commonplace and computer ownership is rising steadily.
2. *Lifelong learning.* The convergence of learning and work that technology can make possible will require greater commitment to lifelong learning from individuals, employers and governments. New policies for the provision of post-secondary education services are needed.
3. *Learner-centred thinking.* Until recently, especially in North America where the monumental function of the campus has been particularly important, universities were mainly built and organized around the needs of the providers. The front entrance of the administration building is often the most impressive architectural feature of the campus. The student entrance is usually round the back. To redesign institutions around the learner is a major paradigm shift. It is also the key to the success of the whole enterprise. Johnstone (1995) has coined the term *learning productivity* to express his view that 'the major problem facing higher education is not excessive costs but insufficient learning'. Increasing learning productivity means having students take more responsibility for their own learning; making the curricula and timetables more focused and purposeful; and training faculty to be mediators of learning rather than better teachers.

   Jack Wilson, the creator of an acclaimed studio course at Rensselaer Polytechnic, expresses the challenge simply:

'The current teaching/learning paradigm is one where the faculty is expected to work very hard (preparing for class and lecturing) while the student sits back and listens. I want to reverse that dynamic.' (Mingle, 1995: 13)

Unfortunately for such a vision, it is not clear that all students want the traditional dynamic reversed. Lisewski (1994), for example, reported student resistance to a move to greater independence of study. This should not surprise us. It is rare for a category of workers to accept, without challenge, that they should become more productive. However, there are academic as well as pragmatic reasons for a greater emphasis on the learner. Conceptions of knowledge are changing. We now believe that knowledge is intimately linked to the historical and personal perspective of the knower and are less confident that we can accurately and objectively represent or mirror reality. Today, as Hall *et al.* (1996: 5) state: a 'focus on the knower, rather than on immutable Truth, is central to our understanding of cognition and the current transformation in education'.

4. *Re-engineered delivery systems.* Making university education genuinely learner-centred is a huge challenge for campus institutions. As we noted from Zemsky and Massy's discussion of academic production processes, technology is usually considered by faculty as a supplement to the existing system and therefore becomes an additional cost. Mingle cites a number of examples, including Wilson's studio course at Rensselaer, where technology has been used in campus settings to engage students in their own learning. He also notes, however, that the comprehensive re-engineering of the delivery of education may require new institutional types. Some models already exist, notably the distance teaching mega-universities that we examine in the next chapter. Another type of mega-university, created by networking many existing campuses electronically, may be about to emerge.

5. *Intellectual assets.* The first requirement of a learner-centred delivery system is good materials from which students can learn. Producing such materials, which should combine pedagogical effectiveness with up-to-date academic content and attractive appearance, is already a major task of the distance teaching institutions. New technology provides the opportunity to combine in a single medium (eg, CD-ROM and, soon, the World Wide Web) intellectual assets that used to be carried on a variety of media (print, video, audio, software). However, the production of good learning materials is expensive. Only if institutions work together in consortia to share the costs of producing quality

materials is new technology likely to improve teaching productivity. Otherwise so-called interactive CD-ROMs, for example, are likely to turn out to be unstructured resource packages, offering information, but no guidance, no teaching and no assessment.

6. *Productivity gains*. Deliberate and determined attempts to increase learning productivity by putting more of the onus for learning on the student will probably succeed, despite initial resistance from some students. It is too early to say whether they will increase institutional and faculty productivity for campus universities because projects are few and evaluative research is sparse. Institutions should monitor carefully where the use of technology does yield productivity gains. The goal is clear. As Williams (1996: v) puts it:

> 'Universities and colleges need to meet further pressure on costs through improved management and the reorganization of teaching and learning rather than by further incremental changes in traditional teaching methods.'

7. *Funding, regulation and accreditation*. Most governments have high hopes of the beneficial impact of technology-based delivery systems on higher education. It is also clear, however, that these systems will disrupt, if not actually destroy, the funding and regulatory arrangements that governments have put in place. Universities will soon be able to reach and teach students all over the globe. Should the government of the jurisdiction in which a university is headquartered take any interest in the quality or the funding of its operations elsewhere in the world? What about the student who pays taxes in one country but, for good and sufficient reasons, studies with a university in another without leaving home? Do governments and universities welcome the free markets in education and training that international narrow- and broadband networks with home connections will promote?

In fact, arrangements for the public funding of higher education are already evolving to reflect new realities. According to Williams (1996: v):

> 'Direct government financial support for universities and colleges is closely related to the idea of higher education as a public service. It has a long tradition in most of Europe and in public universities and colleges in the United States, but, as in Britain, governments around the world are beginning to consider it more efficient to fund higher education by "buying" the outputs, and channelling public funds via the students, rather than subsidising the inputs.'

Hasn't this changed?

In some countries, notably the USA, accreditation arrangements are a serious barrier to the greater use of technology. These arrangements, which have evolved in the context of campus teaching, attach great importance to input measures (eg, library holdings; class size; faculty qualifications) that are unhelpful in assessing the quality of technology-based teaching. To quote Hall *et al.* (1996):

> 'By restricting "acceptable" distance learning programs to extended classroom efforts, the accrediting agencies have acted as a barrier to innovation and expropriation of distance learning as part of any new learning paradigm.'

It is perfectly possible for accreditation arrangements to adapt. The quality assessment arrangements put in place by the Higher Education Funding Council for England, for example, cope with both distance teaching and campus instruction.

These are, however, difficult issues. At the beginning of this chapter we pointed out that in recent years governments have tended to want to exercise more control over their universities, not less. Technology-based delivery systems will make it much more difficult to pursue this policy. Universities are likely to experience a period of funding and regulatory turbulence as their governments develop policies for a new world. To judge by the list of questions for policy-makers with which Mingle concludes his paper, this policy development will be a slow process.

Summary

The majority of the world's universities carry out most of their teaching activities on a campus. This chapter has looked at the challenges such institutions face from demography, changing political attitudes to higher education, and rapidly evolving technological infrastructures.

In the developing world demand from potential students far outstrips the capacity of the existing campuses whereas, for higher education in the industrialized world, supply and demand are broadly in balance. Nevertheless, universities face similar challenges all over the world, especially in relation to governments which want to see higher education become less expensive so that policies to encourage lifelong learning can be affordable. Many governments believe that universities will become more efficient if they take advantage of the information infrastructures now being built.

The response of universities to these challenges is influenced by their previous investment in campus facilities and by an ethos that resists seeing university teaching and research as a production process. Furthermore, universities are having difficulty sustaining their academic and administrative cores as specialist centres and ancillary activities proliferate in response to social pressures. We cited the University of Utah as an example of a large research university that is working to sustain the integrity of its core by protecting the quality of its undergraduate programme, extending its outreach activities and competing for students.

New educational systems will be created by technology-based teaching. They will eliminate geographical and jurisdictional boundaries, integrate academic and real-world concerns more closely, and give students wider and more affordable choices.

The key challenge for campus universities is to change from a teacher-centred model of education to an approach that emphasizes learning productivity – and to carry students with them. The challenge for governments is to develop policies for a world in which traditional funding methodologies and quality assessment procedures for higher education will no longer work.

In the next chapter we examine a very different set of institutions, the mega-universities that enrol tens of thousands of students at a distance and have adapted their teaching methods and organizational structures for that purpose.

Chapter 3

The Mega-Universities

What is a mega-university?

We define a mega-university as a distance-teaching institution with over 100,000 active students in degree-level courses. Table 3.1 lists the 11 institutions that met these criteria in 1996 (ICDL, 1995). Table 3.2 provides some basic data but should be used cautiously in making detailed comparisons between them. The data supplied by the institutions for budgets and numbers of students, graduates or staff are not always calculated on the same basis. Profiles of all the world's mega-universities are given in the Appendix.

The definition of a mega-university combines three criteria: distance teaching, higher education, and size. Each is intentionally restrictive. First, although many universities now offer both distance and classroom teaching, we have only designated as mega-universities those institutions where distance education is clearly the primary activity. In this way the special organizational arrangements established by such institutions to use technology for teaching at a distance stand out more clearly. Second, although tertiary and secondary distance education institutions in the same country may share common features, the student profile, the nature of degree-level study and the research missions of universities make them distinctive. Finally, setting a threshold of 100,000 active students is an arbitrary way of selecting institutions that should be able to demonstrate economies of scale and competent logistics.

Table 3.1 *The mega-universities*

Country	Name of institution	Established	Abbreviation
China	China TV University System	1979	CTVU
France	Centre National d'Enseignement à Distance	1939	CNED
India	Indira Gandhi National Open University	1985	IGNOU
Indonesia	Universitas Terbuka	1984	UT
Iran	Payame Noor University	1987	PNU
Korea	Korea National Open University	1982[1]	KNOU
South Africa	University of South Africa	1873[2]	UNISA
Spain	Universidad Nacional de Educación a Distancia	1972	UNED
Thailand	Sukhothai Thammathirat Open University	1978	STOU
Turkey	Anadolu University	1982	AU
United Kingdom	The Open University	1969	UKOU

Notes
1. As the Korea Air and Correspondence University.
2. As the University of the Cape of Good Hope.

Why study the mega-universities?

The previous chapter looked at issues facing universities that now carry out most of their teaching on campus. Such universities feel growing pressure to develop technology-based course delivery systems using the information infrastructures now evolving in many countries. If they respond to such pressures they may have to change their approach to teaching so that it more closely resembles distance education, notably in becoming more learner-centred.

We shall examine the dynamics of distance education in the next chapter. In this chapter our interest is in the mega-universities as institutions and their roles in the academic life of their countries. They are mostly new institutions that have quickly become the largest universities in their national higher education systems. Moreover, they operate differently from other universities in many ways, not least in the way they have redefined the tasks of the academic faculty and introduced a division of labour into the teaching function. The achievements of the mega-universities pose a challenge to conventional academic practice because they show that a different approach to teaching can be more successful than lecturing.

Table 3.2 *The mega-universities: basic data*

Abbrev. name	Students in degree programmes	Annual intake	Graduates per year	Budget $US million	% of budget from[5]		Unit cost[6]	Academic staff		Total staff (f-t)
					Fees	Grant		(f-t)	(p-t)	
CTVU	530,000[1]	77,000	101,000	1.2[4]	0	75	40	18,000	13,000	43,000
CNED	184,614[1]	184,614	28,000	56	60	30	50	1,800	3,000	3,000
IGNOU	242,000[2]	91,000	9,250	10	42	58	35	232	13,420	1,129
UT	353,000[2]	110,000	28,000	21	70	30	15	791	5,000	1,492
PNU	117,000[3]	34,950	7,563	13.3	87	13	25	499	3,165	2,169
KNOU	210,578[2]	100,000	11,000	79	64	36	5	176	2,670	670
UNISA	130,000[2]	60,000	10,000	128	39	60	50	1,348	1,964	3,437
UNED	110,000[2]	31,000	2,753	129	60	40	40	1,000	3,600	2,023
STOU	216,800[2]	103,130	12,583	46	73.5	26.5	30	429	3,108	1,900
AU	577,804[2]	106,785	26,321	30[7]	76	6	10	579	680	498[7]
UKOU	157,450[2]	50,000	18,359	300	31	60	50	815	7,376	3,312

Notes
1. 1994 figure.
2. 1995 figure.
3. 1996 figure.
4. Central (CCRTVU) unit only.
5. Student fees/government grants.
6. Unit cost per student as percentage of average for other universities in the country (approx.).
7. Open Education Faculty only (full-time academic staff figure for whole University).

It would be natural for established universities to regard these mega-universities as unwelcome upstarts and to question whether large-scale distance education is consistent with fundamental academic values. Now that all universities are exploring the possibility of teaching at a distance some argue that large institutions dedicated solely to distance teaching are no longer necessary. Others argue that because of their size and their commitment to industrial methods the mega-universities will not be nimble enough to survive in a post-industrial age. Since this claim has been made by people with direct experience of mega-universities (Bates, 1995: 242; Raggatt, 1993; Rumble, 1992) some people now expect the eventual demise of the mega-universities. This chapter may assist judgements about their likely longevity. Is their present competitive advantage a temporary phenomenon?

Whatever their future, the mega-universities have already achieved a double breakthrough. By increasing university capacity dramatically while lowering costs sharply they have created a rare discontinuity in the evolution of higher education. A simple comparison shows the scale of their achievement. The 3,500 colleges and universities in the USA have an enrolment of 14 million students and annual spending on higher education is around $175 billion (Gifford, 1995). This represents an average cost of $12,500 per student. The 11 mega-universities enrol 2.8 million students for an aggregate budget of around $900 million, which is less than $350 per student. This shows why the practices of the mega-universities will help to satisfy part of the burgeoning demand for university education in the next century at costs affordable to individuals and governments.

Although the mega-universities share important successes they are not a homogeneous set. A particular mega-university may resemble institutions outside the group more closely than its sister mega-universities. Spain's UNED, for example, has more in common with the slightly smaller German FernUniversität than it has with China's CTVU system. Several features of the UKOU are more like Quebec's Télé-université than France's CNED. Just as practice in campus universities varies, so does the approach of the mega-universities. Reviewing this variety may indicate where the innovations of the mega-universities can best contribute to the renewal of universities generally.

This chapter draws on the profiles of the individual mega-universities in the Appendix to identify common features and priorities for further development. These 11 institutions are in a dynamic stage of evolution. What will be the role of changing technologies in pursuing their current priorities? Will new technologies enhance the competitive advantage of these institutions? Will the next generation of learning technology increase the divergence between the mega-universities and campus institutions or will there be a convergence towards common approaches to teaching and learning?

Why were the mega-universities established?

Rumble and Keegan (1982: 204) made an early attempt to identify the distinguishing features of some of the mega-universities and Keegan (1994b) pursued the topic a decade later. What is the role of these universities and how is it distinct? The names countries gave their mega-universities shed light on their expectations.

Five countries (France, India, Korea, South Africa and Spain) are explicit about their institution's national role. The most straightforward case is South Africa, where UNISA (University of South Africa) is simply named for the country, of which it is the oldest university. The other four in this group have included the word 'national' in the title of their mega-universities. In the remaining institutions the national remit is no less strong for being implicit. Even in Turkey, where the original intent was to encourage many institutions to operate at a distance, the national role of the Open Education Faculty of Anadolu University (AU) is now recognized – and AU accounts for half of all the country's university students.

But the common feature of all the mega-universities is that they use the technologies of distance education to promote open learning. France, Iran and Spain focus on distance education (or distance teaching) in the institutional name, whereas China bases the name on the primary medium used (broadcasting and television). Five countries (India, Indonesia, Korea, Thailand and the UK) refer to their institutions as 'open universities'. This term entered the language with the creation of the Open University in the UK in 1969 – although that institution was originally called the University of the Air (Perry, 1976) when the idea was floated. Its planners thought the name of the university should reflect the aims it was to pursue (opening access to higher education) rather than just one of the means it would use (broadcasting).

Current roles in national policy

Governments created their mega-universities with particular policy goals in mind, above all to increase access to higher education at low cost. No doubt they saw this as a worthy mission but only in a few cases (eg, IGNOU, STOU, UKOU) was an attempt made to give the new institution high status within the national university network. Today all governments are finding that their mega-universities are extremely useful policy tools for a quite different purpose. As countries compete to bring to their people the personal benefits of better communications and the economic dynamism of the information superhighway, their mega-universities are a precious asset.

Three examples illustrate the mega-universities' contemporary role. The Korean government has asked KNOU to operate a cable TV channel as part of Korea's information superhighway policy (Han, 1995: 104). The Chinese government has asked CTVU to provide tertiary education for technicians in rural enterprises (Wei & Tong, 1994: 126). Through its Knowledge Media Institute the UKOU is the British leader in research and development on the large-scale use of new technology for education and training.

There are, of course, pros and cons in the mega-universities' roles as tools of national policy. Universities have historically sought independence from government in order to avoid inappropriate restrictions on academic activity. The particular interest of governments in the affairs of the mega-universities may indeed constrain their options for development. On the other hand, it may also give the institutions greater opportunities to influence government policy on a range of issues.

How should the relations between governments and the mega-universities develop in future? Governments could derive even greater benefit from their mega-universities by reviewing their policies in two specific areas and by moving to output-oriented funding policies.

The first specific area is regulation. For example, the mega-universities of France and Thailand could serve their societies better if their governments gave them greater freedom to manage their affairs. In France CNED needs the latitude to develop its own fees strategy and staffing policies. Thailand's STOU should be freed from the line-item allocation of its state grant. Second, some governments have such excessive expectations for the cost advantages of their mega-universities that they force them to operate suboptimally. This is especially the case in Korea, where KNOU can hardly be expected to perform well at its current staffing levels. More generally, given the convergence of distance and conventional methods, governments should cease applying different funding formulae to them. Instead, starting from the present historic base, they should allocate growth monies to those institutions, of whatever type, that can deliver most cost-effectively the higher education outputs sought by government. Alternatively, as suggested in the previous chapter, they should direct public funds to students rather than to institutions.

Access to communications facilities

Most of the mega-universities have privileged access to certain communications facilities, especially those controlled or regulated by government. The partnership between the UKOU and the British Broadcasting Corporation is the best example. STOU and AU also have access to the national broad-casting networks in Thailand and Turkey. UT has a special arrangement for Indonesia's post offices to act as admission points (ICDL, 1995).

In competitive terms ready access to media and networks that reach people all over the country is clearly an advantage. There is, of course, a danger that the mega-universities might use such media more for their availability than for their effectiveness and be slow to explore new technologies. In any case, as media and communications networks multiply and government involve-ment in this arena decreases, the institutions will have to act more inde-pendently in securing access to the media they need. Such action will be a priority because all the mega-universities, without exception, now wish to have greater access to satellite and/or terrestrial broadcasting for TV and/or radio.

Linkages to the rest of higher education

Although most mega-universities were consciously separate from the rest of their countries' higher education systems in their early days, they are now integral to those systems. IGNOU has, in addition to its distance teaching role, a mandate as an apex body for the promotion, coordination and maintenance of standards in distance teaching in all Indian universities (ICDL, 1995: 5). In 1992 the UKOU joined a common funding regime with all other UK universities and took over the validation function of the Council for National Academic Awards (CNAA) (Daniel, 1995: 402). Through this post-CNAA activity the UKOU is the degree-awarding body for some 8,000 students in 50 campus-based tertiary institutions.

However, the mega-universities do not always fit easily into state higher education funding systems designed for campus teaching. There is a particu-lar challenge when such systems devolve decision-making to a regional level. After Spain and the UK regionalized the public funding of higher education, UNED and the UKOU became, in a sense, the only truly national univer-sities in their respective countries. They do not fit neatly into regionalized funding systems.

Nevertheless, integration between distance teaching universities and other universities will continue to deepen, partly because student behaviour now demands it. For example, the percentage of students simultaneously enrolled at Athabasca University, Alberta (a distance teaching university) and one or other of the region's conventional universities has risen from 14% to 40% in less than ten years (Powell & McGuire, 1995: 455). Quebec's Télé-université has a similar experience (Marrec, 1995). This trend will undoubtedly affect the mega-universities and oblige them to develop facilities for processing high volumes of credit transfer applications if they have not already done so.

An advantage of close links with the rest of the tertiary system is increased awareness of distance education and the curricula of the mega-universities amongst students of all universities. This may lead some of them to opt for a mega-university course later in their careers. A disadvantage is that such links may constrain curricular innovation by encouraging the mega-universities to concentrate on distance versions of the courses already offered widely in other universities. Indeed, some mega-universities (eg, France's CNED, Iran's PNU and Spain's UNED) already teach curricula defined at the national level for all institutions. This practice appears, unfortunately, to reduce academic vitality as well as institutional costs.

Most mega-universities have made major contributions to academic publishing in their countries, especially where they operate in a language not widely spoken outside the country. Thus AU, PNU and STOU have greatly increased the volume of quality academic material available in Turkish, Persian and Thai respectively. Smaller distance teaching universities (eg, the Open University of Israel) have made similar contributions.

What of future priorities? The mega-universities are increasingly embedded in the institutional networks of their countries. As governments seek to increase the availability of distance education by exploiting their existing investments in campus universities they may be tempted to set up new institutions whose purpose is mainly to coordinate distance teaching activities across universities. The proposals for a Western Governors University in the USA and an African Virtual University are along these lines. This may create a new type of network mega-university with many quasi-autonomous nodes.

Reviewing the impact of the current mega-universities suggests, however, that to conceive a mega-university simply as a means of managing and coordinating the activities of existing bodies and agencies is short-sighted. Such an organizational formula may be less cost-effective than at first appears. The energy that drives the successful mega-universities is the academic relationship between staff and students within 'their' university. At a minimum a mega-university needs to have a direct relationship with the students for whom it exists and sufficient staff to give it reasonable independence of action. Failure to meet this condition appears to be a source of weakness for the Chinese mega-university. The currently fashionable concept of a virtual university, that simply networks existing universities in new ways, will fail unless it can evoke the personal commitment from students and staff that is the basis of an academic community.

Students

The mega-universities all have large numbers of students but the profiles of their student bodies differ. At the UKOU, for example, most students are working adults who study part-time, whereas in the CTVU (China) they are mostly adults being paid to study full-time. Other Asian mega-universities enrol significant proportions of school-leavers. The overall trend, however, is towards similar, but diverse, student profiles across the mega-universities. Those institutions that focused on adults are now attracting more young students, whereas the mega-universities originally created for young school-leavers now have a majority of students in employment with a higher median age (Park, 1995: 327). Their common characteristic is to attract students whose needs are not well served elsewhere. Many pay special attention to the needs of students with disabilities.

At a time when all universities are courting adult students the mega-universities are working to protect their traditional appeal to such people. 'Your second chance to get a degree' could have been the early motto of the mega-universities. Today it might be: 'your first choice for lifelong learning'.

Student performance

For students to make mega-universities their first choice they must believe that their studies will be successful. They want to complete their courses and gain benefits in employment. What does the record show?

The Appendix provides data for some institutions. They reveal wide variations in completion rates. There are universities where the majority of students succeed (CTVU, UKOU) and others in which only a minority complete their early courses (KNOU, UT). For the students who do graduate from mega-universities the prospects are good. Over 70% of UKOU graduates reported that they had derived 'great' or 'enormous' benefit from being Open University students (Department of Education and Science & The Open University, 1991). The success rate of graduates from the mega-universities in Iran, Thailand and the United Kingdom in gaining admission to postgraduate programmes in other universities is among the highest in their respective countries.

It is also clear that, independently of academic achievement, employers value the qualities of motivation, personal organization and perseverance that study at a distance develops. Furthermore, there is a growing appreciation in industry and business that, by combining work and work-related study, people learn at a deeper level and apply their knowledge more effectively.

This, combined with cost factors, explains why distance education is becoming the preferred mode of study for degrees like the Master of Business Administration.

Curricula

There are some similar trends in the evolution of the curricula of all mega-universities, notably towards a more vocational focus. A striking example is IGNOU (India) which has changed its academic profile significantly since 1990. Its priority has moved from degree programmes in the liberal arts towards diploma and certificate programmes in applied subjects. Distance education tends to strengthen the relationship between learning and work. Another example is provided by the 200,000 AU students, three-quarters of them in full-time employment, who are studying in 17 vocationally-oriented diploma programmes.

The mega-universities benefit from the economies of scale that flow from teaching large numbers of students. This makes it particularly important for them to teach in subject areas of high demand. Their role as instruments of government policy is also relevant. For example, in 1992 the UK government asked the Open University to develop a teacher training programme for mature graduates in subjects and regions where there was a teacher shortage. By 1995 it enrolled more teacher trainees (2,500) than any other UK institution.

Research

Research is a fundamental element of the mission of universities. Within the academic community the performance of the mega-universities in research is an important yardstick for judging their credibility. How do they rate?

With the possible exceptions of France's CNED and China's CTVU, all the mega-universities consider research to be part of their mission. However, it is too early to judge their research performance. Most of these institutions are less than 20 years old. A research tradition takes time to establish and in its first decade each mega-university had to focus single-mindedly on creating a large and novel teaching system. Furthermore, the number of full-time academic staff in each mega-university (except China's) is tiny in relation to the student body and small in relation to the institutional budget.

Notwithstanding these caveats, research in the mega-universities is developing. The University of South Africa has the best research library in the country, one reason why posts at that institution are sought after by faculty wishing to focus on research. In Spain UNED is rated in the top group of Spanish universities on the basis of its research. The UKOU was placed in the top third of universities in Britain's 1992 national research assessment exercise. Research of national or international eminence was found in all of its faculties and, with more than 1,300 doctoral students, the UKOU is heavily involved in research training.

Cost-effectiveness

Over a decade ago Rumble and Keegan (1982: 220) noted that 'distance teaching universities can be cost-effective in comparison with conventional universities but that this may not necessarily be the case'. They added that,

> 'with the exception of the UKOU, none of the distance teaching universities covered in this book has yet proven their ability to produce graduates at an average unit cost significantly below that of conventional universities in their country.'

Since that time many studies have established the superior cost-effectiveness of the mega-universities, but not necessarily of smaller distance teaching institutions or of the distance programmes of conventional universities. For example, a government review of the UKOU in 1991 compared its costs per graduate with those of three other institutions. The UKOU's costs were significantly lower: between 39% and 47% of the other universities' costs for ordinary degrees; between 55% and 80% for honours degrees (Department of Education and Science, 1991; Department of Education and Science & The Open University, 1991: 67).

Loing (1993a) states that the cost of education in France through the CNED is half that of conventional methods. For CTVU, Wei and Tong (1994: 113) report that the average cost per student is '43 to 51 percent of conventional colleges and universities, though this calculation is not especially reliable'. These figures, taken from Wu Xiaobo (1993: 76), may be compared with those of Ding Xingfu (1993: 95), who argued that the per student costs of the CTVU system were between 25% (humanities) and 40% (science and engineering) of those of conventional universities.

The role of distance education in the renewal of the wider university enterprise will depend critically on its cost-effectiveness with present and future technologies. The mega-universities must not only maintain but enhance their cost-effectiveness if they are to provide an attractive model. This requires attention to effectiveness as much as to costs.

For example, the Chinese, Indonesian, Korean and South African mega-universities all operate at low costs per enrolled student but acknowledge the priority of putting greater emphasis on teaching effectiveness so that more students can complete their courses and programmes. Teaching focused solely on content exposition is a common academic problem and the mega-universities that contract out much of their course preparation experience it acutely. Students complain that the materials do not teach well. A focus on making learning productive is even more important for the mega-universities than for campus universities, because less back-up is available when a topic is poorly explained. In this spirit, South Africa's UNISA is experimenting with the development of courses in teams. In Korea KNOU hopes that teaching with new media will yield greater emphasis on course design. In Korea, South Africa, Spain and Thailand the mega-universities also hope that new communications facilities will make it easier to provide the improved tutorial and student support they seek.

Operating systems

There are many similarities between the operating systems of the mega-universities. Rumble and Keegan (1982: 222) distinguish two major operating sub-systems, for courses and students, and note the importance of logistic and regulatory functions. We prefer a simple analogy with a three-legged stool. The mega-universities depend on systems that support three outcomes: good learning materials, effective student support, and efficient logistics. In Chapter 5 we use a more detailed approach, known as the 'value chain', to identify the key activities of the mega-universities.

In campus teaching, and in the distance teaching programmes of some campus universities, the same individual is responsible for all three of these outcomes. In mega-universities there is a division of labour. Materials design and production is centralized and carried out by multi-skilled teams. The organization of two-way communication with students in the form of individual tuition or group meetings is a distinct and major task. Finally, the division of labour and the complex interactions of distance teaching make the components of the system highly interdependent. Organizing the flow of information and materials efficiently is a basic requirement.

New technology can contribute to the enhancement or degradation of each of these three key elements. Its leverage on the logistics that are vital to the success of a mega-university is especially important. CNED, UNED and UT are all seeking ways of speeding up mail communications. They and a wider group of institutions look forward to improved computer networks.

Production processes

Production processes are a key difference between the present operating methods of campus universities and the mega-universities. In the previous chapter we summarized Zemsky and Massy's (1995) interpretation of the production processes of campus universities based of the economic thinking of John Stuart Mill and R W Shephard. The mega-universities are closer to Shephardian than Millian concepts of production. However, recent discussion of their production processes has adopted a Fordist framework.

The polemic about Fordism, neo-Fordism and post-Fordism in distance education began with Peters' (1973) view that correspondence education is 'the most industrialized form of instruction'. This led a number of authors to criticize the mega-universities for having a Fordist approach to education and to urge that they move to neo-Fordist or post-Fordist paradigms.

Rumble (1995a; 1995b; 1995c) has performed a service by reviewing these criticisms carefully. He found that the tenets of Fordism are an imperfect fit to the practices of the mega-universities. A telling example of the mismatch between Fordist principle and distance education practice was given by Sparkes (1984). He showed that as the media of distance education become more sophisticated, academic productivity, as measured by the ratio of the student-hours of work generated for each hour of academic input, is decreasing steadily. This must represent a real drop in productivity unless the newer media allow students to learn more efficiently and/or enable the institution to reach commensurately larger numbers of students.

Rumble's analysis of how the mega-universities operate against criteria such as division of labour, product variability and vertical integration is a useful starting point for seeking improvements to their productivity. While certain practices of neo-Fordism and post-Fordism would be likely to improve the performance of the mega-universities, Rumble pointed out that the authors who advanced these nostrums had not concerned themselves with cost-effectiveness or any form of quantitative analysis.

A theme of this book is that the world of the 21st century will require dramatic improvements in the cost-effectiveness of higher education. Although the mega-universities have already set a new standard, much more is required. We return to this question in Chapter 5 where Porter's (1985) concept of the value chain will be used to discover where universities should focus in redesigning themselves for greater cost-effectiveness.

Quality and recognition

We observed in Chapter 1 that the reputation of universities among ordinary people relies heavily on measures such as the age of the institution, its wealth and the exclusiveness of its student intake.

The mega-universities are young institutions set up with the explicit purpose of breaking the perceived link between quality of education and exclusivity of access. Furthermore, they enrol very large numbers of students. Although some mega-universities give closer personal tutorial attention to students than conventional universities (Rickwood, 1993: 13), the size of the mega-universities, as well as the term 'distance learning', mean that acquiring a reputation for quality is a slow and difficult process.

The low status of correspondence study a generation ago is still a handicap. Indeed, in 1970, just when the era of the mega-universities was beginning, Mitford (1970) published an article in *Atlantic Monthly*, 'Let us now appraise famous authors', that was a devastating exposé of the racket then masquerading as one of the best-known US correspondence schools. She herself later described entertainingly how that article caused a flurry of regulation of the correspondence teaching industry (Mitford, 1979).

For the mega-universities to acquire good reputations, both in academic circles and with the general public, is a process that rightly takes time. Substantial progress has already been made, for which other mega-universities tend to give the UKOU considerable credit because it has performed well. The national processes of quality assessment introduced in the UK in 1993 have helped. The UKOU is one of only a small minority of British universities to receive 'excellent' ratings for most of its teaching.

Other mega-universities are also making good progress. In 1992 the Indian University Grants Committee commended the programmes of the IGNOU (India) as equivalent to those of other universities. The STOU (Thailand) won the award for institutional excellence of the Commonwealth of Learning and the International Council for Distance Education in 1995.

There remain, however, many problems of performance to be tackled. Park (1995: 329) reports that 90% of students admitted to the Korea National Open University drop out after they try one or two semesters. His view is that 'educational services for students can not be satisfactorily provided and consequently many students are dissatisfied with the quality of KNOU's education'.

Can new technologies improve the performance and the reputation of the mega-universities? Can they add glamour to institutions? France's CNED, for example, has done much to modernize its old-fashioned image by conducting satellite video conferences with secondary schools. Ultimately, however, a secure reputation must be based on strong performance in the central function of teaching students.

The experience of the last 20 years indicates that distance education can free itself from the low status associated with correspondence education. Institutions in both east (Thailand's STOU) and west (the UKOU) have acquired good reputations even though other mega-universities in the same regions complain that the culture is unfavourable to distance education. STOU and the UKOU have a number of common features which help to explain their success: good course materials, tutorial and regional support networks, a rich media mix, significant graduation rates, appropriate staff numbers, vibrant research activity and the culture that goes with a sense of academic community. The mega-universities with a reputation to build should note these characteristics.

International roles

Many of the mega-universities have significant and growing international roles. AU has a centre in Germany to serve 3,000 students from the large Turkish community there. Other institutions have a broader reach, not only serving expatriates from their own country overseas but also attracting a wider clientele. CNED (France), UNED (Spain), UNISA (South Africa) and the UKOU all number their overseas students in thousands. IGNOU (India) is actively developing an international reach. Now all the mega-universities – indeed all universities – face new opportunities for international expansion as the tiny proportion of the world's population with networked computers at home starts to grow rapidly in the 21st century. Landfall in a new world is imminent. My colleague Geoff Peters calls this new 'country' 'Windownesia'.

Implications for campus universities

The mega-universities have allowed countries to expand access to higher education much faster than would otherwise have been possible. The lower unit costs of the mega-universities, compared to conventional campus universities, have impressed policy makers. Because distance education has been the basis of the mega-universities' success many governments now encourage the development of distance education. Quite understandably, they promote it not only in the mega-universities but also in the campus universities where most of their public funds for higher education are spent. From the perspective of campus universities the appearance of a third generation of distance education technologies, the knowledge media, offers the chance to adapt for the future by making a clean start in a new era of distance learning.

This trend in public policy, combined with the growing availability of the knowledge media, will change the environment for the mega-universities. These institutions had little competition from other providers of higher education at a distance until about 1990. Since then a brisk market for this form of learning has begun to develop in many countries. The entry barriers facing an institution wishing to offer distance education through the older technologies (eg, print, video) are now substantially lower than when the era of the mega-universities began a generation ago. With the modern technology of the World Wide Web it now seems possible to offer distance education throughout the globe, albeit only to the tiny fraction of the world's population that currently has access to this technology. Most people in the world have yet to make a telephone call.

The previous chapter identified the challenges facing campus universities and examined how they might use technology effectively to deliver their programmes. The technologies available for distance education are changing fast and distance education is evolving with them. In the next chapter we present the essentials of distance education in order to help both campus universities and the mega-universities develop this form of delivery in ways that play to their respective strengths.

Summary

This chapter has examined the common features of the mega-universities, a remarkable group of institutions that have risen rapidly to prominence in their respective countries because of their size, their cost-effectiveness and their capacity to cater to the lifelong learning needs of a wide variety of people. It has examined the reasons for their establishment and noted the ways they use national communications networks to reach students throughout their countries.

As they have grown these mega-universities have played an increasingly integral role in the higher education systems of their countries. With governments and employers now encouraging campus universities to adopt the methods of distance education, all types of universities will need to work together more closely and many of their programmes will have a greater focus on lifelong learners in the home and the workplace.

The mega-universities have made considerable progress in establishing their reputations with the public and their credibility within the academic community. However, these gains cannot be taken for granted. The rapid expansion of distance education now under way in universities of all types could tarnish the new image of this mode of learning unless close attention is paid to quality.

The mega-universities differ from campus universities in their production processes. The operations of the mega-universities owe much to industrial methods whereas academic processes on campus are more akin to a cottage industry. It is likely that neither approach will be particularly well suited to the third generation of distance education technologies: the knowledge media.

Chapter 4

The Essentials of
Distance Education

Introduction

The two previous chapters have shown that greater use of technology will
be central to the renewal of universities. Any exploration of the potential of
technology in teaching and learning leads fairly directly to an examination
of the development of distance education. This does not mean simply
exchanging one instructional mode for another. It means combining learning that is independent of place with the excitement of the best experience
on campus. Hall *et al.* (1996) put it more formally:

> 'Lest we be misunderstood, this shift is not a move from campus-based to
> distance learning. Rather it is a shift to an integrated, networked model that
> gives to the student both the initiative to learn and the access to the necessary
> learning resources. It lessens the control of the campus and strengthens the
> integrity of the distance model.'

Since the distance model is much less common than conventional teaching
it will be helpful to put it in context. This chapter describes how distance
education became what it is today, places it in the wider framework of higher
education, and asks whether new technologies might make it more or less
competitive.

Porter (1985: 3) insists that in assessing the competitive advantage of an organization you must look first at the attractiveness and the structure of the industry to which it belongs. A successful organization must have a strong position in an attractive industry. Its profitability will depend on the structure of its industry as much as on its own particular merits. Industry structure also determines the threat of substitute products and the barriers that face new entrants.

We begin, therefore, by showing how distance education fits into the global enterprise of education and training. Clarity about the nature of its various forms is a precondition for clarity about its place in public policy and the future of universities. Distance education has evolved as a function of time, place and technology, so it now means different things in different countries. Americans most often use the expression to describe the linking of students in remote classrooms by simultaneous video conference. For example, the US Congress Office for Technology Assessment defines distance learning as: 'linking of a teacher and students in several geographic locations via technology that allows for interaction'.

Elsewhere in the world distance education usually refers to people studying at home using a variety of asynchronous communication media. According to South Africa's National Commission on Higher Education (1996):

'Distance education is the offering of educational programmes designed to facilitate a learning strategy which does not depend on day-to-day contact teaching but makes best use of the potential of students to study on their own. It provides interactive study material and decentralised learning facilities where students can seek academic and other forms of educational assistance when they need it.'

To give an holistic picture of the role and potential of distance education we need to view it from several angles. We shall summarize its historical development, examine the contribution of earlier technologies, compare the pedagogies of distance education and look at its economic structure.

History

The teaching methods used in the early Christian church illustrate different approaches to education and training and some key concepts of modern distance education. Christ taught face to face in small and large groups. Teacher and taught had to be present at the same time; what is now called 'synchronous communication'. St Paul, however, who had the challenge of instructing a dispersed community, developed a method of distance education. He wrote letters to individual churches and asked the local church elders to read them to their community when it assembled for worship. The analogy with the tutors and study groups of modern distance education is clear. Since each copy had to be hand-written and many church members were illiterate, there was little opportunity for individuals to study St Paul's letters at home. St Paul directed his approach to groups. It was a forerunner of the remote-classroom approach to distance education. From St Paul's standpoint, communication was asynchronous because he was not present when his letters were studied. However, for the church groups communication was synchronous because they were together when they listened to the reading of the letters and discussed them.

Two technological developments – the invention of printing and the introduction of universal postal services – allowed distance education to reach individuals in their homes or places of work. Asynchronous communication between individuals for educational purposes became possible. These innovations came together in England in the mid 19th century and led quickly to the offering of courses by correspondence. The earliest offerings ranged from Shorthand (Britain) through English (Sweden) to Mining Safety (USA). Some universities in Australia, Canada and the USA made correspondence courses available alongside their conventional programmes before the end of the 19th century. Russia developed a strong tradition of correspondence education in the 20th century.

The essence of remote-classroom education is a synchronous relationship between an individual teacher and a number of groups of students. In contrast, the essence of correspondence education is a direct but asynchronous relationship between an institution and an individual student, who receives printed material in the mail and returns homework assignments, also by mail, for correction and comment by the institution. Because the focus is on teaching individuals, rather than groups, correspondence education does not require fixed study timetables. Students can usually begin courses when they choose and study at their own pace.

Another variant of distance education began in Britain in 1836 when the University of London introduced its external examination system. The original aim was to offer a credible examination service to people studying in small colleges. However, the proportion of candidates preparing themselves for the examinations by private study grew steadily. Commercial correspondence colleges saw an opportunity to help these people. By the end of the century over 60% of those graduating in Arts through the external examination system had studied with the (private) University Correspondence College (Bell & Tight, 1993: 50).

Correspondence education continued to develop steadily in the 20th century. School systems in Canada, Australia and New Zealand introduced correspondence tuition for children they could not serve by conventional methods. Representatives of these programmes convened the first meeting of the International Council for Correspondence Education (ICCE) in Victoria, British Columbia in 1938. For the next three decades ICCE's constituency also included the commercial and military correspondence schools and the correspondence branches of university continuing education departments.

Public sector institutions used a variety of terms, including home study, external study, independent study and guided study instead of the expression 'correspondence study', probably because the dubious ethics and poor quality of some commercial correspondence schools gave the term an undesirable image.

Between 1960 and 1990 the evolution of distance education accelerated as a result of both technological and political developments. Two innovations were of note: the use of telecommunications to link remote classrooms and the enrichment of correspondence education by the integration of other media, beginning with television.

Telecommunication with remote classrooms

The development of telecommunications produced a new interest in the remote-classroom method of distance education, notably in the USA. The American land grant universities had a tradition of serving people in the rural areas. A leader among them was the University of Wisconsin whose president challenged his staff in 1907 to extend 'the boundaries of the campus to the boundaries of the state' (Parker, 1984: xiii). Until the 1960s, however, universities had to fulfil such ambitions through a combination of correspondence courses and travelling lecturers.

The arrival of effective audio teleconferencing technology allowed an instructor to offer a course at numerous sites simultaneously. The University of Wisconsin implemented such a system in the 1970s. Soon afterwards satellites could transmit video signals to remote classroom networks. Since then this form of distance education has developed steadily, especially in the USA. A good example is the National Technological University, a consortium of engineering schools which offers graduate-level courses by satellite across the USA and internationally.

Diversification of media for correspondence tuition

Policies of widening access to tertiary education, combined with the arrival of public TV and radio broadcasting networks, led to the modernization of correspondence education. The primary locus for this development was the UK Open University. Helped by strong political support, the UKOU's founders created an institution that quickly earned a high reputation for quality and effectiveness. As well as diversifying the media used for course materials the institution also set up a regional tutorial network to provide each student with a locally based tutor for their course.

Synopsis

The history of distance education reveals three salient features:

- There are two basic approaches to distance education: remote-classroom teaching (synchronous communication) and correspondence study (asynchronous communication).
- Distance education encourages the division of the processes of teaching and assessment into separate operations that may then be carried out by distinct individuals or institutions in different locations.
- Technological developments have determined the progress of distance education.

Technology

It is helpful to trace the evolution of distance education in terms of the technologies on which it has drawn. According to Holmberg (1977), distance education operates by conducting a 'guided didactic conversation' between the institution and the student. The separation of institution and student in both time and space requires the use of media for communication between them. Distance education has evolved by the progressive incorporation of additional media into the earlier versions of correspondence tuition and remote-classroom instruction.

Four broad groupings of technologies have influenced the development of distance education to date:

1. the combination of printing and the post in correspondence tuition;
2. the mass media of broadcasting;
3. personal media;
4. telecommunication systems.

Now the combination of computing, telecommunications and the cognitive sciences, called by Eisenstadt (1995) the 'knowledge media' (and also known as 'third generation' distance education technology) is heralded as potentially the most significant mutation so far. Bates (1995) has provided an excellent survey of the strengths, weaknesses and costs of the various technologies now in use.

Correspondence tuition: the foundation

Correspondence study has provided a robust and adaptable foundation for subsequent developments. A large majority of the world's distance students still do most of their work through print and correspondence tuition. Over a decade ago this led Rumble and Keegan (1982: 212) to observe:

> 'In retrospect the distance teaching universities, taken as a whole, have been marked by a curious mixture of public identification with and stress on the use of educational broadcasting and the playing down of their actual basis in correspondence teaching and the use of print.'

As institutions come to terms with a new generation of technology it is also instructive to note the assumptions of the planners of the UK Open University. The report of the Open University Planning Committee (1969: 6) stated:

> 'It is, however, neither practically possible nor pedagogically sound to rely on broadcasting as the principal or exclusive means of instruction in an operation designed to provide disciplined courses at university level... The only method of individual instruction capable of being made available everywhere, and capable of indefinite expansion as new needs arise, is correspondence tuition, which can readily incorporate these new techniques (i.e. broadcasting).'

The longevity and reliability of correspondence tuition suggest that the new technologies which most closely match its characteristics merit particular attention.

The mass media (broadcasting)

The previous section has evoked the paradox of the broadcast media. For Harold Wilson, the political founder of the UKOU, the use of the mass medium of broadcasting for educational purposes was an end in itself. He thought this powerful medium of communication was too precious to be used solely for entertainment. The charter of the UKOU therefore directs it to conduct 'teaching and research by a diversity of means such as broad-casting and technological devices appropriate to higher education'.

The UKOU continues to broadcast programmes, especially on television, for some 20 hours per week. Since the British public knows it best for this use of the mass media, the University consistently resists attempts to cut its airtime or move its programmes to less popular viewing slots. This contrasts with the findings of Bates (1982) who reviewed the use of educational media in 12 distance-learning systems and reported a general move away from broadcasting at that time.

The key to this apparent paradox is that the UKOU and other universities use media with multiple objectives in mind. One of the charter obligations of the UKOU is to 'promote the educational well-being of the community generally'. By broadcasting its TV and radio programmes to the general public, the UKOU provides an informal educational service to a much larger audience than its registered student body. The highest annual enrolment on any single UKOU course module is 9,000 whereas, over a three-week period, several million viewers watch UKOU TV for at least 15 minutes (Acaster & McCron, 1994: 7). There are about one million 'hard-core' viewers of the University's programmes.

Its substantial presence on the broadcast media has helped the UKOU to recruit students and to acquire a high academic reputation. Annual Gallup surveys (Open University, 1995a) show that over 90% of British adults are aware of the UKOU, a very high figure for any institution. Broadcasting helped to create this level of awareness. Many viewers, finding they enjoyed and understood the UKOU programmes, decided to become students. Academics at other institutions, judging that the UKOU programmes were professional and up-to-date treatments of their subjects, viewed the institution with respect.

It would be wrong to conclude, however, that the main function of UKOU broadcasting is general education and publicity. Registered students, many of whom are otherwise isolated, say that viewing the programmes makes them feel part of a learning community. This explains why many of the students who record the programmes on video-cassette recorders (VCRs) also watch them at the time they are broadcast (Acaster & McCron, 1994: 6). Broadcasting also obliged the UKOU to create a paced study regime with identical start and finish dates for all students in a course. This was a break with the more liberal unpaced tradition of correspondence education that has helped the UKOU achieve high completion rates.

Nevertheless, broadcasting requires universities to be clear about the outcomes they wish to achieve. This will be equally true for the newer forms of broadcasting, through satellite, cable, and the Internet, that we shall examine later. If the sole purpose of using audio-visual media is to enhance the learning of registered students, it is better to make them available as audio-cassettes, video-cassettes or CD-ROMs. This partly explains why the development of personal media has been so helpful to distance education.

The personal media

During the 1980s the term 'personal media' came into use to describe equipment, such as personal computers (PCs), audio-cassette players and VCRs, which gave students with this equipment at home greater autonomy and flexibility in their studies. The rather gradual adoption by students of the personal media – faster for VCRs, slower for PCs – posed a challenge to universities seeking to use them for home study. The mass-media, by their nature, facilitate and equalize access besides lending themselves to econo-mies of scale. The personal media do none of these things until all students are in possession of the relevant equipment, which can take many years.

The growing use of the personal media also reinforced the view that simple media can be very effective in distance education. For example, Bates (1982: 11) concluded that for the UKOU 'the greatest media development during its twelve years of existence has been the humble audio-cassette'. Audio-cassettes are popular with administrators because they are inexpensive. Academics feel they have more control over the making of audio-cassettes than of broadcasts. Students find cassettes convenient and informal: 'like a personal tutorial with the course author'. Sound generates a feeling of togetherness.

Since Bates conducted his study the most important development in personal media at the UKOU has been the personal computer. The introduction of the home computing policy now called the 'personal computing policy' by the UKOU has been reviewed by Jones *et al.* (1992) who conclude that it has been remarkably successful even though British households did not acquire computers as fast as originally expected.

Telecommunications

The rapid improvement of telecommunications in the last two decades has been helpful to both types of distance education: correspondence study and remote-classroom teaching. Moreover, the pace of telecommunications developments continues to increase as services are privatized and deregulated around the world (Cairncross, 1995). It appears that some developing countries will be able to leapfrog previous generations of telecommunications technology and equip themselves with modern systems in the next decade. As Cairncross (1995: 39) puts it: 'The death of distance will mean that any activity that relies on a screen or a telephone can be carried out anywhere in the world'.

In the correspondence mode of distance education the main impact of telecommunications has been to enhance tutorial contact with students. For example, at Athabasca University, Alberta, which has enjoyed a rich telecommunications environment since its creation in the 1970s, the telephone has always been a primary means of communication between tutors and students. The University pays for the installation and rental of a second telephone in the tutor's dwelling for this purpose (Daniel & Meech, 1978: 95). Daniel and Turok (1975: 133) noted that in the early 1970s the DeVry Institute, a large American commercial correspondence school, received some 2,000 student calls per day on its toll-free telephone line.

Countries like the UK, where telephone ownership and a telephone culture have developed more slowly, are only now beginning to use telecommunications intensively. UKOU students, for example, are steadily switching to the telephone, instead of the mail, for their administrative communications with the institution. This poses a challenge to an institution which finds that it is better organized for handling letters than telephone calls (Edwards *et al.*, 1995).

Another important product of telecommunications development is the fax machine. This allows institutions to speed up the turn-round of student assignments, a core element of the effectiveness of any teaching system. The UKOU provides fax machines for the homes of its UK-based tutors who teach students in continental Europe. In the Los Angeles Community College District more than one-third of telecourse students submit their assignments by fax (McClatchey, 1995: 124).

In addition to its use for one-to-one communication the telephone is now used regularly in conference mode to link students in tutorial groups. Again, such audio teleconference tutorials have been commonplace in Canada for years. Only in the last decade has the UKOU made systematic use of this technology, notably for its more dispersed students in Wales and Scotland (George, 1994).

Improved telecommunications have been helpful to institutions operating in the correspondence mode. For the remote-classroom mode of distance education they have been essential. Indeed, until telecommunications promoted its renaissance, the theorists of distance education tended to ignore this component of the field. Keegan's (1980) definition of distance education included only 'the possibility of occasional meetings for didactic and socialisation purposes'. Yet, for example, Taylor and Carter (1995), in a survey of the diverse distance education scene in Australia, report that institutions in several states now use audio conferencing and video conferencing regularly with remote groups of students.

These technologies are particularly attractive to campus universities seeking to develop distance education activity. Classroom instructors believe they can adapt relatively easily to the demands of teaching over audio or video links. As the costs of telecommunications decline, remote classroom teaching will be an increasingly viable option even where numbers are small. Furthermore, desktop publishing makes it easy to produce attractive instructional materials to supplement the teleconference sessions.

These technological changes contribute to an important trend documented by Jenkins (1995). Surveying the OECD countries she showed that there has been a 'rapid, recent and substantial change in numbers of universities providing distance education'. In Canada, where 42 of 69 universities are now providers, this represents a 50% increase in eight years. The proportions of universities offering distance courses in some other OECD countries are: France: 40%; Sweden: almost all; UK: 75%; USA: almost all (Jenkins, 1995: 427). Any monopoly that the mega-universities may once have had in distance education is now gone.

The knowledge media

Institutions offering any form of distance education now face a further wave of technological change. The coming together of telecommunications, television and computing is producing a media environment for distance education that is more than the sum of its component elements. Eisenstadt (1995) describes this environment as the knowledge media. It denotes the convergence of the learning and cognitive sciences with computing and telecommunications technology. Behind this new term is the belief that with the 'knowledge media' the conventional, rather static, notion of 'content' will become less important than the dynamic means of accessing, sharing and creating knowledge that are now available. By providing a medium for conversation, a delivery mechanism and a means of circulating digital objects, the knowledge media honour both the community and conversational paradigms that are central to the idea of a university (Brown & Duguid, 1995). The implications of the knowledge media will be examined in a later chapter.

Synopsis

Reviewing the use of technology in distance education leads to the following conclusions:

- Correspondence education is a robust and effective form of instruction.
- Universities that use broadcasting have to make trade-offs between multiple objectives.
- The acquisition of equipment by students is a key factor in the introduction of new technology for home study.
- Technologies that are popular with students, academics and administrators are likely to be successful.
- Students are increasingly turning to telecommunications for communication with their institutions on academic and administrative matters.
- Video conferencing technology is attracting conventional institutions to offer distance education of the remote-classroom type.
- Technological developments have reduced the entry barriers to distance education so that economies of scale are no longer always a prerequisite.

Pedagogy

As distance education has evolved, so have the roles of student, teacher and institution in the teaching system. We noted above that as recently as 1980 distance education was defined primarily in terms of the correspondence tradition (Keegan, 1980). In view of the increasing importance of remote-classroom approaches, Moore's earlier and simpler definition is now more inclusive: according to Moore (1973), distance education is the 'family of instructional methods in which the teaching behaviours are executed apart from the learning behaviours'.

In reality, distance education no longer has a distinct and common pedagogy. The pedagogy of synchronous remote-classroom teaching resembles the pedagogy of classroom teaching more than it resembles the pedagogy of asynchronous correspondence teaching. With one exception (China) the mega-universities all derive from the correspondence tradition of distance education.

Correspondence education

The aim of correspondence education is to create a genuinely student-centred learning system. It is to deliver, at a place and time chosen by the student, an effective learning environment. This involves providing the student with study materials and helping the student to learn by correcting and commenting on the student's exercises. Correspondence education is thus a blend of independent and interactive activities (Daniel & Marquis, 1979). The student works independently on the course materials (reading, writing, conducting experiments, viewing audio-visual material) but inter-actively with a tutor on the assignments and, possibly, with other students at group meetings.

A key strength of correspondence study is its flexibility for both student and institution. The course materials are portable and, because the student relates to the institution as an individual, communicating by mail and/or telephone, there are few constraints of time and place. For the institution the system is flexible in two related ways. It permits a division of labour (eg, course authors and course tutors can be different people) and it can be expanded rapidly with economies of scale. Economies of scale give corre-spondence education another strength: operating with large numbers of students provides the resources needed to produce high quality learning materials. This is a key competitive advantage of the mega-universities.

The major perceived weakness of correspondence education is the extent and immediacy of interaction. In the context of the technologies of the 1970s, Daniel and Marquis (1979) noted that attempts to increase the interactive component of correspondence teaching (eg, through face to face tutorial sessions) usually had two potential drawbacks: they reduced the possibilities of economies of scale and they placed extra constraints of time and place on the student. For this reason these authors considered that the key challenge in designing a correspondence study system was 'getting the mixture' of independent and interactive activities right.

Some years later Daniel (1983) returned to this theme to ask whether some of the home electronic systems of the 1980s could produce the advantages of effective interaction for the student while conserving the economic structure of independent activities for the institution. This ques-tion will be of even greater significance with the knowledge media. Interac-tion is a crucial but slippery concept in distance education. As Mason (1994: 25) wrote:

'The word "interactivity" is currently used in a wide variety of ways. The obvious meaning – communication between two or more people – is by no means the only one.... Much of what passes for interactivity should really be called "feedback" – to the organization or the teacher. It would be useful if the word "interactivity" were reserved for educational situations in which human responses – either vocal or written – referred to previous human responses. The educational value of any specific interactive session could then be seen in terms of the degree to which each utterance built on previous ones.'

More recently Bates has made a helpful distinction between individual and social interaction:

'there are two rather different contexts for interaction: the first is an individual, isolated activity, which is the interaction of the learner with the learning material, be it text, television or computer programme; the second is a social activity, which is the interaction between two or more people about the learning material. Both kinds of interaction are important in learning.' (Bates, 1995: 52)

A key issue is the cost-effectiveness of the means used to create contexts for interaction. The conclusion of the Daniel/Marquis analysis was that it is usually costly to have to compensate, by providing more social interaction, for learning materials that are poor at generating individual interaction with the learner. Social interaction, whether it be with the originator of the learning material, a tutor, or other learners, is important in its own right, but more expensive to provide.

Remote-classroom teaching

The characteristic strengths and weaknesses of remote classroom distance education are almost the reverse of those identified for correspondence education. This is a teacher-centred approach to distance education in the sense that it takes classroom teaching as its starting point and attempts to make it possible for a teacher to instruct a number of classes simultaneously. The communications networks used to link the classrooms can be more or less sophisticated, the most common variants being:

- audio teleconferencing;
- audio teleconferencing with a second audio network used to transmit graphics (eg, on electronic whiteboards);
- slow scan television to deliver the instructor's image and voice with a separate audio network for use by students asking questions;
- video conferencing with separate audio lines for questions;
- multi-point video-conferencing.

In all of these configurations the role of the students more closely resembles their role in a single conventional classroom than in a correspondence study system. To achieve success and student satisfaction, however, remote-classroom systems have found it necessary to modify conventional classroom practices. For the teacher this means special training in the use of the equipment and attention to instructional design, especially techniques for making remote oral interaction effective. For the student it means having access to more and better written study materials than would usually be provided for a classroom lecture on campus. Hence remote-classroom distance education leads its practitioners to adopt, in a modest way, some of the approaches characteristic of correspondence teaching.

The strength of the remote-classroom approach is its potential for inter-action between student and teacher and between students. Whether this potential is achieved, and whether the interaction is pedagogically effective when achieved, depends greatly on the skills of the instructor. Special techniques are required to make interaction effective in a face-to-face teaching session involving more than, say, 100 students in one classroom. They are even more necessary when such numbers are dispersed in multiple sites.

On the criterion of flexibility, remote-classroom systems have a strength and a weakness. The strength is that instructors can update content easily, as they would for a regular class. The weakness is that students are still constrained by obligations of attendance at a set time and place, even though their local remote classroom may be more convenient than the central campus.

Flexible learning

As conventional institutions adopt various techniques of distance teaching, some are using the term 'flexible learning' also called 'multi-channel learning' (Anzalone *et al.*, 1995), to describe their activity. The aim is to augment or replace conventional classroom activities with a range of technologies such as interactive multimedia, computer-mediated conferencing, and e-mail. The strengths of this approach are flexibility and interactivity. A weakness, according to Taylor (1995), is that it does not yield refined study materials. The role of specially prepared materials is, of course, a matter of controversy. For example, Bell and Tight (1993: 3) argue that such materials are not essential and that authors such as Lewis (1990) place too much emphasis on this component of distance education.

The adoption of distance education by campus universities should en-courage universities dedicated solely to distance learning to assess their competitive advantages. By emphasizing that distance education is simply a component of the wider enterprise of education and training, this develop-ment also counters the tendency to claim that distance education is a separate academic discipline (eg, Holmberg, 1986). Attempts to define distance education in a distinctive way have led to 'idealization and unreality' (Bell & Tight, 1993: 6) and, in any case, have tended not to accommodate the growing activity of remote-classroom distance education.

As many conventional universities become dual-mode institutions and offer some courses through distance education, the mega-universities will need to understand what special strengths they bring to the form of education that they have pioneered.

Synopsis

Key features of the pedagogy of distance education are:

- 'In traditional education a teacher teaches. In distance education an institution teaches. This is a radical difference' (Keegan, 1980: 9).
- The correspondence tradition of distance education is student-centred and based mainly on asynchronous communication and interaction.
- The remote-classroom approach to distance education is teacher-centred and based mainly on synchronous communication and interaction.
- The term 'interaction' is not used in a consistent manner in distance education.
- The knowledge media may bring the correspondence and remote-class-room traditions of distance education together.

Economy

Bringing down the costs of education and training has usually been an aim of distance learning systems. That is their relevance to the search for a more cost-effective model of mass higher education for the 21st century. The mega-universities are of particular interest because they have already achieved impressive cost advantages over traditional teaching methods. Whether the knowledge media will make small-scale distance education less costly than classroom instruction is one of the most important questions for the future of higher education.

Cost structures

Over 20 years ago Wedemeyer (1974) expressed the economic expectations of distance education systems as follows:

> 'As an operating principle, the system is capable, after reaching a critical minimum of aggregation, of accommodating increased numbers of learners without a *commensurate* increase in the unit cost of the basic learning experiences: i.e. costs must not be directly and rigidly volume sensitive. After reaching the necessary level of aggregation, unit costs should show a diminishing relationship to total systems costs.'

In making this statement Wedemeyer had in mind distance education systems in the correspondence tradition. The economics of remote classroom instruction are different. Whether that approach is cost-effective at large volumes is another important question. The analysis of China's Television University system in the Appendix provides some pointers.

Wedemeyer's description of the economics of distance education is another way of saying that this is an industrialized form of education where the ratio of fixed costs to variable costs is much higher than in pre-industrial production by craft work. A car factory is a good analogy. The marginal cost of producing an extra car is tiny compared to the investment in design, development and tooling required for each new model.

For example, Wagner (1977) claimed that in 1976 the ratio of fixed cost to variable cost per student was about 2000:1 in the UK Open University compared to 8:1 in conventional universities. The implication of these figures, which is central to the industrial approach in general, is that distance education is less costly than classroom teaching where the numbers studying a particular topic are large. The vital question is, how large?

As an increasing number of universities offer courses at a distance they will want to know the values of two key economic measures of their activity. The first is Wedemeyer's 'critical minimum of aggregation' after which unit costs begin to drop. This corresponds to point A in Figure 4.1, which shows in a highly schematic way the variation of unit costs with student numbers in distance learning systems.

The second figure of interest is the enrolment level beyond which the cost of teaching students at a distance is less than the cost of teaching them in conventional ways. This is point B in Figure 4.2, which is another purely schematic representation comparing the growth of total institutional costs with student numbers for distance learning systems and traditional methods.

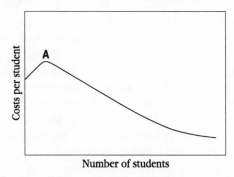

Figure 4.1 *Schematic representation of the variation of cost per student with student numbers*

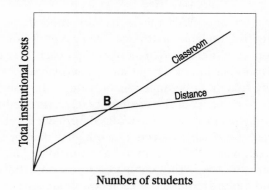

Figure 4.2 *Schematic representation of the growth in total institutional costs with student numbers for distance learning and classroom teaching*

Cost comparisons depend crucially on the assumptions made. The early polemics on the costs of distance education (Mace, 1978; Wagner, 1973; 1977) duly explored the merits of calculating output as full-time students, graduates or some measure of value added. Wagner (1977) showed that the average annual recurrent cost per full-time undergraduate at the UKOU was less than one-third the cost at a campus university, and the cost of a UKOU graduate was less than half. Nearly two decades later, Peters and Daniel (1994), using a different type of analysis, showed that cost comparisons were still strongly in favour of the UKOU.

The data presented in Table 3.2 (p.31) show that all 11 mega-universities are more cost-effective than the campus universities in their jurisdictions on normal measures of output. The more interesting questions, therefore, concern distance education on a smaller scale. Snowden and Daniel (1980) examined the case of Athabasca University and found that with 2,000 full-time-equivalent (FTE) students (8,000 course enrolments) its costs were within the range set by comparable programmes at Alberta's three conventional universities. Marrec (1995) reported that Québec's Télé-université, with nearly 2,200 FTE students, had slightly higher costs than the province's campus universities. Yaari (1996) calculated that the Open University of Israel, with 10,000 FTE students, taught twice as cost-effectively as one of the country's large conventional universities.

The key point behind such comparisons, however, is that as Wagner (1977) stated, it is possible to make a distance teaching system 'as expensive or as cheap as the planners wish'. It is natural that those operating such systems set themselves an appropriate cost target for their particular environment and aim to hit it. The key economic variables they can manipulate for this purpose are the media used, the number of courses, the cost of producing and maintaining those courses, the number of students, and the extent of tutorial support.

Wagner expressed the total cost equation for the UKOU in the simple form:

$$C = a + bx + cy$$

where:
C = total cost;
a = fixed costs;
x = number of courses;
y = number of students;
and b, c are constants.

For Athabasca University, Snowden and Daniel (1980) derived a slightly more differentiated total cost equation:

$$C = a_1x_1 + a_2x_2 + by + c$$

where:
C = total cost;
a_1 = course development costs per credit;
x_1 = course credits in development;
a_2 = course revision/maintenance/replacement costs per credit;
x_2 = course credits in delivery;
b = delivery costs per course enrolment;
y = course enrolments;
c = institutional overheads.

Such equations emphasize the importance of achieving a good balance between independent and interactive learning activities. For a given set of courses the most direct way to reduce the marginal costs per additional student is to cut delivery costs, which usually consist largely of interactive tutorial services. However, since such services may help to make the institution attractive to students, a better approach may be to offer fewer courses and/or to spend less on developing and maintaining them.

The arrival of the knowledge media gives new topicality to the distinction between course development and maintenance costs in the Snowden/Daniel equation. Many assume that these media will change the nature of course production. Instead of investing heavily in the first version of a course and then allowing it to run with only minor revisions for a number of years, people envisage cheaper initial development and more extensive revisions between annual offerings. Only experience will show whether this will cut total costs. The wider point is that costs per student change with student numbers in quite different ways for the various media now available. Figure 4.3, derived from Bates (1995), brings together data for a range of current technologies.

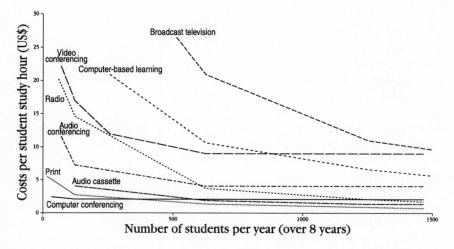

Figure 4.3 *Variation of per student costs with student numbers for distance teaching technologies*

Since Bates did his costings technological development has taken another important turn with the emergence of the Internet as the new computing platform. It now appears that the use of Java language applets in distance education could reduce costs to students significantly. The key economic point is that Internet software is the ultimate example of an industry where manufacturing and distribution cost virtually nothing – all the costs are in design. The usual industrial law of diminishing returns, as size breeds inefficiency, may no longer apply.

Working with a widening range of learning technologies with very different cost structures will be a challenge to all universities offering distance education or technology-based teaching. Making rational trade-offs within a technology strategy requires evidence about the instructional effectiveness of different media. Such evidence will also help institutions make use of one sure-fire method for reducing costs, which is to buy courses ready-made from other institutions instead of developing them in-house.

Synopsis

The economy of distance learning systems displays these features:

- Correspondence education has a higher ratio of fixed to variable costs than traditional teaching. In this respect it resembles industrial production.
- Large distance education systems (eg, the mega-universities) are more cost-effective than traditional teaching methods.
- For given production inputs, distance education allows a greater variety of outputs than traditional methods.
- Key variables determining the total cost of a distance education system are: number of students; number of courses; cost of course development (eg, richness of media mix); cost of course maintenance; and cost of delivery (eg, extent of tutorial support).

New technologies breed new questions:

- If new technologies lead the mega-universities to redistribute investment between initial course development and more frequent revisions later, will this improve cost-effectiveness?
- Can remote-classroom teaching bring significant improvements to the cost-effectiveness of higher education?
- As we noted in Chapter 3, distance teaching materials based on the knowledge media (eg, CD-ROM) require more academic development time than earlier technologies (eg, teaching text, audio-vision). Will there be a commensurate improvement in cost-effectiveness?

Summary

This chapter has reviewed the essentials of distance education through its two main traditions of remote-classroom teaching and correspondence study. Distance education, which relies on the use of various technologies, has introduced the notion of the division of labour into the teaching process. We traced the evolution of the use of technology through correspondence tuition, the mass media of broadcasting, the personal media, telecommunications and the knowledge media. There is no common pedagogy of distance education because the tasks undertaken by teachers are very different in each of its two traditions. However, there is now some convergence between these traditions, giving rise to the concept of flexible learning. This development will affect the economics of distance education. Simple notions of economies of scale in distance education are no longer always valid because unit costs vary with student numbers in different ways for the technologies available now and on the horizon.

Chapter 5

Universities and Competitive Advantage

Renewal and competition

In Chapter 1 we identified some of the pressures that are leading universities all over the world to develop an agenda for renewal. Subsequent chapters examined the particular forces for change in campus universities and in the distance teaching mega-universities. Many universities now see new technologies, both systems and hardware, as an important part of their strategy for change. In particular, recent technological developments appear to make elements of the approach to teaching and learning known as 'distance education', described in the previous chapter, particularly appropriate.

Fundamentally, the drive for renewal is the desire of all universities to maintain or enhance their competitive advantage. All operate in a changing competitive environment where not only other universities, but a congeries of disparate organizations, undertake activities that span the spectrum of teaching, research and service to the community that is the mission of higher education. To develop appropriate strategies for this environment it is helpful to understand more clearly the elements of competitive advantage.

Porter (1980; 1985) has provided a general framework for analysing the dynamics of competitive advantage in organizations. A strength of his work is that it helps to bridge the gap between strategy formulation and implementation. Universities are complex organizations. They must be able to translate their overall competitive strategies into the specific action steps needed to gain competitive advantage. It is instructive to review higher education within Porter's framework.

Most universities are non-profit bodies in the public sector. However, the notions of competitive advantage and superior performance are as real for them as for firms in the private sector. Indeed, many of them now depend more on student fees and other income than on funds from the state. For this reason we shall often use Porter's terms (eg, buyer, industry, profitability, firm) rather than the more euphemistic language of the public sector.

Although our concern is the competitive advantage of universities as total organizations, we shall focus particularly on issues related to the use of technology for distance education. Interest in this mode of learning now unites most of higher education, so the concerns of campus institutions and the mega-universities are converging. In examining the role of technology in competitive advantage the mega-universities are especially interesting because of their prior experience of the strengths and weaknesses of technology in distance education. These mega-universities also worry about their future competitiveness.

A decade ago Daniel (1984) reviewed the future of distance teaching universities in an international perspective and identified some emerging challenges to their continued success. Rumble (1992) expressed concern over the 'competitive vulnerability' of these institutions as many campus universities began to teach at a distance. Keegan (1994a) responded to Rumble with a summary of the competitive advantages of the distance teaching universities and stressed that size was a key factor in their competitiveness. Will size continue to be such an asset if the mega-universities adopt a new generation of teaching technologies?

Competitive advantage: key concepts

The competitive advantage of an organization grows out of the value that it creates for its buyers, either in terms of low prices or unique benefits. The successful organization is able to capture some of the value it creates for its buyers, thus remaining profitable. Competitive strategy is the search for a favourable position within an industry on these criteria. We make the assumption that the key industry for most universities is the education and training sector of their home countries. It is no longer appropriate to consider distance education as a distinct industry and probably never was. Governments fund it alongside other forms of teaching and students increasingly move between campus and distance modes, gaining equivalent qualifications.

An important consideration for higher education institutions in the state sector is that they serve two types of buyers: the government and the student (sometimes including the student's employer). The relative financial importance of these two buyers varies widely between universities around the world. Governments are now minority providers of funds for most of the mega-universities and for many campus universities in the USA. Nevertheless, it is important to give value to the state buyer. If a government thinks that its universities are not adding value to the community it can make their life difficult in various ways.

We address the issue of value to the buyer more fully later. Suffice it for now to note that the two principal buyers, student and state, may judge value in somewhat different ways. Furthermore a state's funding mechanisms may not be entirely consistent with its declared criteria for value. For example, the system of state funding for UK universities encourages them to be low-cost providers but not the lowest-cost provider (Daniel *et al.*, 1994: 17).

The state's role is an instance of Porter's fundamental principle that the competitiveness of an organization depends as much on the structure of its industry as on its own attributes. The five competitive forces that determine industry profitability are:

- the bargaining power of buyers;
- the bargaining power of suppliers;
- the threat of new entrants;
- the threat of substitute products and services;
- rivalry among existing firms.

The structure of the education and training industry has changed considerably in recent decades. For the growth of distance education four important favourable trends have been:

- growth in demand from working adults for part-time education;
- readiness of governments to invest in education;
- development of communication media, both mass media and personal electronic devices;
- availability of computing systems to support complex logistics.

Other trends have created a more competitive industry:

- growing numbers of universities offer part-time and distance courses;

- business and industry have expanded in-house training schemes;
- government funding formulae encourage competition between institutions.

Judgements about the overall attractiveness of the education and training industry must still be made on a country-by-country basis. Universities, both individually and also collectively through their national organizations, try hard to influence the structure of their industry – with mixed success.

Within its industry an organization can seek competitive advantage in two ways: cost leadership and differentiation. To be a low-cost provider an organization must exploit all sources of cost advantage. That often means offering standard products without frills. Seeking advantage through differentiation means finding a niche in the industry where the organization can offer something unique that buyers will value. Bowman and Asch (1996: 41) call this 'perceived use value'.

A third generic strategy for competitive advantage is focus. This can be either a focus on cost advantage or a focus on differentiation in a particular target segment of the industry. Both variants depend on differences between the target segment and other segments of the industry. This may mean buyers with unusual needs or special requirements for production or service delivery.

The success of the mega-universities

This analysis helps to explain the competitive success quickly achieved by some of the mega-universities. Most were built on a strategy of differentiation focus. Their purpose was to serve a limited segment of the clientele for higher education, namely adults who wished to study without leaving their work and places of residence. This strategy had two benefits. First, it proved to be a rapidly growing clientele. Second, to serve these people the mega-universities developed techniques of distance education derived from the remote-classroom tradition (in China) and the correspondence tradition (elsewhere). These techniques yielded economies of scale. The result today is that within their national higher education systems the mega-universities have the competitive advantages of both differentiation and cost leadership.

Interestingly, both strategic ambitions were held by politicians when the UK Open University was set up. Harold Wilson, who launched the idea, wanted to increase access to higher education for working adults (differentiation). Margaret Thatcher, who saved the infant institution when her political colleagues might have strangled it, wanted to use it to reduce the costs of higher education (cost leadership).

Combining cost leadership and differentiation gives an unusual degree of competitive advantage, creating an unstable situation that may not last. According to Porter (1985: 19) there are three conditions under which such a favourable situation occurs.

1. *Competitors are 'stuck in the middle' without a clear strategy.* This may be true of campus universities that 'differentiate' into part-time or distance education without much attention to costs or logistics. For example, many campus universities find it difficult, because of timetabling difficulties, to integrate full- and part-time students in classroom courses. Such integration could be easier with technology-based learning methods which may, therefore, enable such universities to develop clearer generic strategies.

2. *Cost is strongly affected by market share or relationships.* It is easy for mega-universities to take for granted the economies of scale derived from large market share that give them their cost advantage. Three trends threaten that advantage: updating courses more often as subjects change more rapidly; offering more courses (with fewer students per course) as students' interests diversify; and using a more expensive mix of media as new devices become fashionable. Important interrelationships (for example that between Universitas Terbuka and the Indonesian post office) also contain lessons. Universities should be looking to establish partnerships with potentially important future suppliers before competitors get in first. France's CNED has done this through its association with the telematic town of Futuroscope. Korea's KNOU has acquired its own cable channel. Many campus universities have privileged relationships with high-technology companies.

3. *An organization pioneers a major innovation.* The mega-universities did introduce a major innovation that gave lower costs and differentiation at the same time. However, the ideas of distance education are simple and easy to communicate. Even if they were not, the mega-universities have facilitated the transfer of know-how by hiring tens of thousands of their campus competitors' staff as part-time academics. However, fortunately for the continuing competitiveness of the mega-universities, it is still easier to design a large distance education system than to implement it effectively. Twenty years ago the technologies required to produce multimedia course materials were barriers to new entrants. Today, desktop publishing and cheap video equipment have lowered this barrier. The logistical challenges of providing tutorial support to large numbers of students and assessing their work remain more of a barrier.

Implications

The implications for the mega-universities are that they must pursue all cost-reduction opportunities that do not sacrifice valuable differentiation, and all differentiation opportunities that are not costly. They must present a moving target to competitors by investing continually to improve their position. For the mega-universities to continue to achieve competitive advantage by combining cost leadership and differentiation may create internal tensions. The qualities that help an organization maintain cost leadership are frugality, discipline, tight controls, minimal overheads, economies of scale, attention to detail and dedication to the learning curve. These may not sit well with the qualities that foster differentiation such as creativity, innovation, individuality and risk-taking. Sustaining both cultures within their organizations is a challenge for the leaders of the mega-universities.

For campus universities the balance of effort would probably be rather different. Cost reduction is unlikely to be a successful strategy, at least in the short term, because existing campus infrastructures still have to be paid for. However, these universities have ample opportunities for differentiation because their key strength is the variety of academic staff on whom they can call. Furthermore, reputable campus universities start with the tradition of a strong relationship with their alumni as well as with their local and national communities. They must, however, be alert to a potential danger. For traditionalists, exclusivity and quality go together. If alumni value their degrees partly for their rarity as positional goods they may not appreciate seeing their *alma mater* use technology to become a mass-teaching university. They will not want 'their' brand name diluted.

Blurring the institution's generic strategy is not the way to rise to the challenge of competition. Porter (1985: 25) insists that the organization's generic strategy must be at the heart of its strategic plan. Industry leadership is the effect, not the cause, of competitive advantage. Sustaining competitive advantage means choosing a successful generic strategy.

The tensions generated by pursuing cost leadership and differentiation will be strongly felt by universities as they try to apply new technologies in support of these strategies. Effective use of information systems and technology for logistics will require the qualities that support cost leadership. Taking the lead in applying the knowledge media for teaching and learning will require the innovating qualities that create differentiation. The people with these different skills must work in tandem, just as the equipment and software for both logistics and learning should appear seamless across the institution.

The value chain

Competitive advantage cannot be determined by taking an holistic view of the organization. A firm's performance is the result of many separate activities, each of which can contribute to its relative cost position or be the basis of differentiation. Porter (1985: 33) has coined the term 'value chain' to describe the disaggregation of an organization into its strategically relevant activities. Value chains for firms in the same industry may differ in competitive scope. This is the case for the mega-universities, which deploy their human, financial and physical resources differently from campus universities and have achieved competitive advantage by doing so. In examining the value chains of universities we shall concentrate first on the ten mega-universities that have developed from the correspondence tradition.

There is a generic value chain for all firms that is represented in Figure 5.1 (p.76). Porter distinguishes five primary value activities: inbound logistics; operations; outbound logistics; marketing and sales; and service. There are also four support value activities: procurement; technology development; human resource management; and firm infrastructure.

In attempting to construct a value chain for the mega-universities we have used data for the UK Open University. The breakdown of the UKOU's work into value activities would have much in common with a similar analysis of the nine other correspondence-based mega-universities. There would, however, be some variations in the activities included (eg, France's CNED does not tutor or examine most of its students).

Until recently such a representation of the institution would have been difficult to achieve because the notion of activities, as distinct from organizational units, was poorly developed. A change in its funding regime in 1993 obliged the UKOU to calculate the costs of its activities more directly (Peters & Daniel, 1994). Table 5.1 breaks down the operation of the UKOU into 40 activities (within the four main functions of teaching, research, institutional management and student support) and lists their associated costs as percentages of total costs. It also shows the staff (full-time) and non-staff costs for each activity as a percentage of the total costs in these categories.

Another strand of this work was developed by Bowen (1994) whose aim was to bring business strategy and academic strategy together. In this connection he juxtaposed Porter's value activities with the Open University Strategic Plan (Open University, 1994a) in what he called a 'fishbones' analysis in order to determine where the application of technology would have the most useful effects.

Table 5.1 *Breakdown of costs by activity for the UK Open University (1991)*

Activity	Percentage of costs		
	Staff	Non-staff	Total
Curriculum planning	1	0	1
Planning new teaching systems	1	0	0
Academic quality control	1	0	1
Course production – undergraduate	8	1	4
Course production – higher degrees	1	1	1
Course production – non-degree	1	1	1
Course production – support	13	25	20
New student systems	0	0	0
Learning materials distribution	2	3	2
Tuition and counselling	3	10	7
Tuition and counselling staff management	4	2	3
Residential schools	6	13	10
Continuous assessment	4	8	6
Examinations	3	2	2
Sub-total teaching	**48**	**66**	**58**
Develop research plans	1	0	0
Pursue research opportunities	0	0	0
Research – institutional and teaching development	4	1	2
Research – non-teaching related	7	2	4
Research – support	3	2	2
Sub-total research	**15**	**5**	**9**
Prepare institutional development strategies	1	0	1
Public relations, general promotion, etc	2	1	1
Develop marketing plans	0	0	0
Secure funding (government, etc)	0	0	0
Staffing plans and policy development	1	1	1
Governance and committee support	1	1	1
Physical infrastructure	4	12	8
Budgetary management, etc	4	1	2
Purchasing activity	1	0	0
Audit activities and procedure	0	0	0
Produce management information	2	0	1
Staff recruitment and management	4	1	2
Market and promote courses	2	2	2
Market and sell to non-registered students	1	0	1
Develop and maintain major systems	2	1	1
External income-generating projects	1	0	0
Sub-total institutional management	**26**	**20**	**23**
Student systems policy and plans	1	0	1
Student registration, etc	3	2	2
Information, advice, support to customers	4	4	4
Collect fees	1	0	0
Award financial assistance	0	2	1
Award accreditation	1	1	1
Sub-total student support	**10**	**9**	**10**
External duties	1	0	0
Grand total	**100**	**100**	**100**
Overall breakdown	**43**	**57**	**100**

However, allocating the UKOU activities in Table 5.1 to the nine categories in Porter's generic value chain did not produce a very discriminating analysis. Nearly half the activities, as measured by cost, fell into the category of 'operations'. We therefore developed a generic value chain that fits the mega-universities better. It is based on the functional analysis of the UKOU produced by the Scoping Study Team charged with laying down the structure of the University's information systems strategy (Open University, 1993). This combines the breakdown of activities with an analysis of information flows. It serves to highlight the linkages between activities that provide further levers for competitive advantage (Porter, 1985: 75).

From this analysis we included three types of support activities in the generic value chain:

- direct, plan and manage the institution;
- provide institutional infrastructure services;
- human resource management.

For the primary activities we took the five other functions identified by the Scoping Study Team, namely:

- carry out research;
- develop educational materials, courses and programmes;
- provide educational services logistics;
- carry out marketing and sales;
- provide educational services.

The resultant generic value chain for the mega-universities is represented in Figure 5.2. Distributing the activities listed in Table 5.1 between the primary and support activities in this value chain is straightforward. This makes it easy to see how the UKOU's spending is divided between the different value activities. We present the results in Figure 5.3 using Porter's method of presentation. The area of each horizontal or vertical bar (for support and primary activities respectively) in relation to the area of the whole diagram represents the costs of those activities as a proportion of the UKOU's 1991 budget. Each activity is further broken down into staff costs (full-time) and non-staff costs.

For comparison, Figure 5.4 attempts a similar analysis for a campus-based research university. We cited the example of the University of Utah in Chapter 2, and Figure 5.4 is derived from its expenditure data (University of Utah, 1995a) which was presented following the guidelines of the National Association of College and University Business Officers. We noted earlier that the primary value activities of mega-universities do not correspond neatly to the primary activity categories of Porter's generic value chain. The same is true for campus universities where, for example, the notion of inbound and outbound logistics is less salient than for a manufacturing firm. Figure 5.4 therefore splits the primary value activities of the University of Utah into five categories that match the realities of its institutional mission.

The most important contrast between Figures 5.3 and 5.4 is the volume of ancillary activity conducted by campus-based research universities in addition

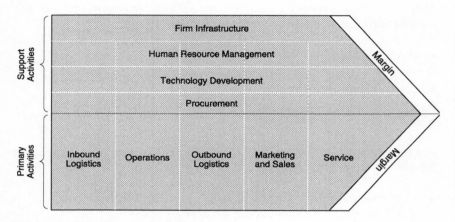

Figure 5.1 *Porter's generic value chain*

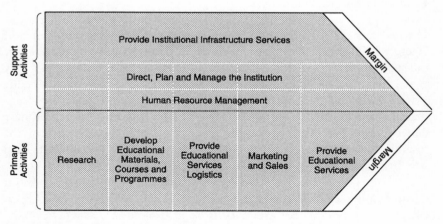

Figure 5.2 *A generic value chain for the mega-universities*

to their core mission of teaching and research. This means that such universities must retain competitive advantage across a much wider range of endeavours than, say, the mega-universities, which are too young to have developed extensive ancillary services to the community outside their core activities. Some of the ancillary activities of campus universities could, of course, be outsourced. This provides an incentive to demonstrate regularly that the university gains competitive advantage by running them itself.

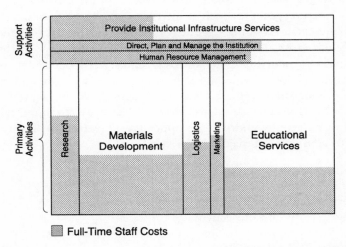

Figure 5.3 *Breakdown by total cost with each activity category divided into staff and non-staff cost (UKOU 1991 budget)*

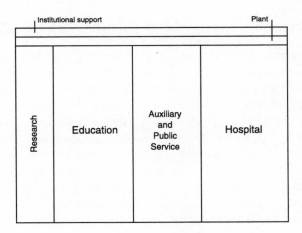

Figure 5.4 *Breakdown by total cost in activity categories (University of Utah, 1995a)*

The value chain and cost advantage

The value chain is the basic tool for pursuing cost advantage. Indeed, cost analysis is also important for differentiation, which tends to raise costs and will not yield the desired value for the buyer unless these are controlled. The approach is to analyse the costs of each value activity within the categories shown in the value chain, concentrating on the most costly activities and those whose costs are increasing most rapidly. For the UKOU, Figure 5.3 provides a starting point for such an analysis. Comparing this diagram with similar representations of the value activities for lower-cost mega-universities such as South Africa's UNISA and Spain's UNED would show clearly where the UKOU was incurring its higher costs. Similarly, the pattern of teaching, research and service activities at other campus universities would differ in detail from the pattern at the University of Utah shown in Figure 5.4.

Cost behaviour depends on cost drivers. These are structural causes of the cost of an activity and may be under the university's control. Porter (1985: 70) identifies ten major cost drivers:

- economies or diseconomies of scale;
- learning;
- pattern of capacity utilization;
- linkages (between value activities);
- interrelationships (eg, sharing value activities across units);
- integration (in-sourcing);
- timing;
- discretionary policies;
- location;
- institutional factors (eg, regulations, staffing structures).

Comments on three of these will serve as examples. First, the mega-universities claim to benefit from 'economies of scale'. While this may be true of their operations as a whole, all are likely to have some value activities that show diseconomies of scale. Second, 'discretionary policies' are determined, in most universities, by diffuse and participative decision-making processes. It is easy for such processes to promulgate policies, in the name of quality, that raise costs more than they raise the value to the buyer. Third, the most ancient campus universities in each country created an image for the traditional academic community with the 'timing' of their entry to the market as first movers. Similarly, the mega-universities established a brand name for distance education at lower cost than later competitors.

Often several cost drivers operate within a particular activity. From this it follows that an organization can gain a cost advantage in two ways: by controlling cost drivers and by reconfiguring the value chain, which is now known as re-engineering (Hammer & Champy, 1993). Having identified a potential route to cost advantage, it should be tested for sustainability. There should also be a check that any erosion of differentiation that goes with the cost advantage is acceptable.

The value chain and differentiation

Like cost advantage, differentiation can occur in any value activity in the value chain. The most important type of differentiation is that which buyers value. The tendency for differentiation to increase costs must be watched. By analogy with cost drivers, Porter (1985: 124) has identified drivers of uniqueness. These are:

- policy choices (eg, the UKOU's elimination of prerequisites);
- linkages (eg, using the Internet to link student and university activities);
- timing (eg, CNED's image in France as a video conference pioneer);
- location (eg, cities attractive to international students);
- interrelationships (eg, links with telecommunications providers);
- learning and spillovers (eg, strength in mathematics spilling over into computing science);
- integration (eg, in computer systems);
- scale (eg, a large university may be able to field a better football team);
- institutional factors (eg, a relationship with a union that allows a university to recast job descriptions in helpful ways).

As universities make choices about differentiating through technology the question of what is valuable to the buyer will be fundamental. All universities aim to create competitive advantage for the buyer through their courses. As media evolve, first the distance teaching universities and then campus institutions will expect their students to acquire various technological devices for use at home (eg, video cassette recorders, computers, modems, set-top boxes) so that they can take advantage of the new possibilities. Ideally the student will see the use of this home equipment for coursework as a way of getting more value from the purchase and not as an imposition. The next chapter draws on the experience of marketing high technology products to identify factors that make technology purchases attractive to students.

Differentiation is an area where buyers' perceptions of value are crucial. The signals that an institution sends to buyers through its reputation, its image and the appearance of its product should reflect this. Some universities are now signalling their intention to lead in the application of new technologies to higher education. One key category of their buyers, namely their governments, seem pleased with this development. The same may be true of their students. However, the costs that technology-rich teaching strategies could place upon students should make universities blend signals and reality carefully.

Porter identifies various potential pitfalls in a differentiation strategy and it is easy to imagine universities tumbling into several of them as they introduce new technologies into the teaching and learning process. The pitfalls are:

- uniqueness that is not valuable (eg, will students value courses on the Internet once the novelty has worn off?);
- too much differentiation (eg, enthusiastic academics simply confusing students with too many media);
- too big a price premium (eg, will the mega-universities be able to maintain economies of scale with new technologies?);
- ignoring the need to signal value (eg, adult students may be sceptical about the benefits of, say, CD-ROM-based courses);
- not knowing the cost of differentiation (for the mega-universities this would be particularly dangerous in the two largest cost areas of the value chain, materials development and educational services);
- focus on the product instead of on the whole value chain (eg, technology may present advantages for universities in their administrative operations as well as in activities involving students directly);
- failure to recognize buyer segments (eg, the increasingly heterogeneous student bodies of most universities will pose a challenge for any strategy to change teaching technologies).

All this suggests that universities should pay very close attention to their buyers and to their buyers' own value chains in developing their technology strategies. Attention to the costs of differentiation will also be vital. Activities that do not fit with the chosen differentiation strategy may have to be abandoned.

Technology and competitive advantage

Technology is a major lubricant of competition. Changes in technology transform the structures of industries and are great equalizers. Although the education industry has traditionally been rather impervious to technological developments this may now be changing. Certainly there is an expectation of change in distance education. Technology is not important for its own sake. It is only important if it affects competitive advantage and industry structure. Many 'hi-tech' industries are less profitable than their 'low-tech' counterparts. Today technology is pervasive in all firms and almost any technology can affect competitiveness.

The value chain is the tool for understanding the link between technology and competitive advantage. By technology, of course, we mean procedures and systems as well as machines. Every activity in the value chain uses technology to combine purchased inputs and people to produce output. This applies as much to support activities as primary activities. Today information technology permeates the value chain. For this reason Porter (1985: 168) found it helpful to distinguish between information technology and office/administrative technology because office functions are easily overlooked. This distinction is hard to sustain today when, in many organizations, all employees have similar workstations on their desks and are linked to the same rich systems environment. This trend serves to remind us that technology is a major source of linkage within the value chain. For universities, as we noted above, the interdependence of the university's technology and the student's technology is an increasingly important linkage between two value chains.

Technology affects competitive advantage if it influences the firm's relative cost position or differentiation. It is likely to have an impact on both, since technology influences cost and uniqueness drivers and is also influenced by them. The mega-universities have used information technology in a sophisticated manner to support their complex logistics. Links with broadcasting organizations made some of the mega-universities proficient at teaching through television and radio.

Tests of sustainable advantage

Four tests determine whether technological change will give sustainable competitive advantage:

- Does the change itself sustainably lower cost or enhance differentiation?
- Does the change move cost or uniqueness drivers in the firm's favour?
- Does pioneering the change yield 'first mover' advantages over and above the benefits of the technology itself?
- Does the change improve industry structure?

Technology and industry structure

For universities it is particularly important to consider the impact of technological change on industry structure. Broadly speaking, we are dealing with the specific application to education of widely available technologies. How other institutions use them in education will determine whether industry structure changes in damaging ways. Technology can affect industry structure by its impact in a number of areas:

Entry barriers. We have already noted that current methods for the physical production of course materials (eg, desktop publishing) have lowered the entry barriers to distance education and reduced the advantages of operating on a large scale.

Buyer power. Before very long a well-equipped student may be able to access from home the electronic offerings of a large number of educational institutions.

Supplier power. The multiplication of broadcast TV channels may decrease the power of broadcasting authorities. For the moment, however, our survey of the mega-universities shows that these suppliers still have the power to frustrate ambitions for more air time.

Substitution. The development of multimedia educational materials by a range of public institutions and private-sector suppliers will enable universities to buy components of courses for less than the cost of developing them in-house.

Rivalry. The Internet has given thousands of individuals and institutions the chance to dabble in the business of supplying distance education. The entry barriers are low but, fortunately, so are the exit barriers. This segment of the industry seems unlikely to structure itself in a manner inimical to universities that are prepared to invest in developing and supporting quality products.

Industry boundaries. Technological change will expand the boundaries of the distance education segment of the education and training industry. It has already done so geographically. By enhancing the quality and attractiveness of courses it will bring more customers into the market. Another effect is the widening set of interrelationships between distance education and the media, computing and communications industries. These changes in structure present more opportunities than threats to universities.

Industry attractiveness. The above list suggests that distance education is seen as a particularly attractive segment of an attractive industry. This is bringing in new players, but if universities are clear about where their competitive advantages lie this should not damage them.

Issues in developing a technology strategy

In the final chapter we shall address the implementation of technology strategies in universities. Here are some of the questions that a university should ask about technology in formulating a strategy.

What technologies should it develop?

Chapter 7 will identify technologies that could help universities achieve priority goals, taking into account the implications of the value chain.

Should it seek leadership in these technologies?

In most areas universities will seek to be leaders in the application of technologies rather than developers of the technology itself. This type of leadership role is straightforward for the non-teaching functions. France's CNED, for example, can already claim to be a leader in the large-scale use of telephone technology for enquiry handling. The UKOU is at the front of the field in the use of electronic publishing technology. In the USA Carnegie-Mellon University sets the pace in using digital techniques for archiving audio-visual materials.

When technology is used for teaching at a distance the leadership issue is more complex because providers must rely on equipment owned by the student. In general this is more likely to be trailing-edge than leading-edge hardware. However, the time gap between leading edge and trailing edge is closing. Furthermore, what counts is less the hardware than the way it is used. The mega-universities, for example, will wish to lead in the large-scale use of domestic electronic technology for the purposes of higher education. The earlier point about signalling is also relevant. The image of some of the mega-universities is closely linked to the successful use of media in higher education. To lose this image would be to lose an element of competitive advantage.

How should it obtain the necessary technologies?

It will be simple for universities to obtain some of the new technologies they will wish to use in future (eg, software). Others, such as satellite broadcasting, CD-ROM and interactive broad band networks, they will want to develop on the basis of interrelationships. This is a complex area, not least because of uncertainty in the industries concerned about how patterns of use will develop. Given the costs of developing good courseware it would appear to be essential for universities to work together in producing and using such materials. This goes against established competitive habits and a reluctance to admit to teaching a course that was 'not invented here'. However, the critical mass achieved through consortia arrangements may help universities to maintain dialogue with key suppliers of technologies of potential competitive advantage to them. Risk can be reduced by sharing development costs and securing a larger market. In this arena the advantages of maintaining the role of what Porter (1985: 186) calls a 'first mover' appear to be considerable and may compensate for some loss of autonomy.

When a firm elects to be a first mover in a new technology it often has to educate its buyers and help them with switching costs. Resmer *et al.* (1995) have reported on the strategies developed for this purpose by the US universities that require all students to have their own computers. A policy of helping with switching costs has been pursued for some years by the UKOU which subsidizes the acquisition of computers by students who could not otherwise afford them. More recently it has equipped the homes of the executive members of its student association with computers and communications equipment so that they can conduct the business of the association by computer conference. In this way the UKOU accelerates the take-up of new technologies by students and gains experience in applying them effectively on a large scale.

Formulating a technology strategy

In summary, the following steps are required to turn technology into 'a competitive weapon rather than a scientific curiosity' (Porter, 1985: 198):

- identify all the distinct technologies and sub-technologies in the value chain;
- identify potentially relevant technologies in other industries or under development;
- determine the likely path of change of key technologies;
- determine which technologies and potential technological changes are most significant for competitive advantage and industry structure;
- assess the firm's relative capabilities in important technologies and the cost of making improvements;
- select a technology strategy, encompassing all important technologies, that reinforces the firm's overall competitive strategy;
- reinforce business unit technology strategies at the corporate level.

The next chapter examines what might make technology attractive from the students' point of view. Parallels between university students and consumers should not be taken too far. Universities require their students to work hard without giving any advance guarantees of success. However supportive the atmosphere which the university creates, students remain *in statu pupillari*, to use the Latin term to emphasize the longevity of the tradition. It is always possible that the university will judge that they have failed to meet the required standard despite the tuition fees they have paid. For this reason students are likely to make pragmatic and utilitarian judgements about the advantages of any learning technologies that are proposed to them.

Summary

Maintaining or enhancing competitive advantage in a changing environment is the central purpose of university renewal. We have applied Porter's (1980; 1985) analysis of competitive advantage to universities, with special attention to the likely impact of the technologies of distance education on competitiveness. Porter's approach begins with the notion of creating value for buyers. Students and the state are two key buyers for universities.

There are three strategies for gaining competitive advantage: to lower costs; to differentiate; or to focus on a niche market and seek either cost advantage or differentiation there. Some of the mega-universities achieved success quickly because they combined low cost with valuable differentiation. However, an organization cannot expect to maintain this unusual degree of competitive advantage. Already the structure of the higher education and training industry is changing as more campus universities offer courses at a distance.

Competitive advantage must be sought by detailed attention to an organization's value-creating activities. Porter's notion of the value chain has been adapted to the activities of universities in order to identify where the drive for competitive advantage should be focused and to compare the pattern of value activities in campus and distance teaching universities.

The most important drivers of cost and differentiation were identified. The success of a differentiation strategy depends crucially on the perceptions of buyers, especially so when a university's move into distance teaching requires students to acquire special equipment at home.

Finally, technology plays a major role in competition through its effect on an industry as a whole. Looking at the impact of technology on competitive advantage allowed us to identify key issues that technology strategies for universities must address.

Chapter 6

Making Technology Attractive

Will students want it?

The central theme of the previous chapter was that universities gain competitive advantage by creating extra value for their buyers. Employers and governments are important indirect buyers of higher education and training and they seem to be enthusiastic about greater use of technology in university teaching. But the direct buyers are the students. What is valuable to them?

Competitive advantage can be achieved by cutting costs or providing a distinctive product. Universities that incorporate new technologies into their teaching hope to score on both fronts. For the foreseeable future, however, differences in teaching methods will be more obvious to students than reduced costs, especially as they may face the additional cost of buying new devices for their homes.

New uses of technology can change industry structure in ways that give some organizations competitive advantage. If changes to the structure of higher education make it more attractive to students, then the earliest universities to adopt those changes may benefit from being seen as 'first movers'. Industry changes can also increase the power of the buyers. For example, well-equipped students may soon be able to access from home the electronic course offerings of a wide variety of institutions and pick and choose between them.

Students will assess carefully the signals they receive from universities that

urge new technologies upon them. Does the university have a solid reputation? Does it have a reassuring image? Above all, does its new teaching
'product' carry conviction? Porter's framework for seeking product differentiation warned us that innovators can get carried away in various ways. As
The Economist (1996b) noted:

> 'Jean-Louis Gassée, who used to run Apple Computer's research labs, has
> called it "Silicon Valley sophism": the assumption among the wired élite that
> a new technology will take off "because it would be cool if it did." Examples
> include virtual reality, personal digital assistants, and practically everything
> dreamt up at the Media Lab of the Massachusetts Institute of Technology.
> These innovations thrill boffins but make little impact on consumers.'

A survey conducted in Britain (Campaign for Learning, 1996) showed that
technology still ranks low when people are polled on their favourite methods
of learning. The question 'Which of these learning tools do you prefer to
use?' drew the following responses:

books 67%;
lecturing 36%;
videos 36%;
CD-ROM/Computers 19%;
audio-tapes 11%;
Internet 7%;
none of these/no preference 3%;
none of these/don't want to learn 3%.

People display a healthy scepticism. A new educational technology may be
unique, but does it teach better? Will the array of new devices and media
simply create bewilderment? Is the extra cost worth it? Has the university
bothered to explain to students where the benefits for them might lie?

Converting university teaching to technology-based systems is an expensive process. Where can institutions look for evidence about the likely
reactions of students to new methods and for advice about how to maximize
the chances that students will adopt them? The adoption by businesses and
individuals of high technology products, particularly those that represent a
discontinuous innovation, holds obvious parallels. What can we learn from
that experience?

Moore has summarized and structured a wealth of experience of the
introduction of new technology – both success and failure. His book,
Crossing the Chasm (Moore, 1991) looks at the challenge of marketing high

technology. It starts from the fact that brisk initial sales of a new product often do not lead on to success in the mass market. This finding translates readily into a nightmare scenario for a university undertaking the techno-logical transformation of its teaching: it is acclaimed by the first students, publicizes its apparent success, and only later discovers that most students are indifferent or hostile to the change.

Moore shows how particular industries have successfully crossed the *chasm* between an initial group of buyers and the larger mass market. In a second book, *Inside the Tornado* (Moore, 1995) he argues that penetration of this later market occurs in a succession of phases. A challenge for the supplier is that the strategies needed for success change radically between the different cohorts of buyers.

There are parallels between the industrial experience reported by Moore and the likely experience of universities seeking renewal through new technologies. For many students, perhaps especially those of campus uni-versities, the new methods will represent a discontinuous innovation. The reactions of buyers to discontinuous innovations are the theme of Moore's work. What lessons does it have for the role of technology in lifelong learning?

The technology adoption life-cycle

The focus of Moore's attention is the technology adoption life-cycle. Like many phenomena the adoption of new technology follows a Gauss (or bell) curve if one plots the numbers of people adopting a new technology against time. His analysis starts from the key finding that, at least for some high technology products, this is a segmented bell curve with potential time gaps between adoption of the product by different categories of people. This is represented schematically in Figure 6.1.

Moore distinguishes between successive groups of adopters:

Innovators: the enthusiasts who like technology for its own sake.
Early Adopters: who have the vision to adapt an emerging technology to an opportunity that is important to them.
The *Early Majority* are the pragmatic solid citizens who do not like the risks of pioneering but are ready to see the advantages of tested technologies. They are the beginning of the mass market.
The *Late Majority*, who represent about one-third of available customers, dislike discontinuous innovations and believe in tradition rather than pro-gress. They buy high-technology products reluctantly and do not expect to

like them. The refrigerator is their ideal model of a technological device. The light comes on automatically when the door is opened, the food stays cold, and the user does not have to think about the equipment.

The *Laggards* do not engage with high technology products – except to block them. They perform the valuable service of pointing out regularly the discrepancies between the day-to-day reality of the product and the claims made for it.

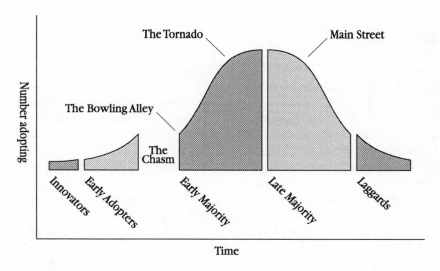

Figure 6.1 *The technology adoption life-cycle*

For Moore the most important time gap in technology adoption, which he calls the chasm, is between the early adopters and the early majority. Many high-technology companies have disappeared after their product foundered in this chasm. This sad fate usually comes as a nasty surprise because sales volumes start to rise rapidly at the end of the early adoption phase. Then, just as the company is gearing up for increased production, sales suddenly dry up if the early majority does not buy.

The analogy with the use of technology-based teaching methods by universities is clear. Some students will always be attracted to new technology for its own sake (the innovators). Others will quickly see the potential for more convenient and efficient learning (the early adopters). The key question is, will the pragmatic solid citizens, on whom the success of the university depends, be attracted to form an early majority of users?

This is a pressing question for some institutions. A real example shows that the stakes can be high. In 1996 some 17,000 of the UK Open University's

150,000 degree-credit students were using on-line computing from their homes in their studies. Moore reports that the innovators and the early adopters, taken together, account for about one-sixth of the whole market. This implies that the Open University has yet to cross the chasm in the adoption of on-line computer use from home. However, the University's projections of over 30,000 students on-line by 1998 assume that it will cross the chasm soon. Will this assumption prove correct?

Crossing the chasm

How does an organization cross the chasm? Moore's studies show that a general assault on the mass market does not work. Just as kindling wood is needed to start a log fire and a beachhead in Normandy was essential to the D-Day invasion of Europe in World War II, so an organization needs first to create a niche in the mass market from which it can expand. The aim is to begin by dominating that niche.

Finding a niche is made easier by the strength of the professional communities found among the pragmatists of the early majority. Translators, for example, talk to other translators and news of a technology that is helpful for translators will spread quickly through their professional network. It is easy to imagine certain groups of students constituting a niche in an analogous way.

There are two approaches to creating a niche market. First, it can be based on an application. Universities that introduce a policy of requiring students to have their own computers often implement it first in the engineering faculty where computers have direct application to the subjects being studied (Resmer et al., 1995). The second approach, which Moore calls thematic, creates a niche out of an advance in the technology itself. Computer-mediated conferencing is an example of a thematic niche. Students at home enjoy being able to communicate with other students for purposes both related and unrelated to the courses they are studying (Jennison, 1996).

However, finding a niche for a new product in the mass market relies ultimately on informed intuition. By definition there are no existing data on how a particular niche will receive a brand new product. Moore recommends developing scenarios by assessing, for example, what a particular delivery technology could give to distinct groups of students in the way of useful applications. The purpose is to tune a particular combination of the value triad of technology, students and application into a powerful value proposition. If that is achieved those students will have a compelling reason to adopt the technology.

In the context of the renewal of higher education such a 'must-have' value proposition could be based on one of three elements:

1. It creates a previously unavailable capacity that makes learning dramatically easier, or more productive, or more enjoyable.
2. It radically improves the productivity of the university on a critical success factor that is already well understood.
3. It visibly, verifiably and significantly reduces current total overall operating costs.

There are, of course, technologies that universities could adopt for their administrative or research operations that might satisfy one of these conditions. Such a decision would, however, be within the university's control. In this chapter our focus is on the adoption of technology by students, something which the university cannot directly control. From the student perspective the compelling reason to adopt a technology would be some version of the following general value proposition:

'The use of technology X in course Y, by making my learning more efficient, productive and enjoyable, will greatly increase the likelihood of my passing the course well and no other university can match this quality at this price.'

The whole product

Another key to finding and dominating a specific niche in the early mass market is the notion of 'the whole product'. Products can be perceived by buyers in different ways. First there is the generic product that is sold in the box. Then there is the expected product. This is the minimum product that will work and the one that naive consumers think they are buying (eg, toys that come with batteries; electrical products with plugs; computers with monitors). Next on the scale toward the whole product comes the augmented product which includes everything needed to maximize the chance of satisfying the buyer's needs. Finally, there is the potential product that includes the possibility of growth as more ancillaries and enhancements come on to the market.

It is vital to progress along this continuum of perceptions towards the whole product as the market objective moves from left to right in the technology adoption life-cycle. The 'techie' innovators are happy to develop their own ways of using a new product. They may take the generic product apart and re-configure it for their own needs. The pragmatists, however, want a whole product that works. Whole-product planning should be the centrepiece of attempts to create niches, within the wider student body, that can serve as beachheads for expansion to the majority.

The analysis of the components of distance education in Chapter 4 helps to identify the difference between generic and whole products in technology-based higher education. A generic product, for example, might be certain textual elements of a course made available over the Internet. The whole product would be an integrated learning system that included all components of the course and the human interaction required to create a supportive environment for learning.

Sadly, as extra levels of buyer value are added, the developing whole product resembles the layers of an onion. The volume of each successive layer increases as the cube of the onion's dimension. It is impossible to include all the features that might give all pragmatists compelling reasons to buy. Hence the need to focus on some promising niches, ie, to begin by using technology to make particular courses or services highly attractive to specific groups of students.

For universities developing technology-based teaching the most difficult challenge is not to lose sight of the need for a whole product when developing niche applications. Often it is less challenging to established practice to begin by applying technology to the teaching of part of a course rather than the whole course. The idea is to take a concept that is commonly found difficult to teach (eg, phase diagrams in materials science) and develop and make available a learning package for all who teach that topic within a larger course. This has been the approach of the UK's Open Learning Foundation, a university consortium whose purpose is to share the costs and benefits of developing learning materials. It was also the aim of the Teaching and Learning Technology programme of the UK's Higher Education Funding Councils, which provided funds for universities to work together in applying technology to the teaching of a range of disciplines.

Such an approach fits nicely with the traditional academic view that technology should be a useful addition to traditional teaching rather than a substitute for it. That, of course, is its fundamental weakness. First, it adds costs rather than reducing them. Second, and more importantly for our argument in this chapter, it is burdensome for students working at home. If such students are to find their personal investment in technology worthwhile, they need to use it extensively throughout the course. In this sense it is helpful to interpret the drive to a whole product as the imperative of focusing technological applications on whole courses and programmes.

From the bowling alley to the tornado

This first part of the early majority market is nicknamed by Moore 'the bowling alley' (see Figure 6.1). The institution should aim to move from one niche to another in this mainstream market towards widespread general adoption. 'Each niche is like a bowling pin, something that can be knocked over in itself but can also help to knock over one or more additional pins' (Moore, 1995: 27). The key task is to become the market leader in each niche.

At this stage a campus university offering a technology-based course in a particular discipline is likely to be perceived as a market leader in the application of new teaching technology to that subject, rather than a leader in technology-based education generally. For example, the National Technological University of the USA offers instructional television courses by satellite to highly skilled engineers requiring updating. It is perceived as a leader in this niche but has not, as yet, tried to go beyond it. Bates (1995: 115) suggests that this particular technology would not, in any case, be successful outside this very special group of students. A university that is already focused on distance teaching also has to choose niches in which to start using new technology. Cost considerations make it unrealistic to imagine launching a new instructional strategy based on a new medium (CD-ROM for instance) across all subjects simultaneously.

Niches should be chosen using several criteria. First, they should be areas where the new technology can make a real difference for students, giving them a compelling reason to adopt it. Second, the niche should not be so big as to overwhelm the institution. Third, some thought should go to ordering the niches so that knocking over one bowling pin (niche) increases the chances of knocking over the next. Although the idea of the niche approach is to focus sharply on the needs of particular students, it should not customize each application so much that synergy with future niches is lost.

Moore argues that the bowling alley calls for vertical marketing, meaning an approach based on the particular application of interest to the customers (eg, the manipulation of paintings for students of art appreciation). This is in contrast to horizontal marketing based on the technology. It is possible, of course, that if a particular home technology required is also attractive to the rest of the family the student may welcome an excuse to acquire it.

The organization that develops whole products successfully in a series of niches may create a *tornado* as the mass market takes off. Moore explains the appearance of tornadoes, in industrial settings, by a change of focus from *economic* buyers to *infrastructure* or *technical* buyers. Prior to this point individuals make purchases that suit their own applications. Now those responsible for the overall infrastructure of the firm (eg, in information technology) enter the field. These people are always looking out for new paradigms but they are also pragmatists. To defuse the tension of worrying about when to commit their organization to an innovation they communicate intensively, which creates a herd instinct.

The result is that these infrastructure buyers often move together in adopting a new technology; they tend to pick the same vendor; and they like to make the change fast. That is why large numbers of customers enter the market simultaneously, swamping the supply systems and creating a frenzy. The ensuing tornado is an exceptional condition. Universities competing hard for enrolments might relish creating a tornado of demand from students, but how would the notion of a mass market tornado apply to technology-based university teaching? The answer is different for the remote classroom and correspondence traditions of distance education.

For universities teaching through remote classrooms the concept of an infrastructure buyer has some meaning. Institutions watch each other and, if some see others gaining benefit through the use of, say, video conferencing, they might be tempted to buy similar equipment. It is unlikely, however, that the phenomenon would be frenzied!

In the correspondence tradition, where students study at home or in the workplace, the nearest thing to infrastructure buyers would be firms that sponsor large number of their employees as students. Employers are keen on technology-based teaching and to become the preferred supplier of continuing education opportunities to a number of large firms is an attractive proposition for any university. Families keen for an excuse to buy a new device (eg, the latest set-top box) could also be a surrogate for infrastructure buyers.

It is also possible to imagine some elements of a tornado developing as a result of decisions by students themselves. Technology-based education derived from the correspondence tradition frees students from geographical constraints in their choice of institution. It is conceivable that large numbers of them might pick a particular institution offering a new approach. Indeed, this appeared to happen with the UK Open University which, from the time it pioneered multimedia distance teaching in the 1970s, has always received more applications than it can accept at the fees it charges. However, given the pent-up demand for higher education among British adults, this phenomenon was really the creation of an *application* niche, based on need, rather than a *thematic* niche based on the intrinsic attractiveness of the technologies used.

The rules that Moore outlines for handling a tornado market suggest that the Open University's inability to be open to all its applicants might apply to any university that experienced a dramatic increase in demand. Moore's rules for the tornado market are:

- Ignore the customer.
- Just ship.
- Extend distribution channels.
- Drive to the next lower price point.

When a tornado occurs in the industrial sector customers simply want to be supplied. They want the new commodity and the focus has to be on getting it to them as quickly, easily and cheaply as possible. That means not changing the product fundamentally during the tornado and not neglecting any potential distribution channel. In the tornado phase products become institutionalized and commoditized. This puts strong downward pressure on price, which in turn brings in more customers. Said Moore (1995: 84), 'If the leader snubs a new price point, then the market will go to the clone. The lesson is clear: *tornado markets will be served*. It is never a question of *if*, it is only a question of *who*'.

Each of these rules for a tornado market is uncomfortable, if not abhorrent, for university teachers. Ignore the students? No, we proclaim our care for them. Just ship? No, we want to individualize learning. Extend distribution channels? No, it's *our* credits that are valued, franchising our courses is suspect. Drive to the next lower price point? Surely, in higher education what has low cost has low value?

The irony is, of course, that in periods of very rapid expansion of student numbers, such as occurred when university enrolments in the UK increased by 53% between 1988 and 1993, campus universities do follow these rules without many scruples. Customers are 'ignored' in ever larger classes. Admission requirements are lowered to increase intakes. Courses are franchised into community colleges. The unit of resource is driven down. It may be that students would be served rather better in a tornado of growth based on new learning technologies – but the rules for sustaining the tornado are difficult for any university to proclaim as its policy.

In all markets, however, tornadoes eventually end. Firms are unwise to assume they can step onto a new tornado when the old one begins to slow down. The mega-universities achieved something of a tornado market with the use of the mass media in their early years. They and other universities may create another tornado with the knowledge media, but all would be wiser to plan instead for 'Main Street', Moore's term for when a new paradigm begins to settle in.

On to Main Street

Success in the tornado meant ignoring the customer, but in Main Street the focus comes back to the user. By this stage, in the commercial world, there is a commodity market with low prices. The challenge for suppliers is to find niche extensions of the commodity market, which they do by 'mass customization'. This requires perceptive design alterations rather than technology breakthroughs. The user does not need more advanced solutions, but more accommodating ones. However, in contrast to the bowling alley, the resource to develop new applications painstakingly through partnerships with customers is not available. The discipline for marketing in Main Street is:

- Make an offer.
- Learn from it.
- Correct your mistakes.
- Make another offer.

The key is to build learning into the offer mechanism. What makes this phase easier is the latent value still unused in the product. In the tornado phase, marketing only profiles a tiny proportion of the things that, say, a personal computer or a link to the Internet, can be used for. In the Main Street phase niche customers can be taught to appreciate more of the value inherent in the product.

Some disturbing implications of the technology adoption life-cycle for organizations can be illustrated by summarizing the role of market segmentation in the different stages we have described:

- In the early market you do not segment, you follow the visionaries.
- To cross the chasm and negotiate the bowling alley you must segment. That is the basis of the whole product strategy.
- Inside the tornado you must not segment, you ship standard product to get market share.
- On Main Street you segment again, but not as you did in the bowling alley.

Similar reversals occur in other areas of business strategy such as competitive advantage, strategic partnerships and organizational leadership as a technology moves through the adoption life-cycle.

Competitive advantage

Creating value for the buyer is the key to competitive advantage. Treacy and Wiersema (1995) identified three value disciplines that produce different kinds of value for customers:

- product leadership;
- operational excellence; and
- customer intimacy.

The optimal combination of these disciplines changes though the technology adoption life-cycle. To interest the early adopters of a technology, product leadership is the key quality needed. Then, in developing niches on the other side of the chasm, this has to be combined with customer intimacy as applications are developed into whole products. If progress down the bowling alley leads into a tornado, product leadership remains important but customer intimacy must be traded for operational excellence. The challenge now is to get the product out in volume and working. Finally, on Main Street operational excellence must be maintained, since this is still the mass market. But the product is now a commodity, so product leadership is less important than a new attention to customer intimacy that seeks niche extensions in the phase of mass customization.

A more general way of expressing this is that there are four domains which customers can value: technology, product, market and company. The domain of greatest value to the customer changes in moving through the technology adoption life-cycle. Innovators and early adopters value technology and product, whereas in the mass market the favoured domains are market and company. This implies that the proper strategy has two stages. First, an organization develops an early market by demonstrating a strong technology advantage and converting it into product credibility. Second, it develops a mainstream market by demonstrating market leadership and converting that into company credibility.

Pragmatists and conservatives are the majority of customers. If they focus on the market and the organization then the way the organization positions itself becomes very important. The aim of positioning is to make the product easier for the customer to buy rather than easier for the company to sell. As Moore puts it: 'The goal of positioning is to create a space inside the customer's head called "best buy for this type of situation" and to attain sole, undisputed occupancy of that space'.

Such positioning has four components: a claim, solid evidence of leadership, communication, and feedback/adjustment. The claim is the hardest element to get right because there always seems to be too much to say. (This is especially likely to be the case for universities offering technology-based courses!) To avoid this trap Moore suggests the lift (elevator) test. Can the organization explain the virtues of its new approach in the time it takes to go up in a lift? Without a succinct claim, marketing, R&D and dealings with partners are unlikely to be well focused. One way to produce a two-sentence claim is to fill in these blanks:

For (target customer)
Who (statement of need or opportunity)
The (product name) *is a* (product category)
That (statement of key benefit; ie, compelling reason to buy)
Unlike (primary competitive alternative)
Our product (statement of primary differentiation).

Universities embarking on technology-based teaching could benefit by obliging those proposing new delivery strategies to develop a convincing claim along these lines before approving the project!

Strategic partnerships

One of the conclusions of this book is that as universities harness technology to the process of renewal they will need to operate in a variety of partnerships: with other institutions of higher education; with network providers; and with suppliers of equipment. The same is true in high-technology industry, where open systems architecture, in particular, leads firms to strike strategic alliances with each other. However, some of these relationships are fairly transient because the demands on partnerships also change radically on progressing through the technology adoption life-cycle.

Some of the basic principles of strategic partnerships in industry carry over directly to the relationships that universities may develop with other bodies:

- The purpose of a strategic partnership is to achieve leadership in a particular market segment by focusing on the whole product needed to secure the number one position.
- Partnerships formed in the absence of the focal point of a whole product are unmanageable and have huge opportunity costs. Progress towards a whole product is the critical feedback mechanism of partnership. This is a vital point for universities. Collaboration between institutions will be

an essential part of the process of coming to grips with new teaching technologies. However, given the academic predilection for seeing technology as an add-on to existing practice and not a substitute for it, people will tend to shy away from developing whole products (ie, whole courses or programmes). Unless this nettle is grasped, frustration and unproductive expense will be the principal products of many attempts at inter-institutional collaboration.

- In a partnership the firm that controls the customer relationship has the greatest leverage. This principle explains why the dynamics of partnerships change in successive phases of the technology adoption life-cycle. The locus of power tends to move as follows:
  - in the early market power lies with the technology provider and those who can integrate it into a useful system. Partnerships aim at helping visionary customers develop their applications (eg, the adaptation of a computer conferencing system for use by students in a teacher training programme during teaching practice);
  - in the bowling alley power moves into the hands of the ringleader of the niche market attack (eg, art historians providing academic input to the design of a CD-ROM on that subject);
  - in the tornado power is with the big suppliers, who will tend to shed partners at this stage;
  - finally, on 'Main Street', power shifts to the distribution channel. This can create tensions in the partnerships between producers and distributors as the distributors fight to get prices down. In higher education this tension is often present when one institution franchises its offerings through another. It will be a risk as partnerships emerge between universities that have good distance education course materials and others having technology-based delivery systems.

Organizational leadership

The changes in business strategy that must occur as an organization takes products through the technology adoption life cycle are a challenge to its leadership. Moore suggests that organizations should think of themselves as theatre troupes in which people can play various roles and team up in different ways. This is an area where the oft-criticized management style of universities, with its preference for academic consensus, may become a strength. To quote Moore (1995: 235):

'But there is another property of consensus management that is typically overlooked. Within its fora of continual, sometimes seemingly incessant, team meetings, leadership, power and influence can shift back and forth subtly without disturbing the management hierarchy. Decision-making gravitates towards expertise rather than the job title without challenging the latter's authority. Thus product and customer champions can come to the fore during the bowling alley, and systems champions during the tornado, and the group as a whole, knowingly or not, succeeds in navigating the changes of strategy that hypergrowth markets impose.'

Whether the development of technology-based delivery systems by universities leads to hypergrowth markets or not, it will certainly bring radical changes to the academy. The following comment is worth taking to heart:

'A commitment to trust is mandatory if the leadership strategies of consensus management and decentralized operations are going to work.... The paradox of trust is that by intelligently relinquishing power, one gains it back many times over. Once you reach your personal limits, this is the only economy of scale that can help – and hypergrowth markets will push you to your personal limits faster than most other challenges'. (Moore, 1995: 237)

Summary

When universities move to technology-based teaching methods, students are likely to face additional expenses as well as the challenge of change. Making the new delivery systems attractive to students is therefore a crucial element of any technology strategy. This chapter has drawn heavily on the stimulating studies by Geoffrey Moore of the technology adoption life-cycle in order to suggest how to make new teaching technology attractive to students.

The key lesson is that the early enthusiasm of some students may not be a good guide to the reactions of the majority. To attract the majority a university must apply technology to the teaching of particular subjects so that students' learning is more effective and enjoyable. This means producing a whole product that integrates course materials and tutorial support. The expertise acquired by 'conquering' a number of subjects successfully and developing whole products can then lead to success with the majority of the student body.

If students find technology useful in particular courses they will gradually acquire enthusiasm for the idea of technology-based learning. If this is done well the university will gain competitive advantage by being perceived as a reliable first choice for such courses.

Chapter 7

The Knowledge Media

Introduction

This chapter explores how a new generation of media could contribute to the process of university renewal. Figure 7.1, derived from work by Simon Buckingham-Shum, recalls how media have shaped our concept of knowledge throughout history. Today's new technologies, which Eisenstadt (1995) has dubbed the 'knowledge media', are emerging from the convergence of computing, telecommunications and the learning sciences. They are also known as 'third generation' distance education technologies. We shall use Eisenstadt's term for two reasons. First, the potential role of these technologies in university renewal extends beyond distance education. Second, Eisenstadt and others make ambitious claims for the knowledge media, arguing that they can change the relationship between people and knowledge in a qualitative fashion. The previous history of the application of technology to education is littered with exaggerated claims that subsequently proved untenable. It seems appropriate, therefore, to examine the potential of these new technologies against demanding criteria. Calling them the knowledge media reminds us of the claim that they will make a difference not merely of degree, but of kind.

We begin by summarizing the agendas for lifelong higher learning and university renewal. If the knowledge media are to make a real difference they must help institutions and students address these issues. What are the salient issues?

How Media Shape Knowledge

ORAL CULTURES
Knowledge: "You know only what you can recall";
knowledge is dramatized; repetitive; concrete;
situated; participatory; personal; historically fragile.
Culture: intellectually conservative; prominence of
ritual and story-telling; wisdom associated with
people.

WRITING
Knowledge: not restricted to human memory
limitations; abstract; decontextualized;
reproducible.
Culture: primacy of mind over emotions;
contemplative tradition.

*Writing
leads to
abstract
reasoning*

PRINTING
Knowledge: infinitely reproducible; objective and
precise; indexible; referenceable.
Culture: scientific rationalism; development of
highly refined linguistic/literary styles.

RADIO/TV
Knowledge: instantaneously accessible; soundbite
sized; image   based; passively absorbed;
increasingly packaged and filtered.
Culture: expects knowledge and opinions on tap;
beginning to lose meaning in the data.

GLOBAL HYPERMEDIA
Knowledge? transient (digital); changeable;
perspectivized; interlinked; open-ended; dynamic;
public not private; breadth at expense of depth.
Culture? information-rich (knowledge-rich? wiser?);
loss of linear modes of reasoning; loss of linear
model of history...

Media shape language and thought.
How will globally linked, digital, interactive media shape
the way we formulate, communicate and acquire knowledge?

Figure 7.1 *How media shape knowledge*

The agenda for renewal

We explored the key strategic challenges facing campus universities and large distance teaching universities in Chapters 2 and 3. Despite their differences these two types of institution face many similar problems and opportunities and now share, for example, an interest in the new technologies of distance education. We shall list separately some salient issues that confront each set of universities. From this we can derive a set of common challenges and ask how the knowledge media can help institutions rise to them.

Challenges for campuses

For campus universities the agenda can be summarized in five points:

1. Emphasis on learning productivity is the route to more effective teaching. This will require institutional redesign in order to provide each learner with an experience that integrates, at a personal level, a range of interactions with the rich resources of the university.
2. As the habit of lifelong learning spreads, students will become increasingly diverse. The majority will combine study and employment. Students, who will have a wide variety of academic backgrounds, will expect to choose from an extensive curriculum delivered in a convenient and affordable manner.
3. The notion of an academic community will have to be reconceived with less emphasis on a physical campus as a common focal point. This paradigm shift may strengthen awareness of the core functions of a university and create a new basis for a sense of institutional belonging among students and staff.
4. Universities will need to become increasingly adept at managing collaborative ventures with a wide variety of bodies, including other universities. Such collaboration will be required in order to offer students work-related courses and to make the investments necessary for the preparation and distribution of high quality intellectual assets such as learning materials.
5. Public funds will constitute a decreasing proportion of the financial support for higher education. Direct grants to institutions are likely to be replaced by mechanisms that channel support through individual students. Governments will, however, continue to develop explicit procedures to ensure accountability and quality assurance in universities.

Matters for mega-universities

From the profiles of the mega-universities given in the Appendix, six priorities for their future development emerge:

1. To improve teaching effectiveness and course design.
2. To introduce or enhance tutorial support to students and foster student-to-student communication.
3. To find the right balance between cost, time and quality in course production in order to blend economies of scale with the need to tailor products to serve niche and specialist markets.
4. To improve logistics and scale up the use of new technologies.
5. To develop more participative governance processes.
6. To expand TV and radio broadcasting.

Common concerns

These lists of the challenges now facing two very different models of university reveal large areas of common concern. They can be conflated into the following four general issues:

1. Teaching effectiveness and learning productivity.
2. Reinforcing the spirit of collective endeavour as the geographical dispersion of the members of the academic community increases.
3. Production and delivery of courses and intellectual assets.
4. Scaleable growth and logistics in distributed institutions.

The following sections explore what the knowledge media could do to help all universities address these challenges for the academy in the third millennium. We shall focus particularly on the newer technologies because of the claim that they may make a qualitative difference to learning effectiveness. Bates (1995) has already provided an excellent survey of the role of the more established technologies.

Competitive advantage results from a combination of cost leadership, differentiation and focus. We note, in this context, that the analysis of value chains in Chapter 5 showed that the development of learning materials and the provision of educational services, which relate to all four of the headings listed above, account for much of the expenditures of campus universities on their core functions and for most of the total budget of the mega-universities.

Teaching effectiveness and learning productivity

What are the elements of effective university teaching and high learning productivity? Will the knowledge media help to supply them? In her important book, *Rethinking University Teaching*, Laurillard (1993) points out that since most research on teaching has been done in schools, attempts to apply the results to universities do not usually take into account the specific nature of academic learning.

The essence of academic learning is that it has a second order character. As Laurillard (1993: 5) puts it:

'The central idea is that academic learning is different from other kinds of learning in everyday life because it is not directly experienced, and is necessarily mediated by the teacher. Undergraduates are not learning about the world directly, but about other's descriptions of the world, hence the term "mediated".'

Elsewhere (1993: 26) she adds:

'Everyday knowledge is located in our experience of the world. Academic knowledge is located in our experience of our experience of the world. Both are situated, but in logically distinct contexts. Teaching may use the analogy of situated learning of the world, but must adapt it to learning of descriptions of the world.'

This means that academic knowledge has to be abstracted or represented formally in order to be useful by being generalizable. It follows that teaching must situate knowledge in real-world activity but also create artificial environments that allow the learning of precepts, or descriptions of the world.

In the article where he launches the term 'knowledge media', Eisenstadt also argues that teaching, and especially teaching through the media, too often starts from an impoverished view of what knowledge is:

'Now is knowledge the answer to what fits onto CD-ROMs, what "sits" on a file server, or what "travels" down the information highway? Most emphatically not! Knowledge is an emergent property which transcends the fixed-size-and-space concepts of media and information, just as it transcends the notion that you can impart it to students by "filling" them up from the teacher's "vessel"... knowledge is a dynamic process, a vibrant, living thing, resting on shared assumptions, beliefs, complex perceptions, sophisticated yet sometimes crazy logic, and the ability to go beyond the information given. "Knowledge" is the correct abstraction for describing what people communicate to one another. "Content" is not.' (Eisenstadt, 1995)

From such standpoints university teaching cannot be simply exposition. It must be a rhetorical activity. This means that dialogue and interaction is essential. Laurillard argues that the ideal teaching and learning process is a one-to-one discussion, although not just any one-to-one discussion. This hardly seems a promising starting point for the improvement of teaching effectiveness and learning productivity in universities whose student to staff ratios are headed remorselessly upward.

Other writers, such as Bates (1995: 56), consider the notion that the one-to-one tutorial is the ideal teaching environment is open to argument. However, Bates does agree that assessment of the suitability of different technologies for a particular situation needs to start from a rigorous attempt to define 'good teaching' in that context. He also places great importance on the role of interaction in the learning process but, as we noted in Chapter 4, distinguishes between individual and social interaction in a way that is helpful in the design of distance learning systems.

In order to clarify their concept of good teaching, universities should invest in studies to find out where their students are starting from and what they bring to learning. It also helps if, as in some of the 'open' universities, there is an idealistic commitment to take responsibility for the students' learning. The mega-universities have the benefit of being set up as learning systems and, if teaching is mediated learning, then their use of various media must be an asset. Finally if, as Laurillard holds (1993: 4), the solution to the problem of university teaching and learning productivity lies in a new organizational infrastructure and not in guidelines on how to teach, the framework of distance education provides elements of such an infrastructure.

After stressing the importance of both finding out what students bring to learning and appreciating the complexity of the process of coming to know something, Laurillard reviews traditional methods of developing a teaching strategy. The first, instructional design, she finds deficient because neither Gagné's (1977) original work first published in 1965, nor that of successors such as Romiszowski (1988) have more than a tenuous link with any empirical base. 'Gagné's approach is essentially a logical analysis of what must be the case, rather than an empirically grounded theory' (Laurillard, 1993: 72).

The second method, intelligent tutoring systems design, has similar weaknesses because the assumptions on which such systems are based 'derive from logical analysis, not from empirical studies of students...it is a theory that begins and ends in the mind of the researcher' (1993: 77). The third method, instructional psychology, generalizes widely from a limited experimental base. She argues that the studies on which it is based are 'suggestive rather than prescriptive, and do not promise ever to be more than that' (1993: 82).

Laurillard finds most promise in phenomenography, the final methodology she reviews. The term 'phenomenography' was coined by Marton (1981) to mean 'descriptions of the phenomena'. Knowing the alternative ways that students conceptualize key phenomena, which include the concepts of reality they have already acquired, is clearly helpful to teachers. Although this method generates qualitative rather than quantitative data, and descriptions rather than explanations, it does have the advantage of focusing on the form of interaction between teacher, student and subject matter. For this reason she believes it 'offers the best hope for a principled way of generating teaching strategy from research outcomes' (Laurillard, 1993: 64). This shift in focus, from what the teacher should do to how they must set up the interaction, is consistent with the crucial role of dialogue in academic learning. The notion of teaching and learning as a conversation links Laurillard's conclusion to the work of the late Gordon Pask who formalized it in his conversation theory (Pask, 1976).

We have outlined the development of Laurillard's thinking because it appears to provide the clearest lens through which to examine the claims made for all teaching media, including the knowledge media. She concludes that the learning process must recognize the special character of academic knowledge and be a dialogue between teacher and student that is:

Discursive – teachers and students must agree learning goals, make their conceptions accessible to each other, and give mutual feedback.
Adaptive – the teacher should alter the focus of the dialogue in the light of the emerging relationship between their own and the student's conception.
Interactive – the student must act to achieve the task goal and the teacher must provide feedback so that something in the world changes as a result of the student's action.
Reflective – the teacher must help students link feedback on their actions to the topic goals at every level.

If this type of interactive contract seems somewhat legalistic, Laurillard comments that 'democracy is a serious business'. The essence of the process is that it describes a form of interaction between teacher and student, rather than action on the student. It is also intended to be self-improving.

Figure 7.2 reproduces the conversational framework in which Laurillard identifies the activities necessary to complete the learning process. She then examines a range of media and makes judgements about whether they lend themselves to each of these activities. The results of her analysis are reproduced in Table 7.1. She stresses (1993: 105) that, 'I have selected the main types of educational media and divided them into their canonical forms, the orthodox, unadulterated way of using each one'.

Laurillard made this analysis of the teaching and learning qualities of this particular set of media before the expression 'knowledge media' was coined. Indeed, it was only after 1993 that expressions such as the information superhighway, the Internet, the World Wide Web, Java and CD-ROM came into common parlance. Have these new developments added new media to Laurillard's list that deserve the attention of universities?

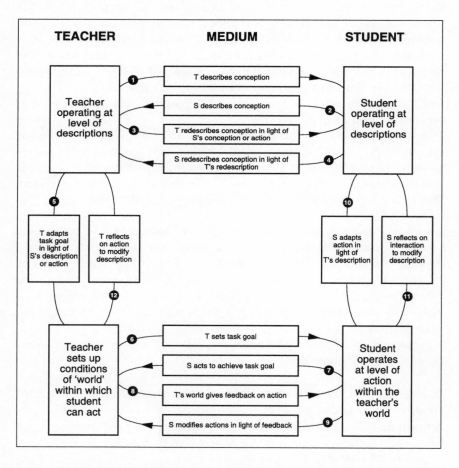

Figure 7.2 *The 'conversational framework' identifying the activities necessary to complete the learning process*

S = Student / T = Teacher	Print	Audio-vision	Television	Video	Self-assessed questions	Hypertext	Multi-media resources	Simulation	Microworld	Modelling	Tutorial program	Tutoring system	Tutorial simulation	Audio conferencing	Video conferencing	Computer conferencing	Computer supported collaborative work
1 T can describe conception	✓	✓	✓	✓	○	✓	✓	○	○	○	✓	✓	✓	✓	✓	✓	○
2 S can describe conception	○	✓	○	○	✓	✓	✓	○	✓	✓	✓	✓	✓	✓	✓	✓	✓
3 T can redescribe in light of S's conception or action	○	○	○	○	○	○	○	○	○	○	✓	✓	✓	✓	✓	✓	○
4 S can redescribe in light of T's redescription or S's action	○	✓	○	○	✓	✓	✓	○	○	○	✓	✓	✓	○	○	✓	○
5 T can adapt task goal in light of S's description or action	○	○	○	○	○	○	○	○	○	○	✓	✓	✓	○	○	○	○
6 T can set task goal	○	✓	✓	✓	✓	○	○	✓	✓	✓	✓	✓	✓	✓	○	○	✓
7 S can act to achieve task goal	○	✓	○	○	✓	○	✓	✓	✓	✓	✓	✓	✓	○	○	○	✓
8 T can set up world to give intrinsic feedback on actions	○	✓	✓	✓	○	○	✓	✓	✓	✓	○	✓	✓	○	○	○	✓
9 S can modify action in light of intrinsic feedback on action	○	✓	○	○	○	○	✓	✓	✓	✓	○	✓	✓	○	○	○	✓
10 S can adapt actions in light of T's description or S's redescription	○	✓	○	○	✓	○	○	○	✓	✓	✓	✓	✓	✓	○	○	✓
11 S can reflect on interaction to modify description	○	✓	○	✓	✓	○	✓	○	✓	✓	○	✓	✓	○	○	○	✓
12 T can reflect on S's action to modify redescription	○	○	○	○	○	○	○	○	○	○	✓	✓	✓	○	○	○	○

Notes:

Microworld: A computer program that embodies rules governing the behaviour of defined objects and their interaction with each other, thus creating a 'little world' in which the user can manipulate objects.

Tutorial program: A computer program that presents information, sets exercises for the student, accepts answers in a specified format and gives feedback on those answers.

Tutoring system (also called 'intelligent tutoring system'): This performs the same tasks as a tutorial program but in a different way: generating the information from a database, generating exercises from rules using the information already collected about the student, and generating feedback from both the database and the student record.

Tutorial simulation: A combination of adaptive and interactive media that provides intrinsic feedback through the simulation element and extrinsic feedback through the tutorial element.

Table 7.1 *Media comparison chart*

Eisenstadt (1995) introduced the term 'knowledge media' to describe the 'convergence of telecommunications, computing and the learning or cognitive sciences'. Even though Eisenstadt's own research is in artificial intelligence, it is clear from the examples he quotes that by the 'learning and cognitive sciences' he means particularly the kind of phenomenographic studies and conversation theory which Laurillard also finds most helpful.

A key supposition in Eisenstadt's description of the knowledge media is that for some media quantitative improvements in performance (eg, in speed, bandwidth, ease of manipulation) create changes in kind, rather then merely of degree, as far as the user is concerned. As Nikita Kruschev once said about nuclear weapons, 'quantity has a quality all of its own'. For Eisenstadt, 'knowledge media are about the capturing, storing, imparting, sharing, accessing and creating of knowledge' and a medium is not just a technical format, such as video or CD-ROM but 'the whole presentational style, the user interface, the accessibility, the interactivity'. This fits naturally with the trend to consider knowledge as constructed socially by individuals through discourse in which they use previously accepted criteria for reaching agreement. As Lincoln (1989: 58) expressed it: 'science is less a statement of truth than a running argument'.

The practical conclusion is that certain media, particularly those which combine a screen and telecommunications, have the potential to mediate more of the teaching and learning activities listed in Table 7.1 than Laurillard indicated when she examined the 'orthodox, unadulterated' way of using them. Putting it another way, increases in telecommunications bandwidth and computing power 'adulterate' some media in ways that are potentially helpful to education.

The word 'potentially' is necessary because Table 7.1 reminds us that much of the potential of the simple media has yet to be exploited by universities. It shows, for example, that the integration of self-assessment questions into a printed text significantly enriches it as a medium for teaching and learning. This is a discovery which most textbook publishers have only recently made. The further addition of an audio-cassette, to create audio-vision, results in a multi-media package that fails only three of Laurillard's 12 key activity tests.

Computer-mediated communication (telematics)

A good example of a medium that now has a much richer potential than its orthodox, unadulterated version of the 1980s is computer-mediated communication, often known in Europe as 'telematics'. France was the first country to introduce popular telematics when, in the late 1970s, it replaced the traditional telephone directories with a database that subscribers could search from home using a simple terminal. Today's computer-mediated communications systems are much more sophisticated and provide a good example of an increase in quantity leading to a change in quality. Three types of computer-mediated communication are of special relevance to universities: e-mail, computer conferencing, and the Internet/World Wide Web. We examine the implications of each of these technologies in turn but the crucial development is that they have now come together in integrated software packages.

E-mail

A message is the basic unit of e-mail. It is a discrete item of text, to which other files (word-processed documents, spreadsheets, etc) can be attached, that is produced by a sender and addressed to one or more named readers. Messages are usually prepared off-line and the sender goes on-line to transmit them. Each message is routed by the system to the addressee's mailbox on the host computer and waits there to be read when the addressee next logs into the system. The addressee can then read the message, reply to it, forward it to others, delete it, file it or leave it for future attention. Most e-mail systems also have a bulletin board facility which gives multiple read-only access to messages and documents.

E-mail is already in widespread use for communication within organizations. The number of messages exchanged by this means between the staff of the UKOU increased from 8,000 per day in 1994 (Bird, 1994) to over 20,000 in 1996. In 1995 the University equipped the homes of the elected executive committee members of its 150,000-member student association with suitable equipment so that they could use e-mail in conducting the business of the association. A year later they judged that the advantages it offered outweighed the difficulties (mostly of reliability).

It is easy to imagine the extension of e-mail to the wider student body. Indeed, once students gain the habit of using computer-mediated communication they will expect to be able to use it for their administrative correspondence with the institution. Its major potential in the academic arena is for the submission and marking of assignments. The importance of rapid and relevant comments on students' assignments is the most reliable research result in distance education. Even distance teaching institutions in countries with efficient postal systems, such as CNED in France, would like to improve turn-round times on assignments. What needs to happen to make the electronic handling of student assignments a reality?

The first requirement, which we examine in the next section, is that students and tutors must have the necessary equipment at home and be prepared to use it for this purpose. The second is that a reliable and pedagogically effective handling system be developed. This must start with the reliability of transmission of the electronic messages. E-mail still goes astray too often for comfort. In his entertainingly sceptical book about the information superhighway, Stoll (1995) reports how he mailed a postcard and sent an e-mail message across the USA every day for two months. The 60 postcards all arrived, with an average transit time of three days. The average transit time of the 55 e-mail messages which reached their destination was 12 minutes, but five never arrived at all. For the UKOU a figure of almost 10% of assignments undelivered would mean the loss of 100,000 student assignments per year on its million-assignment turnover, a clearly unacceptable figure.

Assuming that the delivery of e-mail will become reliable, the UKOU is developing techniques that will make tutors' comments via this medium as useful as possible to students and allow the university to monitor the process and capture the marks awarded. The UKOU considers the marking of student assignments to be a critically important function and tutors are expected to comment extensively on students' work. Central staff monitor a sample of scripts in order to verify that the process is being carried out well with common standards of marking. These processes are being incorporated into the electronic assignment handling system. Efficiency gains beyond the simple shortening of turn-round times may well result.

In 1996 the UKOU conducted a small pilot project for these developments with 330 students, situated all over the world, on two computing courses. To be consistent with the University's equal opportunities policy, *open and equal,* machine specifications were made as wide as possible so that even students with the simplest computers could participate fully (though more slowly). Likewise no particular word-processing package was specified so that students could use their own. The official assignment-handling forms were completed automatically so that tutors needed only to mark and comment on the script electronically. The integrity of the students' work remained intact with the tutors' comments appearing in a different colour. The assignments could be submitted via e-mail or Web page to the University's central office where they were logged and receipt numbers issued. Tutors logged on to the Web page and retrieved, downloaded, marked and uploaded their assignments. Electronic copies of all scripts were retained centrally. The University is evaluating this project and comparing it to its traditional approaches to assignment handling. It is also experimenting with tutorial models. The aim is to have a system that will work well for thousands of students by 1998.

Computer conferencing
Computer conferencing is a development of the basic technology of e-mail that uses the filing and organizing power of a computer to support sophisticated group and many-to-many communication facilities. This has created powerful teaching and learning tools. Indeed, even the infant applications of computer conferencing were described in an early book on the topic as revealing 'a medium which, whilst being essentially one of literary discourse, is also one of interactive, reflective and asynchronous group communication' (Mason & Kaye, 1989: 1).

The asynchronous nature of computer conferencing and the simple home equipment required (telephone, basic computer and modem) make it a particularly attractive medium for universities embarking on distance education. It does not impose constraints of time and place on students. Its unit costs at low volumes are less than those of any other distance teaching medium (see Figure 4.3) although, because these unit costs are almost independent of student numbers, there are no economies of scale (Bates, 1995: 5). This led Kaye (Mason & Kaye, 1989: 3) to claim that computer conferencing,

> 'will ultimately emerge as a new educational paradigm, taking its place along-side both face-to-face and distance education; at the same time it will change the nature of "traditional" multi-media distance education.'

Seven years later computer conferencing has become sufficiently popular with students and tutors at the UKOU for the institution to make a big investment in expanding its use. In 1995 the UKOU required 30,000 students to have access to a computer, of which 5,000 needed to have network access. The comparable figures were 35,000/17,000 in 1996 and are forecast to reach at least 40,000/20,000 in 1997. This is a high rate of growth even though computer conferencing is unlikely to involve a majority of the UKOU's 150,000 students before the 21st century. Reaching the majority also assumes that computer conferencing will not fall into the 'chasm' of the technology adoption life-cycle described in Chapter 6.

A number of articles and reports describe the recent developments in computer conferencing at the UKOU. Selinger (1995) notes its value for communication between trainee teachers who feel 'less isolated by the realization that they are not alone in their negative as well as positive teaching experiences'. Computer conferencing also provides an efficient means of taking student experience into account in revising a course:

> 'it is the intention to monitor the issues that students refer to most often. This will help determine any re-structuring and re-focusing of the course. The free nature of the medium in which students are allowed to discuss any issues that arise for them will contribute to an increased understanding of beginning teachers' needs and there will be a permanent written record of their evolving concerns.'

A survey of UKOU tutors (PLUM, 1995a) in a new course (THD204 *Information Technology and Society*), that uses both CD-ROM and computer conferencing, showed extremely positive attitudes to the computer conferencing in this course, despite negative experience with CoSy, a previous conferencing system. This is another example of the technical development of a medium making a large difference to its perceived effectiveness. The UKOU has already used four conferencing systems, CoSy, Wigwam, FirstClass and HyperNews. Whether to standardize on a particular system could become a controversial issue.

However, computer conferencing also raises interesting issues of teaching and learning as well as course design. Mason (CITE, 1995) has reported on the use of computer conferencing in a fourth-level UKOU course (A423 *Philosophical Problems of Equality*). The academic in charge of the course believed that computer conferencing did provide an answer to a strategic challenge facing all universities that teach at a distance, namely the need to plan courses with fewer resources for smaller populations so that a wider range of topics can be offered. However, she also concluded that,

> 'there is probably a severe limit to the amount of constructive teaching of a subject like philosophy that is possible in a computer conference.... If we can make conferencing work in less ambitious ways, however, the advantages may be enormous.'

Mason also notes (CITE, 1995: 11):

> 'However, students' use of conferencing has revealed a much less palatable fact, which somehow has never been so "visible" before: that many students have a very poor understanding of the course materials. It is generally acknow-ledged that the assessment and examination system in tertiary education is frequently a poor indicator of "deep level understanding". The relatively informal context of computer interactions is often much more revealing. While the lack of understanding as indicated by many of the conference messages on A423 was rather disturbing to the course team, there is no reason to believe that this problem is unique to this course – or to this University! It is simply that the medium of conferencing makes it harder to ignore. Student feedback is more public and conferencing is a more sensitive mechanism for revealing students' real thinking.'

It seems that new technology is making the Open University even more open! Set against the goal of improving the effectiveness of teaching in the mega-universities this feature of computer conferencing is to be welcomed. It does appear to be a medium with high potential for encouraging the adaptation of course materials and teaching to the real experience of students. The effective moderation of a computer conference by a tutor is crucial to making effective the feedback mechanisms that Laurillard claims are essen-tial to academic learning.

A major worry for any university that seeks to extend the use of computer conferencing (and computers generally) is the readiness of students to acquire the necessary equipment. The UKOU therefore surveys its students regularly about their ownership of various technologies and their attitude to acquiring them.

A survey (PLUM, 1995b) of students who enquired about the course THD204 *Information Technology and Society* but did not register found that few had been put off by the equipment requirements. More simply thought it wiser to avoid an innovative course in its first year of offering. However, students who express an interest in a course related to information technology are not likely to be representative of the wider student body. A survey (PLUM, 1995c) of a large sample of a cross-section of all UKOU students revealed that 65% of students had access to a computer in 1995 and that 45% of the remainder would consider buying one if UKOU use increased. In fact, usage is already impressive. In the middle of a holiday weekend, on Easter Day 1996, 6,469 students dialled in to the UKOU system. The following Saturday the figure was 11,603.

As would be expected, however, in an institution that has 150,000 students ranging from teenagers to people in their 90s, there is a minority of students who do not want to see the UKOU extend the requirement for computer use. Porter (1985) talks of the 'failure to recognize buyer segments' as one of the pitfalls of the introduction of new technology. For universities to produce two versions of each course, one using computers and one not, would be very expensive. On the other hand, most distance teaching universities operate on the principle that study should be made as flexible as possible so that people are not excluded. Obviously the long-term solution to the problem is for computers to become cheap, easy to use and an asset to any household, and for other devices, such as video games and set-top boxes, to have peripherals that turn them into computers. Technology seems to be evolving in this direction. We discuss later the implications of the evolution of the Internet network into a versatile computing platform.

Jennison (1996) reported that some students find great value in computer conferencing independently of any course requirements to use it. They welcome the feeling of being part of a tangible academic institution. One wrote, 'I would never come into contact with this rich tapestry of humanity by any other means'. Computer conferencing has been particularly appreciated by those who, for all sorts of reasons, have no opportunity to make contact with fellow students in other ways. Some of the UKOU's 4,000 disabled students, for whom new technology has always been a positive force, are very enthusiastic. The 'lurkers', those who rarely respond or post messages themselves, are just as keen. Wrote one: 'I'm mainly just a lurker but get immense value from CoSy and learn a tremendous amount'. The system includes the Log Inn, a virtual pub, and Jennison recorded nearly 200 non-course-related conferences initiated by the students themselves.

It is risky, however, to generalize from these early enthusiasts. A survey by Haynes highlights the challenge that the computer industry faces:

> 'Persuading Aunt Maud to get intimate with entire networks of computers is perhaps the industry's biggest challenge. A recent survey by Apple found that 85% of respondents were terrified of computer technology – a figure that suggests the PC user who tried to use his mouse as a foot pedal is by no means alone. For computer-literate PC users, Windows may seem perfectly straight-forward; for novices it is an unnavigable nightmare.' (Haynes, 1994: 25)

The computer industry is, of course, aware of the problem. The same author quoted a senior industry figure: 'At the moment, computers don't have artificial intelligence; they have artificial stupidity'.

The convergence of the media may be helpful in giving the computer a place alongside other household appliances. UKOU data show that students acquire electronic equipment readily when it can provide entertainment for the family as well as being an aid to study. This was the case, for example, for video cassette recorders, which were owned by 95% of UKOU students in 1995 (PLUM, 1995c: 8). A survey of the general population of the UK showed that in 1994 the number of families with children having video game equipment overtook those having a computer. In this context the marketing of computers with CD-ROM drives on the basis of their 'edutainment' value is to be welcomed. However, less than 10% of first-year UKOU students owned CD-ROM drives in 1994 (PLUM, 1994).

Another potential source of entertainment is the Internet. Curiosity about this phenomenon may also be an element of motivation for some households to acquire the necessary computing and communications equipment. The Internet and the World Wide Web are also tools of great interest to universities.

The Internet and the World Wide Web

The loose confederation of interconnected networks known as the Internet has been in existence for 25 years. Its growth began to accelerate when it linked up with public and commercial networks in the mid-1980s. Then a phase of explosive development began in 1993 when special software and better ways of connecting documents allowed users to travel the network with pictures, sound and video, simply by pointing and clicking a mouse. This interactive cyberspace, the World Wide Web, began to attract an enthusiastic audience. No communications medium or consumer electronics technology has ever grown so quickly. Usage is difficult to measure because of the decentralized nature of the Internet but Anderson (1995) estimated 20 million users in mid-1995 and suggested that by 1997 'the citizens of cyberspace will outnumber all but the largest nations'. Lycos, a firm specializing in Internet search software, estimated that the World Wide

Web grew from 4.8 million to 7 million pages between April and June 1995 (Bacsich, 1995).

The potential of the Internet is linked to two phenomena. First, Moore's Law (named after the founder of Intel), which says that computing power and capacity double every 18 months. Second, Metcalfe's Law (named after the inventor of the Ethernet standard), also known as the law of the telecosm (Haynes, 1994: 17), which says that the utility of a network to a population is roughly proportional to the number of users squared. The Internet harnesses both these laws at the same time, which will give it a much greater staying power than the fad of Citizens Band radio to which it was at first compared. The Internet's immediate attraction for universities offering education at a distance is that it has the potential to help with the perennial problem of student access to libraries, museums and other resources. In theory the student can use the World Wide Web to bring data and information from all over the world right into the home.

The current reality is more prosaic:

'By comparison with the electronic nirvana of the information superhighway prophets today's Internet is easy to ridicule. Yes, things are difficult to find; yes, 90% of what is available is rubbish. True, information is not the same as knowledge. And quite right; everything takes far too long.' (Anderson, 1995: 21)

Before examining the tension between information and knowledge and the role that the Internet can play in academic learning, we should pause to ask whether these and other shortcomings are likely to be overcome. Will the Internet survive? The problems are real. After a tour of universities and educational technology companies in North America, Bacsich (1995) reported:

'Virtually everyone we met was aware of the limitations and problems of World Wide Web and the Internet generally. We tried accessing our own home pages (at the UKOU) from a number of locations and the speed of access ranged from slow to unusable. However, everyone was sure they could not afford to ignore it, even if not all of them liked it. Most were developing strategies, software or course applications based on the Web; in short they were leading developments, rather than merely following them.'

The challenge facing the development of the Internet is to avoid the tragedy of the commons whereby our farming predecessors overgrazed land with no owner other than the community. Once connection is made to the Internet, use appears to be free. Certainly there are no charges based on either of the telecommunications traditions of charging by distance or by time. However, the bandwidth required by users has gone up sharply with the arrival of multimedia. The capacity needed to store or transmit a 700-page book (1 million bytes) will handle only 50 spoken words, five medium-size pictures or three seconds of video. With multimedia still in its infancy and only 7% of the US population connected in 1995, it is clear that Internet capacity will need to grow dramatically if it is to respond to growing demand. Anderson (1995: 25) discusses how the organization of the Internet might change (eg, a greater role for the telecommunications companies, payment for priority use) and concludes that the Internet will evolve and muddle through because:

'ubiquitous, open networking seems as fundamental to civilization's needs in the first half of the 21st century as ubiquitous, open roads did in the first half of the 20th. The lesson of the Internet is simple and lasting: people want to connect, with as little control and interference as possible. Call it a free market or just an efficient architecture: the power of open networking has only just begun to be felt.'

With their own growing commitments to ubiquity and openness, universities should find the Internet a congenial partner. However, the manner in which they use it will need careful thought because there are some obvious pitfalls. One is that since universities that teach at a distance become significant publishers, they will need to have a clear policy about use of their intellectual property. Once a document is on the World Wide Web there is no chance to control or even monitor its copying or onward use. As Anderson puts it (1995: 22): 'For publishers who still see a threat in the photocopier the Internet looks like the end of the world'.

For this reason and the sheer convenience of books and print materials universities will probably wish to continue to send at least part of their distance learning course materials to students in physical form. For what, then, should universities use the Internet? The obvious answer is for resource-based learning, but that is too glib. To quote Laurillard (1995: 206) again:

'multimedia designers are now promulgating the idea of the importance of student control over their learning, and there is a sudden interest in "resource-based learning". It has a lot more to do with the limits of computers and the complexity of learning than it does with pedagogical high-mindedness. It is a time-consuming process to address students' needs: far easier to make the material available and give them the navigation tools to find their own way through it. But beneath the rhetoric of "giving students control over their learning" is a dereliction of duty. We never supposed that students could do that with a real library; why should they be able to do it with an electronic one?'

This follows an earlier chapter in which Laurillard examines the claims made for hypertext and hypermedia, which are a key feature of the World Wide Web. Hypertext is text whose interconnectedness is made explicit and navigable. The interconnections are defined by the author (or the user) in the form of links between words (or longer passages) in the document. Clicking on the word makes the connected word appear. 'Words' can also be chunks of audio or video material, hence the extension of the idea to hypermedia.

In her book Laurillard uses the term 'interactive' to mean something that provides intrinsic feedback on the user's actions, such as a computer system that changes its behaviour according to the learner's input. In this sense hypertext is 'no more interactive than writing in the margins of a book' as the system remains neutral to whatever the student does. Because it connects associated items of information, hypertext is a good information retrieval system, but this very fact makes it inimical to academic knowledge.

> 'Academic knowledge... is not reductive; it is unitary, indivisible. In education we want to preserve the relationship between what is known and the way it comes to be known, so the notion of a fragment of information has no place in that kind of analysis.... If there is any relationship between knowledge and information it is contrastive, the one unitary/holistic, the other elementary/atomistic.' (Laurillard, 1993: 123)

In their book on the Java programming language, Freeman and Ince (1996) highlight the same problem from a different perspective:

> 'It is very difficult to build interaction into an Internet application. Most of the applications that have been developed tend to give the impression of being interactive. However, what they usually involve is just the user moving through a series of text and visual images following pointers to other sections of the text and visual images. The most one often gets with the vast majority of Internet applications is some small amount of interactivity, for example an application asking the user for an identity and a password and checking what has been typed against some stored data which describes the user.'

These reflections suggest that universities have an important teaching task in helping their students get value out of the Internet and the World Wide Web. To the extent that a link to the Internet will be part of the registration package for all university students in the future, they will be free to browse it at their will. They will find that like the real world, the on-line world contains too much information to make sense of. It will be up to universities to help them make sense of all this information by providing systems that respond to learners, teach navigation skills, answer frequently asked questions, and constitute a gateway service. If this is done well, institutions may find a further market for such services in the rest of higher education. Universities also have a role in solving the technical problems of the Internet, for example in reducing delays by the use of caching and mirror sites (*The Economist*, 1996c).

Universities will pay special attention to the World Wide Web sites they maintain themselves. It is too early to forecast the format of such sites because the capabilities of the Internet and the Web are still evolving. For example, 1995 saw the development of real-time audio broadcasting over the Internet. The market leader, Progressive Networks' RealAudio, sold its first 100,000 player licences in three months. Audio-cassettes and audio-vision are teaching media whose effectiveness in distance education is well-established. The idea of having a bank of course-related audio items available on the Internet might well be attractive for the mega-universities. Ironically, the UKOU adopted the lecture format, one of the oldest academic methods, for its first high profile venture into audio on the Internet. This was a lecture on Fractals, delivered worldwide on 11 October 1995, and was the inaugural event of the Knowledge Media Institute Stadium, an experiment in large-scale telepresence.

Revisiting the Internet a year after his earlier survey, Anderson (1996) remarked that it is evolving in 'dog-years' (ie, seven years growth for each human year). This makes it very difficult to predict its future impact. Anderson is convinced that we are seeing a major paradigm shift. It is not just that the Internet is cheap and open, although those characteristics make it particularly congenial to universities. He holds that the Internet (and Intranets – the private organizational networks that are even bigger in aggregate) is transforming software by becoming the new computing platform. Crucially, for universities committed to wide student access, the Internet is breaking the cycle that requires more and more computing power to run ever more complex software. As the saying goes, 'Intel giveth and Microsoft taketh away'.

The key innovation has been the Java language, which allows the writing of small programmes, 'applets', that reside in the network until needed. Because of this, Java is more than a language: it is also itself a computer. The implication for universities is that students will be able to have access to enormous computing power without having to invest large sums in their own equipment. For Anderson (1996: 10) this is a revolution: 'The arrival of the Internet was the blinding flash of an H-bomb. Java is the shockwave that follows, toppling buildings and flattening trees'. This arrival of this shockwave may be a defining moment in the development of technology-based university teaching and learning.

Synopsis: universities on-line

E-mail, computer conferencing and access to the Internet are already available as integrated software packages. Turning these information technologies into true knowledge media will require determined work by universities. Their greatest initial asset is that they satisfy the desire of distant students to communicate with each other.

As more individuals have good and productive experiences with computers and user interfaces continue to improve, the present fear of computers among some students is likely to disappear. The price of adequate personal computing equipment is unlikely to rise in real terms and, with the arrival of Java, may fall sharply. Furthermore, Cairncross (1995) predicts that early in the 21st century the price of telecommunications will fall dramatically and cease to vary significantly with distance. If it happens this will present remarkable opportunities for computer conferencing. A university could maintain a network of tutors all over the world and encourage each to augment their general tutorial competence with specific skills for teaching particular concepts. Students could then be directed to particular sub-conferences to get help from tutors experienced in dealing with the various problems encountered with difficult topics. It seems also that the revolution of the Internet in higher education has barely begun.

Stand-alone multimedia

Most of the mega-universities already call themselves multimedia distance teaching systems. Until now, however, the various component media of those teaching systems have come on separate supports. It is now possible to combine several of the media that deliver a particular set of course materials on a single support, CD-ROM being the leading current technology for this purpose. One conclusion is that universities that produce distance learning materials should be arranging to keep all their intellectual assets (print, diagrams, audio, video, software) in digital form so that they can readily be re-configured for new delivery systems.

In principle, anything that can be put on a CD-ROM can be downloaded to a personal computer over an appropriate connection from a distant server. In practice, the idea of providing students with CD-ROMs specifically made for their particular course is likely to prove attractive, at least in the short term. In a substantial survey of multimedia technologies directed at business readers, Hagel and Eisenmann (1994) suggested that 'networked multimedia applications will tend to lag behind those that are "standalone" – that is can run on a single PC or video game console'. This is likely to be even truer outside North America where it is a safe working assumption that it will be at least a decade before 90% of homes have access to interactive broad band facilities. (In the UK overall telephone ownership is only just over 90% of households and this figure falls to below 50% for disadvantaged groups. Serving such groups is part of the mission of the UKOU and the other mega-universities.) However, the delivery of audio and video over the Internet is developing very fast. As we saw in the last section, the Java language will turn the Internet into a vast CD-ROM. Universities should keep their choice of networked or stand-alone delivery systems for their multimedia courses under constant review.

The CD-ROM market is an infant business where the present products are primitive compared to what is likely to come. One weakness is the limitations of most home versions of personal-computer technology, which can make viewing pictures or video or listening to sound from a CD-ROM somewhat irritating. The other shortcoming arises from the inexperience of those who authored and published the first CD-ROMs. Reviewing the titles then available, *The Economist* (1994) found that the best CD-ROM adaptation to date was the *Oxford English Dictionary*. This was partly because of the quality and quantity of the data (which it shared with the printed edition). However, what

> 'sets it apart and makes the choice of CD-ROM much more than just a means of storage, is the addition of an unusually flexible, bespoke searching programme that enables the user to isolate almost any variable... and conduct on a whim, with perfect accuracy, arcane analyses that might otherwise have taken months.'

Early results from experimentation with CD-ROMs in the UKOU also lead to the conclusion that students value highly the facility to search text. In terms of Laurillard's taxonomy of media, a CD-ROM that allows sophisticated searches is a reasonably interactive medium. Until the capacity of both CD-ROMs and home computers increases substantially, institutions may be wise to devote most of their course-related CD-ROMs to text and graphics rather than video.

Recreating the academy as a community

Campus universities worry that as they have grown and diversified the sense of academic community has been lost. We noted in Chapter 3 that such universities are now concerned to integrate students more fully into academic life by better coordinating the roles and efforts of all staff.

The mega-universities are concerned to create a sense of academic belonging among students for very practical reasons. The considerable differences between these universities on the criteria of student retention and achievement have no single cause. It is generally true, however, that student performance and satisfaction correlate well with the richness of the media mix that the institution employs and the personal support it gives to students through live, face-to-face interaction. These measures, in their turn, are closely related to the resources available to the institution. The desire to provide more tutorial support to students is explicit in the plans of the Indonesian, Korean and South African mega-universities, while those in Spain and Thailand intend to use video conferencing to enrich the work of their study centres.

Campus universities embarking on distance teaching tend to focus first on producing learning materials. They should also give attention to student support and opportunities for student-student interaction. To the extent that resources for these developments may have to be found by cutting back on other activities, the cost-effectiveness of tutorial provision is a key factor. Can technology help?

Tutorial support

It is too soon to expect automated tutorial systems to play a significant role in the teaching strategies of the mega-universities. In her discussion of adaptive media, which include tutorial programmes, tutorial simulations and tutorial systems, Laurillard (1993: 162) writes:

> 'Tutoring systems would be the acme of all the educational media, if they existed. They address all aspects of the learning process I have defined as being necessary. They are difficult to develop and contribute more to progress in AI (Artificial Intelligence) than they do to education.'

This suggests that although universities should follow these developments and experiment with tutorial simulations in some of their courses, they should base their tutorial provision on people. How do they select the tutors and how can technology help the tutors?

Campus universities can draw on a large pool of faculty and graduate teaching assistants to support their students. Most of the mega-universities, however, were set up in order to remedy a shortage of university-trained people in their country. It followed that university-trained people who could act as tutors were also in short supply, especially in rural areas. For this reason, and in order to help establish their academic credibility, some mega-universities (eg, IGNOU) turned to distinguished academics in local universities to organize regional tutorial services. Other mega-universities simply judged that tutorial provision was not practical or affordable.

It is time to review these assumptions because the rapid development of higher education in all countries, and indeed the growth of the mega-universities themselves, have produced a much larger pool of potential tutors. Not surprisingly, the former students of a mega-university can make excellent tutors because they understand from experience the challenges facing other students. In the UKOU's operations in Russia and the countries of the former Soviet bloc, where its management courses are taught in local languages, all tutors have to take their course as a student before being appointed to tutor it. This ensures that they are not only familiar with the content, but also have first-hand experience of the UKOU teaching system.

The technologies most often mentioned as helpful, once a network of tutors is in place, are computer-mediated communication, the telephone and video conferencing. We examine each in turn.

Tutoring by computer
The context for the use of computer-mediated communication in universities was described earlier. There is a palpable enthusiasm for this medium among students, as the following comments testify (both are from messages sent over the UKOU conferencing systems):

> 'I consider the effects of the use of computer-mediated communication for disabled study to be no less than revolutionary. It can change the life of a disabled student by increasing the motivation to study and giving him/her access to other students in a way never before possible. Telephone tutorials have been used by the UKOU to help overcome the isolation, but they are for a limited period, whereas CoSy can be used at any time during the day or night and gives the opportunity for equal say.'

> 'I would much rather be browsing through FirstClass than working. I keep telling myself I will only use it at weekends when the phone charges are cheaper but the lure is too strong. I wonder if it's because like you I'm an OU graduate and it's such a novelty being able to contact other students as easily as we can now. We've had to study on our own for such a long time that this "freedom" is a luxury that other students may not quite understand.'

An academic in the UKOU's teacher training programme gives an example of a student giving such useful help to another that the staff incorporated it into the course:

'A Post Graduate Certificate in Education student in Newcastle, two weeks into her first teaching practice, put out a cry for help (on the computer conferencing system) as she'd lost her voice. Within the hour someone from Bristol came back to say she had the same problem BUT her sister was a speech therapist and had sent her two pages of advice! This was attached. (We now put that in the course materials.)'

All the experience with these systems suggests that the work of the tutor who moderates the conference makes a great difference to its effectiveness. Clearly tutors will need training for this role. It is also clear that computer conferencing is demanding on tutors. However, the systems do allow tutors to save time. For example, instead of explaining the same point separately to a number of students when marking their assignments, the tutor's explanation can be posted on the system and students who need it can be referred to it.

Tutoring by telephone
One-to-one tutoring by telephone is a well established practice in distance education in countries that have a developed telecommunications infrastructure. It seems likely that this will be the situation for all the mega-universities in the first decade of the next century as developing countries leapfrog into the digital telecommunications future. Furthermore, if Cairncross' (1995) prediction is right, and telecommunications charges drop sharply and become essentially independent of distance, then tutoring by telephone will become an option for all institutions.

George (1994) has described how over 2,000 students of the UKOU in Scotland are in contact with their tutors only or mainly by phone; and that groups of these students use over 200 hours a year in audio conferencing. These group telephone tutorials, where students join each other and the tutor by teleconference from their homes, are of particular interest. Like a computer conference they give some economies of scale to the tutor's work while allowing the students to learn from and support each other. The skills needed for successful telephone tutoring are well documented and can readily be acquired (Parker, 1984). Experience shows that a good face-to-face teacher is almost invariably a good and effective telephone teacher (George, 1994: 82). In an interesting innovation, the UKOU is now experimenting with group telephone tutorials for language instruction (French) and intends also to use the telephone for assessing students' oral language skills.

Video broadcasting and conferencing
Television broadcasting is not a new medium. However, the number of channels available for delivering television is rising rapidly and all the

mega-universities now want to expand their TV and/or radio broadcasting. This finding is surprising in view of Bates' (1982) conclusion that there was then a move away from broadcasting in the 12 distance teaching institutions he studied. The reasons for this trend were: the broadcasting organization was separate from the distance teaching organization, which therefore had limited control over the product; transmission time was inadequate in quantity and quality; the institutions could not be sure of reaching their intended audience by broadcasting. Bates found that the cost of broadcasting was not a factor in the decision to use it less. He concluded that the main reason was simply academic distrust of the medium.

Why is broadcasting popular again? First, only one of the 12 institutions surveyed by Bates in 1982 was a mega-university. Size colours the institutional attitude to broadcasting simply because a large institution has more bargaining power with the broadcaster and a greater incentive to reach a large audience. Transmission time is still a problem today but the growth in the number of channels with the development of cable and satellite systems and terrestrial digital TV will shortly ease this difficulty. The Korean mega-university, like a number of campus universities around the world (eg, Carleton University, Canada), now has its own cable channel. The UKOU became part of the BBC's new all-night educational programming in 1995 and CNED is involved with France's new educational TV channel. The potential of broadcasting to reach any intended audience is now high in most countries for terrestrial transmission but very variable for cable and satellite.

Any university planning to expand into broadcasting must be clear about what it is trying to achieve through this medium. In particular, it should clarify what audience(s) it is trying to reach. If the purpose is simply to reach a student audience, as in the Chinese TVU system, then the growth of channels is a good thing because it makes more airtime available. If part of the purpose is to reach the largest possible general, non-student audience the ideal situation is to have enough channels to allow the institution to have good air time, but not to have the audience diluted between too many channels.

Institutions should be clear about the return they expect on their investment in broadcasting because educational television, by itself, does not make money. However, the return on investment could be a combination of student learning, the creation of a sense of academic community among students, enhancing the institution's reputation with the general audience, marketing, student recruitment, public relations, opening up academic work to public view, meeting national educational goals, etc.

In this context research on the drop-in audience for UKOU terrestrial broadcasts may provide pointers to other universities. Acaster and McCron

(1994) reported that in 1993 five million people (more than 10% of the UK adult population) saw at least 15 minutes of UKOU television in a three-week period. However, this figure had dropped to 3.7m by 1994 because, although the UKOU's audience share at its transmission times had gone up, some transmissions had been moved to less popular times. The one million viewers who saw more than one UKOU programme were very positive. They claimed to watch because they found the subjects interesting and said they were looking for educational, rather than simply informative programming. Compared to the people watching other channels at the time the UKOU audience was older and more male.

The same survey also found that students (at any level and with any institution) appreciated the programmes more than people who were not involved in formal study. The most common complaint from viewers was that it was difficult to get information about the schedules of UKOU programming to help in planning their viewing. This complaint was made with even more force about radio broadcasts. Few of the drop-in TV audience had ever heard a UKOU radio broadcast because they had no idea where to look for them among the many networks. Students show a clear preference for audio cassettes over radio broadcasts for course-related purposes. This means that universities must be especially lucid if they develop a radio broadcasting strategy.

The survey data on the UKOU's terrestrial broadcasting may have some validity for transmissions on cable and satellite television. Institutions generally expect production for cable/satellite TV to cost less than terrestrial broadcasting. However, if they seek a substantial drop-in audience (the UKOU attracts between 5% and 12% of the audience of the four UK terrestrial channels for its broadcasts) there will be pressure to level up the production values – and the accompanying production costs – towards network standards. This appears to be happening, for example, in the Mind Extension University satellite/cable channel in the USA. It seems likely that this activity requires a net subsidy from the universities that use the channel (ie, the costs of using cable/satellite are not fully covered by the fees and state grants that enrolled students bring).

The need for clarity about purpose and costings will be particularly important as universities expand satellite broadcasting outside their own territories as part of their growing international reach. The production costs of broadcast TV are likely to deter individual campus institutions from using this medium extensively. There is, however, a case for the creation of consortia to share the investment needed to use this powerful medium to keep the world's academic community in the public view.

Campus universities tend to be more attracted to the use of video conferencing to create remote classroom networks. Bates (1994) has reviewed educational applications of video conferencing technology in North America and his results suggest that institutions should proceed cautiously. There does seem to be a conflict between suppliers, who are eager to provide the video equipment and the telecommunications bandwidth that it requires, and educators who may not always find this a cost-effective teaching and learning technology.

Students do consistently prefer an electronic classroom at a local site to having to travel to another centre. However, Bates found that the instructional preparation time for video conferencing was usually grossly underestimated because teaching and learning methods had to be radically changed to exploit fully the potential of the technology. Indeed, in many of the projects he reviewed, 'it was difficult, given the extra cost and lack of exploitation of the visual medium, to see the justification for using video conferencing rather than audio conferencing'. He concludes:

> 'None of the projects reviewed provided firm evidence that two-way live video-conferencing was more effective than one-way video plus two-way audio, or even the distribution of video tapes for individual use. Indeed, there was some evidence that mature students who were working preferred flexibility to live video interaction, if the latter meant that they had to be in a certain place at a certain time.'

Governance

The governance structures of universities vary considerably, reflecting national cultures. The process for choosing the head of the institution, for instance, can be an election among the academic staff, appointment by government, or appointment by the institution's governing board.

In recent decades the tendency of governments has been to curtail, rather than foster, the notions of university autonomy and participative governance. Business models of corporate organization have become fashionable, although in the early 1990s scandals in some of the UK universities using this model put it out of style there. Since most of the mega-universities are relatively recent government creations, the introduction of participative decision-making structures was not a priority. However, the Indonesian and South African mega-universities have now made it an institutional priority to increase the participation of staff and other stakeholders in the governance of the university.

The governance structures of universities are outside the scope of this book. We simply note that there seems to be some correlation, in both campus universities and the mega-universities, between institutional success and the level of participation of staff in governance. This should not be surprising, for knowledge-based industries work best with management processes based on teams and consensus rather than on hierarchy and authority.

The purpose here is simply to observe that current technologies can facilitate effective participation in governance where it is sought. Examples are:

- the use of audio conferencing to allow staff, students and graduates not based at the central campus to participate in meetings;
- the use of file servers and World Wide Web sites to make university documents available to staff;
- e-mail, which tends to loosen hierarchical processes;
- organizational development technologies, such as Continuous Quality Improvement or the UK's Investors in People programme, which encourage communication on goal setting at all levels of the organization.

Synopsis: the mediated academic community

Many universities would like to re-create a sense of academic community and belonging after a period during which growth and diversification have eroded it. The developing information and communications technologies provide new mechanisms for bringing members of the academic community together. In order to create the environments for intellectual interaction that are the essence of academic community, universities must adapt for their own purposes recent developments in telecommunications and the fast-evolving technology of the Internet. They should not forget the potential of the older technology of broadcasting for informally associating large numbers of people with the academic enterprise.

Production and delivery of courses and intellectual assets

The value chain analyses for the UKOU (Figure 5.3, p.77) show that course materials production is the most costly activity in staff time that a large distance teaching institution carries out. This is a key process for any university wishing to teach at a distance in the asynchronous, correspondence tradition. Any attempt to enhance competitive advantage must, therefore, address this issue.

The goal is not simply to reduce its cost. Some large distance teaching universities have low development and production costs but are unsatisfied with the quality of the resultant courses. The UKOU is generally satisfied with the quality of its courses but each takes so long to make that it cannot produce as many of them as its students would like. The aim must be to produce courses in a manner that gives an optimal balance of cost, quality and development time. In terms of Porter's analysis, universities should seek to achieve both differentiation, in the sense of courses that are more attractive, effective and stimulating than conventional offerings, and cost leadership. This is a tough challenge.

It is clear that new technologies, such as computer conferencing and the Internet, will change the format of university courses taught at a distance. Until now the common practice, in the correspondence tradition, has been to develop materials covering the whole course content and then to run the course for a number of years. The speed of change in many areas of knowledge was already putting strain on this process by requiring regular revisions to the materials. Now, with the ability to provide extra material directly to students through computer conferencing and the Internet, the notion of course materials will become much more dynamic. The future will see more flexible curricula and more independent work by students. The examples given earlier of computer conferencing show that this medium will help the process by making student feedback much more explicit and useful in course revision.

The role of the course team

The evidence indicates that the team approach to course development yields courses that are superior to those produced by individual academics, especially where the individual academic is in another university and working under contract. This evidence, which comes both from student achievement and the judgements of other academics about the intellectual vigour of the product, suggests that developing courses in teams is worth some added cost. By putting the principal academic talents at the centre of the curriculum the course team approach also reverses the tendency, lamented by Zemsky and Massy (1995), for the professoriate to desert the core function of the university. The challenge is to render course team activity more effective at producing good courses quickly at reasonable cost.

This is not, therefore, process re-engineering in the sense of Hammer and Champy (1993), which seeks order-of-magnitude reductions in costs and for that reason has acquired a reputation for being simply a euphemism for down-sizing (see, for example, *The Economist,* 1995). In any case all the mega-universities, except the Chinese TVU system, already have small academic staff complements. The aim should be to produce and deliver more courses without a commensurate increase in staff, rather than to reduce the size of the faculty. Nevertheless, some of the principles of Hammer and Champy's work are relevant.

To the extent that moving to teams rather than hierarchies is a key principle of re-engineering, the course team is a ready-made locus for change. If courses are to become more dynamic entities, whose content and methods will evolve over their lifetimes, a first step is to make the course team explicitly responsible for the course throughout its life. This would be a change from present practice in some cases. At the UKOU, for example, the large production course teams essentially disband once the course is ready. One person, or at most a few individuals are charged with becoming the 'maintenance' course team, whose job is to monitor the offering of the course and prepare the student assessment material required annually. UKOU academics feel this work has low status.

New technology, especially computer conferencing, could facilitate the notion of a 'lifetime course team' by giving academic staff easy access to students. If a course directed students to resources on a rapidly changing database like the World Wide Web, the team would be obliged to stay close to these changes. Furthermore, a more proactive course team would be able to save money and enhance teaching effectiveness by more sophisticated use of computer-assisted assessment.

An important general goal, which Laurillard (1993: 206) has highlighted, is to get a better match between the effectiveness of the media mix for the student and the time spent developing each medium by the course team. She estimates, for example, that UKOU students distribute their study time between the media of print, video, computer, tutorial and essay in the proportions 10 : 1 : 2 : 1 : 3. The academic development time for that distribution of teaching would be equivalent to 60 : 10 : 10 : 1 : 1. This means that writing print and setting essays use academic time most efficiently in terms of study time generated. This may not, however, use the students' time most productively for learning gain.

Another issue is that current technologies, and especially the knowledge media, do not lend themselves to the sort of centralized production facilities that were appropriate for TV and radio broadcasting. This is a helpful development if it puts academics closer to the production process, as desktop publishing has done, and reduces the academic distrust that Bates (1982) found for the broadcast media. It may also help to reduce the tension between productivity for the academic and productivity for the student.

Such decentralization of media development does hold some dangers. The mega-universities may lose economies of scale in the use of media and confuse students by using different systems (eg, for computer conferencing) in different courses. This suggests that all universities developing intellectual assets should take a proactive stance by putting in place shells, templates and software standards that would carry over from course to course. There is also much scope for sharing production resources and this can also facilitate the transfer of know-how, technology and good practice from one course team to another.

Just as information technology has been a key factor in process re-engineering in industry, so it could play a helpful role in enabling the 'lifetime course team' to do its expanded job. If course teams are given the challenge of having courses in the hands of students within a maximum of two years of the decision to offer the course, they will need enhanced project management tools. Up-to-date management information on the progress of the course project, widely available to team members, is a key requirement. Another is an electronic publishing system, possibly linked to computer conferencing software, that gives team members instant access to each other's work. A common technique of re-engineering is to tackle tasks in parallel rather than sequentially. Preparing course materials in this manner will place considerable demands on the coordination of the process.

The challenge of producing good courses faster and cheaper with new media is considerable. It is encouraging that a common finding from industrial re-engineering experience is that carrying out processes more quickly almost always saves money. Achieving the objective of faster course development will require disciplined work planning. At the UKOU, for example, course production was much faster in the early days because the members of each course team were involved in fewer other activities than now. Focusing the work of academics on a smaller number of tasks in any time period seems crucial.

Logistics in dispersed institutions

A consequence of their quasi-industrial structure is that the mega-universities rely on relatively larger administrative and operational systems than campus universities. Porter (1985) showed that in seeking competitive advantage it is just as important to use technology well in support operations as in teaching.

The literature on re-engineering, and particularly its emphasis on the role of information technology in making it possible to recast processes completely, is highly relevant here. We shall comment on information systems, the use of the telephone, and the transmission of materials and assignments between the institution and its students.

Information systems strategy

By the standards of most businesses universities, whether they are based on a campus or teach at a distance, are complex operations. In addition to the sheer density of human transactions they generate, universities operate with considerable ambiguity about the roles of their 'members'. Are students customers? Are the faculty owners or employees?

The mega-universities are large business enterprises. As well as selling a wide variety of products to a large customer population distributed all over their country and beyond, they also have to organize an elaborate 'after-sales service' which involves multiple transactions with each customer. Sophisticated administrative computing systems are fundamental assets to the mega-universities. These institutions must take advantage of each advance in information technology to improve their competitive advantage.

Their administrative computing systems are now so vital to the continued existence of the mega-universities that their upgrading is a serious matter. The UKOU is currently spending some £10 million ($16 m) on a five-year programme to renew its systems. After beginning this work in 1992 with the idea that the main task was to move from a mainframe system to a distributed system, the institution realized that far more was at stake. It therefore recommenced the process, along with a complete review of its information systems strategy using a rigorous methodology (PRINCE) developed by the UK government's computing agency. It was this work that gave rise to the scoping study used to construct the value chain for the UKOU. This fundamental analysis of the information flows within the organization was intended to provide a secure basis for the development of a suite of systems to support institutional operations.

The first major product of this process is the main student record system, CIRCE (Corporate and Individual Records for Customers and Enquirers), which was introduced in 1996. The introduction of such a system provides an institution with many opportunities to review its processes and make efficiency gains. A similar process (GAEL 2) is under way at CNED.

The development of increasingly powerful logistics systems by the mega-universities should provide an incentive for collaborative ventures with campus universities. Twenty years ago the most important competitive advantage of large distance teaching institutions was their ability to manage the complex technologies required for developing good course materials. Now those technologies (video, print, computing) have become cheaper and easier to use, which partly explains the entry of many campus universities into distance education. Today it is the powerful logistics systems required to support large numbers of students nationally and internationally that is harder for campus universities to reproduce. There are obvious complementary alliances to be forged between campus universities that have the academic strength to develop courses in a wide range of disciplines, and the mega-universities whose logistics support systems can handle additional students at very low marginal costs.

Administrative use of the telephone

The teaching opportunities created by the progress of telecommunications have already been explored. There is also a trend in all countries for people to turn to the telephone for their administrative dealings with organizations. Most campus universities in North America already have sophisticated systems for handling phone enquiries and course registrations. Among the mega-universities, France's CNED has been a leader in responding to the greater use of the telephone. This institution, which avoided being in the telephone directory in the 1980s, now has an ultra-modern system for handling thousands of calls per day.

In contrast, the UKOU has only recently realized the importance of updating its practices in this area. An internal report (Edwards *et al.*, 1995) was blunt: 'The failure to exploit the opportunities offered by the telephone is damaging our relationship with present and potential students and customers and at variance with the University's strategic aims'. The report makes clear that the main obstacle to progress is not the technology but working habits and a national culture that have traditionally treated the telephone as an informal means of communication.

Moving materials

E-mail and computer conferencing have real potential to speed up the turn-round of student assignments and improve the feedback given to students. However, even if problems of intellectual property rights on the Internet are resolved, it seems clear that universities operating at a distance will continue to need to ship some course materials to their students. In the mega-universities such shipments are measured in tonnes per day.

Little can be said as a general prescription for dealing with this issue, where problems tend to be location-specific. They also tend, however, to be time-specific, so institutions should keep their distribution mechanisms under constant review. The mega-universities in Spain and Turkey, for example, distribute materials through their local study centres, where students come and collect them. India's IGNOU adopted a similar strategy, renting trucks for the purpose, in 1993. The UKOU hired its own courier to deliver materials in Belgium for a while but now uses the regular mail. Because the mega-universities are very large customers, most national post offices work hard to satisfy their needs, including liaison with postal authorities in other countries.

One recent development, which may have applications for some universities, is the possibility of printing on demand at remote locations (Alexander and Karsh, 1995). Under such a system the document (for example a set of course books) is distributed as a data stream to printers (such as Xerox DocuTechs) at remote sites where the requisite numbers of copies are printed and dispatched. This method could be particularly helpful to universities with substantial student numbers in other countries, where it would eliminate the delays, costs and inconvenience of shipping over national borders.

Summary

Despite their differences, campus universities and the mega-universities share a number of similar strategic challenges. This chapter has focused on four of them: making teaching more effective and learning more productive; producing and delivering course materials and intellectual assets; recreating the academy as a community; and the logistics of dispersed institutions. We have examined how the knowledge media, and some older media like television and telephony, might help universities respond to these challenges.

The linking of students by bringing their home computers on-line could have a powerful impact in all areas and the equipment they need may soon become much cheaper. Universities need to do considerable development work if they are to derive full advantage from opportunities such as on-line tutoring and the Internet. If they are successful these developments could reinvigorate, in on-line universities, the sense of academic community that has declined over recent decades.

The thoughtful and skilled application of new technology also provides important opportunities for universities in their administrative and operational activities. Collaborative ventures that bring together the academic resources of campus institutions with the logistics capacity of the mega-universities have great potential for providing students with a wide choice of well-supported courses.

Chapter 8

Implementing a Technology Strategy

Framework for a technology strategy

This book has explored the role of new technologies in the renewal of higher education. We looked first at the challenges of the changing environment in which universities operate. Taking advantage of technology to develop elements of distance education will be one response to those pressures for many institutions. After describing the essentials of distance education we examined the nature of competitive advantage for universities and asked what would make new learning technologies attractive to students. The previous chapter reviewed current experience of the knowledge media against that background.

In this final chapter we wind these threads together and ask how universities should develop a technology strategy within their planning processes. We first define the framework into which a technology strategy must fit. We then examine the issues campus universities must consider in developing such strategies. Finally, to illustrate the implementation of a technology strategy in a mega-university, we shall describe how the UK Open University has tackled it.

The word 'strategy' has military connotations and derives from a Greek word for general. The *Oxford Dictionary* defines strategy as 'the art of a commander in chief: the art of projecting and directing the larger military movements and operations of a campaign'. For *Webster* it is 'the art of devising or employing plans or stratagems towards a goal'. A 'stratagem', in turn, is 'any artifice or trick, a device or scheme for obtaining an advantage'. We should bear these definitions in mind. Just as a general often avoids the obvious frontal attack, changing the university through technology requires imaginative implementation as well as sensible planning.

Content and process

Good planning requires attention to both the *content* and the *process* of strategy (Bowman & Asch, 1996). How a strategy is derived greatly affects whether it can be carried out successfully, especially in a university. To have a technology strategy disavowed by the faculty, as happened in the USA at the University of Maine, is not a happy outcome.

The content of strategy refers particularly to the level of the organization which it addresses. Corporate strategy deals with the overall aims, scope and mission of the organization. Business strategy focuses on competitiveness and asks which markets the organization should target and how. Operational strategy underpins business strategy at the level of functions and departments. The technology strategy of a university is situated primarily at the level of business strategy and also has considerable implications for some operational strategies. Most universities already have a corporate strategy that provides a framework for planning at other levels.

Bowman and Asch (1996: 3) emphasize that good strategy process combines both appropriateness and commitment. An ideal process inspires strong commitment to a high-quality strategy. At the other extreme, a weak strategy that attracts no staff loyalty is unlikely to have any impact. The intermediate cases, which are more dangerous, are the consultant's strategy: a strategy which is good but generates no feeling of ownership; and the blinkered strategy: a poor strategy that everyone believes in.

The collegial tradition of academic governance makes it unlikely that a technology strategy developed without extensive faculty input would have any impact. Involvement of the university community in developing the strategy is essential if it is not to seem like a consultant's strategy. However, the historic constancy of lecturing methods on campus may make it hard for faculty to imagine strategies that take them outside an intuitive core of shared assumptions and beliefs about teaching methods. Furthermore, almost any technology strategy is likely to challenge habits by requiring changes to the way faculty teach and students learn. There is a real risk of developing a blinkered strategy.

This implies that the development of a university technology strategy requires debate, time and leadership. Those leading the process must inspire a vision of the future that is attractive to all concerned. It is legitimate to create an aura of anxiety in order to generate discussion that increases understanding of the external forces for change. There is, after all, a danger than unless universities become generators of technology-based courses their faculty will gradually become buyers' guides and librarians for materials produced outside the academy. New uses of technology should be linked to shared academic goals and previous experiences of institutional success. Mechanisms for implementation need to emphasize cooperation, teamwork and support. A technology strategy debate is an excellent opportunity to remind all staff of their stake in the future of the university and to obtain renewed commitment. They also need to remember that technology changes rapidly. To wait to act until a fully validated decision has been reached is to miss the point – and the boat.

Industry structure

Chapter 5 summarized Porter's (1985) work on competitive advantage and derived from it some key components of strategy development. The opportunity to provide value to buyers, which is the essence of competitive advantage, depends as much on industry structure as on the attributes of a particular organization. For a university the relevant industry is the education and training sector of its home country. Institutions need to maintain a systematic awareness of trends in that sector whether they plan to have a technology strategy or not. However, developing a technology strategy gives a particular slant to the five competitive forces that determine industry structure:

1. *Rivalry among existing institutions*. The growth of distance education is eroding the geographical constraints on institutional rivalry. People can now study with universities in other countries without ever leaving home.
2. *The threat of new entrants*. Apart from faraway academic rivals, universities may now have to compete with new providers who start from a base in technology rather than education (eg, satellite TV stations, telecommunications companies, software houses).
3. *The bargaining power of buyers*. Rivalry and new entrants may produce dramatic price differentials between institutions. New home technologies and open systems will give students an increasingly wide choice of universities.

4. *The bargaining power of suppliers.* At present technical progress and vigorous competition are driving down the costs of computing and communicating. Nevertheless is it risky for a university to become too dependent on a single supplier of a crucial technology.
5. *The threat of substitute products and services.* Any university that trades the centuries-old tradition of classroom lecturing for new teaching technologies must be aware that technologies continually change.

Routes to competitive advantage

The principal routes to competitive advantage are either cost leadership or differentiation. Technology can help a university travel either route. A challenge in implementing a technology strategy is to balance the discipline and frugality that supports cost leadership with the innovation and risk-taking that yields differentiation.

In order to determine where technology can be applied to greatest effect in reducing costs or creating valuable differentiation a university needs good information on the costs of its activities. This is a weakness in most institutions. In Chapter 5 we applied Porter's concept of the value chain to universities in order to identify key categories of value activities at a macroscopic level. However, for the purpose of applying technology in pursuit of competitive advantage, the costing of activities must be continued at a finer level. Once this is done it may be possible to see how technology could alter particular structural causes of the cost of an activity (cost drivers) or of its distinctiveness (uniqueness drivers). We review some examples relevant to campus universities later.

Skills and resources

An effective technology strategy must start from the skills and resources already available to the university. This is not just a question of the skills and resources in place, but how well they work together and whether the university could create new capabilities by combining them in different ways. Prahalad and Hamel (1990) argued that long-term competitiveness depends on the ability to build core competences, which they defined as 'the collective learning of an organization, especially how to coordinate diverse production skills and integrate multiple streams of technologies'. Such core competences give a university the ability to create exciting courses and learning opportunities. Starting from what the university is capable of doing is likely to provide a more durable basis for a technology strategy than reviewing unmet needs in the higher education market.

Universities should review their capabilities and competences with one eye on their competitors to see where significant competitive advantage might exist. Looking at the scale on which the mega-universities operate, campus universities might well wonder where their own assets for distance education could possibly lie. One such advantage is their academic faculty. Relatively speaking, the academic staff of campus universities are more numerous than those of the mega-universities in each discipline. Most campuses have some academic units with high reputations because striving for international excellence in sharply focused areas is a good way of sustaining academic vitality, especially in small universities (Daniel & Bélanger, 1989).

There is another reason for starting from a university's academic strengths when identifying the capabilities on which to base a technology strategy. Distance-taught or technology-based courses are much more public than classroom instruction. The university should be aware that its total image in the outside world may be influenced quite quickly by perceptions of the quality of these new offerings. It should put its best academic foot forward.

Three points should be made about financial resources. First, technology should be treated as an operating expense, not a capital expense. Inappropriate accounting hinders a technology strategy by focusing too much on large equipment decisions ('we will buy you the right platform'). Second, when implementing a technology strategy it is important to have a special source of funds on which individuals and units can call. Such funds can be managed by those guiding the strategy to create synergy between different initiatives. Third, the formulae and mechanisms that drive the flow of resource through the university should be consistent with the technology strategy. This is another way of saying that the technology strategy should support the overall goals of the university.

Developing a technology strategy tests the effectiveness of a university's collegial decision-making and human resource management. Those institutions with high morale and a collective sense of purpose will have an advantage because the capabilities required for a successful strategy emphasize coordination and integration of activities across the university. Processes for the promotion and preferment of staff should place value on activities that advance the technology strategy. Good relations with unions will be helpful as working practices evolve in the light of new needs.

The development of technology-based teaching provides a nice opportunity to strengthen the relationship between research and teaching. In his important work, *Scholarship Reconsidered: Priorities of the professoriate,* Boyer (1990) urged the academy to break out of the old, rather sterile dichotomy between teaching and research by focusing instead on four facets of scholarship: the scholarship of discovery, the scholarship of teaching, the scholarship of integration and the scholarship of application. A successful technology strategy requires close attention to the scholarship of teaching. Resource for new technology in teaching will be used most effectively if it is obtained through the sort of peer-reviewed and competitive proposal process used for research funding. Innovation in technology-based teaching requires the same care and understanding as the development of knowledge in any other field.

Finally, any inventory of the skills and resources available to underpin a technology strategy must review the university's marketing and operational systems. Has the institution previously marketed itself to the clientele that its technology-based teaching might address? If the intention is to offer such teaching to large numbers of students, can existing operational capacity be scaled up to cope? Our study of the technology adoption life-cycle identified three value disciplines whose relative importance changes at different stages in the cycle: product leadership, customer intimacy and operational excellence. The first two are the most important for success in the early market. This is a reassuring finding for a campus university. It implies that the institution can draw on the strengths of its faculty and its close relationship with an existing student body to develop technology-based courses. Only later, if it desires to reach much larger numbers of students, need it develop operational excellence in the support of distance learners.

In summary, the most important skills and resources for a technology strategy are those capabilities that are durable and difficult to replicate because they combine particular strengths of the university in unique ways.

Organization and culture

The other influence on university technology strategies that merits comment is academic organization and culture. The basis of any organization is the division of its overall task into discrete, specialized activities and the coordination of these activities so that the whole task gets done.

A campus university divides its teaching enterprise into many separate entities (courses) and gives individual faculty members plenty of autonomy in teaching the courses assigned to them. There is specialization by discipline (sociologists teach sociology) but not usually within the teaching activity itself. The academic responsible for the course *plans* the curriculum, *organizes* the resources necessary, *teaches* the material to students and, in some jurisdictions, also *evaluates* their attainment. This is a complex set of tasks. Some coordination is needed between academics with respect to such things as prerequisites and timetabling, but classroom instruction is essentially a robust, decentralized approach to the teaching function that gives individuals considerable independence of action. Clark Kerr's description of a university as 'a federation of independent academic entrepreneurs united by a common grievance over parking' contains an important truth.

However, coordination of teaching activities does occur and it happens in various ways. The coherence of the overall curriculum is ensured by *discussion* within the discipline or more widely. Heads of department usually have a responsibility for the overall *supervision* of student assessment. *Standardization* occurs at the administrative level (eg, 60-minute lectures, registrarial regulations, procedures for ordering audio-visual equipment).

Most technology-based teaching, even teleconferencing to remote classrooms, requires a different balance of specialization and coordination. For large-scale distance education in the correspondence tradition there is such a considerable division of labour that the functions of planning, organizing, teaching and assessing a course may well be carried out by different groups of people. Those charged with developing and implementing a technology strategy must expect that it will challenge existing organizational habits. They may even be accused of premeditated assault on the academic culture!

Such accusations are best countered by ensuring that the technology strategy flows with the grain of the academic culture. First, the collegial processes of governance should be used to the full in developing and implementing the strategy. Second, changes in the organization of faculty work can provide a useful pretext for a wider debate about the nature of teaching, research and scholarship. Boyer's *Scholarship Reconsidered* has already led most US universities to review their criteria for academic promotion and preferment in ways that place greater importance on the teaching and service functions (Huber, 1996). We noted above that sound dispositions for technology-based teaching may have a closer resemblance to the organizational frameworks used for research than those appropriate for classroom teaching. This may be a change, but it is not an assault on the culture of the academy.

Technology strategies for campus universities

Why have a technology strategy?

Few universities yet have a technology strategy at the institutional level. For those that do, such as, in the USA, the University of Minnesota at Crookston and Sonoma State University, a key aim has been to provide universal access to information resources (Resmer *et al.,* 1995). Why should a campus university develop a technology strategy rather than take the more usual route of relying on the initiatives of individual faculty members or their departments?

The short answer is that a *laissez-faire* approach, far from enhancing the university's competitive advantage by giving it cost advantage and valuable differentiation, is likely to increase costs and create excessive differentiation that students will find burdensome. Universities are becoming aware of the need to increase their productivity (Johnstone *et al.*, 1996). The application of technology without a concurrent transformation in the teaching/learning process will be an add-on that will only increase costs. Re-engineering the learning environment will not occur without the development of a technology infrastructure, of which universal student access to the technology is a part.

An institution-wide technology strategy can deliver gains in cost-effectiveness at two levels. Reductions in expenditure on space and equipment are the less controversial of these gains. For example, universities that wish their students to derive maximum benefit from information and communications technology should move away from campus computer labs toward a situation where students have their own laptop computers. Campus computer labs are costly, limited and inconvenient resources that depersonalize the computer. Most faculty would no longer put up with sharing a lab computer instead of having one on their desks, why should students?

The more controversial gain is in teaching productivity. In Chapter 2 we noted the view of Zemsky and Massy (1995) that some substitution of capital for labour in the core teaching function could be essential to the survival of universities. The development of approaches that make such substitution possible may well happen as a result of individual or departmental initiatives but, if the university is to reap advantages from them, an institution-wide strategy is needed. The *studio* model of instruction developed at Rensselaer Polytechnic Institute in the USA is a good example. In this model students work on projects, individually and in teams, in a rich computer-supported environment. The faculty are available for consultation. The result of this approach has been a 10-point increase in student grades, a 20% reduction in cost, and, in the discipline where the model was pioneered (physics), the need for three fewer instructors to discharge the teaching function of the department (Mingle, 1995; Zemsky, 1996a). In such a case an institutional strategy is essential, at the very least to cope with the timetabling issues raised by new course formats, but more importantly to allow the whole university to reap the benefits, in lower costs and valuable differentiation, of a notable advance in practice.

Putting a strategy together: key choices

Competitive advantage is achieved by identifying important value activities and applying technology to carry them out either at lower cost or in ways that buyers find more attractive. The first step in developing a technology strategy is to decide which value activities to target. Here we shall focus on teaching because most universities wish to remain competitive in this core function.

Although a drive for cost advantage will usually overlap with a quest for differentiation it is helpful to distinguish between the two objectives. Does the university seek primarily to reduce the costs of instruction or is it mainly concerned to make its teaching more distinctive?

Cutting costs
The unit costs of teaching can be cut either by adding more students without commensurate increases in expenditure or by making instruction more efficient without changing student numbers. British higher education adopted the first approach, in a striking manner, in the period 1988–94 when student numbers went up by 50% and unit costs went down by up to a quarter. However, this increase in cost-effectiveness did not involve the use of technology in any substantial way. The additional students simply mopped up the spare capacity in the system. UK universities do not believe this phenomenon could be repeated. Future cuts in unit costs, whether student numbers change or not, will require different approaches.

Such approaches can be based on the old technologies of planning as well as on the new information and communication technologies. For example, Zemsky *et al.* (1993) developed a model for estimating how faculty invested their discretionary time and used it to consolidate a curriculum in a way that honoured faculty notions of instructional quality while reducing the demand for instruction. Applying this model to four prestigious liberal arts colleges they showed that:

> 'on the average, each of the institutions could do with 25 percent fewer faculty without crowding a single course and without denying students any of the sequential courses they required for graduation. The simulated reduction in the number of faculty was also achieved without increasing the teaching loads of those who remained.' (Zemsky, 1996b)

Although the silence that greeted this work in 1993 was deafening, the realization among academics that productivity issues have to be faced is now growing (eg, Johnstone *et al.*, 1996). Nevertheless, many universities will be attracted by approaches that bring in more students so that unit costs can fall while maintaining staff numbers. At this point the drive for lower costs intersects with the search for valuable difference.

Driving for difference

If institutions that are already at full capacity with their present teaching methods wish to expand numbers, they have to do something differently. This is likely to involve technology since adding new buildings or satellite campuses is unlikely to lower unit costs. Whatever technological choices they make, and we look at the options below, universities are likely to face scepticism on the part of both faculty and students.

Faculty are used to a craft approach to teaching that involves them in the four activities of *planning, organizing, instructing* and *assessing*. They may resist new approaches that are almost certain to require more development work and usually introduce greater division of labour into the craft tradition – not least by putting more responsibility on the student. Such resistance can be overcome, but it requires an institutional strategy. Development work for new teaching technologies must be allocated and organized so that it is not just an overload. If faculty tasks evolve from lecturing to mentoring or tutoring they will need training for these new roles.

This can be accomplished successfully. The UK Open University has a staff of over 7000 part-time tutors (associate lecturers) whose task is to provide marking and academic support to local groups of students. The University invests around £500,000 ($US800,000) each year in training these associate lecturers, many of whom have full-time teaching posts in campus institutions. A key purpose of this training is to show tutors how to stop lecturing and to act instead as mediators between students and the learning materials for the course. Their task is to add value in those elements of face-to-face contact that students find most useful, for example by facilitating group discussion. The evidence suggests that although many tutors find this transition difficult, once they have made it they derive greater satisfaction from the new role.

Students are likely to be no less sceptical of new approaches. Listening to lectures is less work – and requires less initiative – than participating in a team on a studio course or working through distance learning materials. Here again, an institution-wide approach to 'selling' the new methods to students is helpful. Chapter 6 drew on industrial experience of the technology adoption life-cycle to suggest how technology-based teaching can be made attractive to the mass of students.

Choosing technologies

The purpose of using technology in teaching is to give better value to students (and other buyers like employers and the state). Choices must be pragmatic because technologies change rapidly. A commitment to a particular technology for its own sake is unlikely to yield sustainable advantage. Often universities that made an early commitment to a specific technology (eg, Dartmouth College, USA, to interactive computing, and many institutions to campus cable systems) were no longer perceived as leaders in the following decades.

This implies that we should assess the potential of technology in a generic manner. Chapter 4 described the essentials of distance education and distinguished between its two main traditions: remote-classroom teaching and correspondence tuition. Although these traditions may now be converging, they help provide a conceptual framework for a technology strategy. Universities that use telecommunications to link classrooms will have particular expenditures and organizational demands. Others, that communicate with students, wherever they are, through their personal computers, will face different challenges. To migrate from one technology to its successor within the same tradition of distance education is challenging – but possible. Changing in midstream between the horses of different traditions of distance education is a risky process that could dampen enthusiasm for technology-based teaching.

The basis of a technology strategy is to identify, in the light of the university's core competences, the students technology-based teaching will serve and the programmes it will deliver. If this task calls for distance teaching it should be easy to decide whether remote-classroom technologies or multimedia correspondence tuition are more likely to be appropriate. Sometimes external factors determine the use of technology in advance. When the China TV University was set up, for example, the decision to deliver satellite television to classrooms was already taken. Similarly, any university in the western USA now contemplating an expansion of technology-based teaching may want to take advantage of the facilities that the Western Governors University will provide.

Once the basic goals of a technology strategy are set, universities can use the excellent guide provided by Bates (1995) in selecting the most appropriate media. He suggests seven criteria for decision-making, summarized in the acronym ACTIONS:

Access
Costs

Teaching and learning
Interactivity and user-friendliness
Organizational issues
Novelty
Speed.

We shall comment on these criteria in turn and relate them to the drivers of cost and uniqueness in value activities that were identified by Porter (1985).

Access

Access issues generate the most difficult questions that a technology strategy must address. Ducking problems of differential access by making some technologies optional is not an answer. Doing so discriminates between students and impacts negatively on the cost driver of capacity utilization. Why invest extra resources for the best-equipped students? Access is also a matter of location, which can influence both cost and uniqueness. Ten years ago the costs of providing supported open learning to students differed significantly by location. The costs of the knowledge media vary less with location. Nevertheless, to make a teaching system independent of geography, students in some countries must pay a relatively high price for equipment and connections.

Costs

Figure 4.3 (p.64), which was prepared from data provided by Bates (1995), shows how the costs per student study hour of different technologies vary with student numbers. Scale affects the cost and uniqueness of value activities. Not surprisingly, one-way media have greater potential for economies of scale than multi-directional technologies. For computer conferencing the cost/volume relationship is almost flat. However, since the richness of interaction grows with the numbers using the network, cost-effectiveness does increase with volume. Institutional factors also impact on both cost and differentiation. The flexibility shown by university staff in integrating technology-based teaching into their work is an important influence on the success of a technology strategy.

Teaching and learning

Technologies differ widely in their capacity to present content or inculcate skills. However, as Bates (1995: 6) points out, people are good at learning from a variety of media. He claims this makes teaching and learning less important as discriminators between media than access and costs. The possibilities of linkages between activities in the value chain can also influence cost and uniqueness. For example, because the use of one-way media (eg, print, broadcasting) requires careful preparation, they may provide greater opportunities for faculty to make synergistic linkages between research and teaching than two-way media which call for a more spontaneous style. A multi-directional medium like computer conferencing, on the other hand, allows linkages between materials development and educational services in the value chain (Figure 5.3, p.77) that were more difficult to achieve in distance teaching with older methods.

Interactivity and user-friendliness
In technology-based teaching the issue of interaction is complex. We explored some of the questions it raises in Chapter 7. Two-way media are not always more interactive than one-way media. Properly designed one-way communication can be highly interactive for students at a deep level. However, two-way communication media can help eliminate two long-standing weaknesses of distance education. Computer-mediated conferencing can allow students to communicate more readily with each other and with the university on a range of matters. Students can access a host of previously inaccessible learning resources on the World Wide Web.

These technologies are relevant to two cost and differentiation drivers in Porter's analysis: integration and interrelationships. A high level of integration between the computing and communications systems of the university and its students is now in prospect. Already students can interact closely with administrative systems on-line (eg, course descriptions, registration, exam results). These technologies also provide opportunities for universities to develop useful relationships with commercial firms. Decisions to in-source or out-source services and systems can also influence cost and uniqueness.

Organizational issues
Using new technologies will have a visible impact on the university and so, in a changing world, will maintaining the status quo. The tough challenge for campus universities is that to derive most benefit from technology they must recast the teaching/learning process. Put another way, the forms of technology-based teaching that appear to pose the least threat to current teaching practices also hold out the least promise for reducing costs or yielding valuable differentiation.

In this arena the key cost and differentiation driver is learning. Debate within the academic community, far from tapering off once the technology strategy is developed, should continue at a high level during implementation so that the whole organization learns from the experience. Methodologies from the research function of the university ought to spill over into this activity.

Novelty

In the real world, especially one where technology is considered a capital investment, the novelty of a teaching system may determine its attractiveness to funding bodies. Bates (1995: 13) warns institutions of this trap. First, as noted earlier, technology should be treated as operating expenditure. Second, unless a novel technology proves to be cost-effective, the university will have trouble when soft money runs out. Furthermore, as we saw in Chapter 6, the pragmatic majority of students are not attracted by novelty for its own sake. However, some of the faculty whose energy can provide lift-off to a technology strategy will be enthusiasts for novel technologies. The university should ensure that its discretionary policy choices, which can drive both costs and differentiation, strike the right balance.

Speed

The criterion of speed in the choice of technologies operates at two levels. First, it is desirable to implement a technology strategy quickly while the window of opportunity provided by its supporters remains open. The founders of some of the mega-universities described in the Appendix knew that their institution would not survive unless they got the show on the road smartly. Second, teaching technologies must be chosen with an eye to the frequency with which the material they convey needs to be updated. Timing is a driver of cost and differentiation. While the advantages of being a first mover can be exaggerated, there is much to be said for starting early and learning along the way. A technology strategy that waits for fully validated decisions, ideal technical platforms and perfect learning materials will remain muscle-bound. Those who have already used a technology are likely to make better use of its improved successor than neophytes.

A technology strategy for a mega-university: the UKOU

The mega-universities will adopt the knowledge media, as we call this third generation of distance teaching technologies, at different times and speeds. A crucial factor in their decisions will be the level of economic development of their country and, particularly, the evolution of its national telecommunications infrastructure. To explore the practical issues that arise in implementing a strategy for new technologies we shall take the case of the UK Open University. The UKOU projects that 95% of its students will have networked computers by 2004, which is within the time horizon of its current strategic plan. Given that the essential criterion for technology use, namely student ownership of the equipment, seems likely to be met, the institution is planning its future on that basis.

Most of the mega-universities have had to plan and organize their own start-ups in the last 20 years. Making the transition to the knowledge media will be very different for two reasons. First, whereas institutions could take a 'big bang' approach to their start-up, this will be a gradual transition. Courses using different technologies will run side by side and both must function effectively. Second, as we noted in the previous chapter, course development with the knowledge media does not lend itself so easily to the centralized approach that worked well for the broadcast media. The decentralized nature of knowledge media production is both a strength and a weakness. Academics will have a greater sense of ownership but economies of scale and common standards will be harder to achieve.

This implies that the essential challenge is to achieve a good balance between bottom-up and top-down planning. In the document through which the thousand-member UKOU Senate decided to develop a technology strategy in 1994, the term 'enabling framework' was used to describe the approach.

An enabling framework for technology development

Much of the Senate document (Open University, 1994b) was aimed at creating a common framework for thinking about the role of technology in the UKOU's future. It reviewed the university's past use of technology, explored the new opportunities available, reported on the expectations of students, examined costs, and indicated the next steps to be taken. In some respects, although not presented as such, the paper listed the activities in the UKOU value chain that could be improved by new approaches.

The Senate gave this paper a more enthusiastic welcome than its authors anticipated, indicating that the academic staff were less cautious about the adoption of new technologies than had been supposed. This support legitimized two more concrete initiatives. First, the UKOU Finance Committee agreed to make an investment of £10m ($US16m) from reserves over three years (1995–97) to give impetus to the adoption of new technology. Second, the tasks of the University's five Pro-Vice-Chancellors were rearranged to create a post of Pro-Vice-Chancellor (Technology Development).

The INSTILL investment

The general purpose of the investment from reserves, known as the INSTILL project (Integrating New Systems and Technologies into Lifelong Learning) (Open University, 1995b) was twofold. First, it gave greater reality, tangibility and legitimacy to the technology strategy. Second, it provided some resources to support activities. The INSTILL investment was never intended as the main source of funds for the introduction of new technology. Indeed, the UKOU spends £10m every year on information technology alone. However, given the decentralized nature of the activities being promoted, it was important to have resources on which projects could draw.

Under the INSTILL scheme funds were allocated under seven general headings with considerable flexibility for spending within each heading. The seven areas and amounts were:

1. £1.5m to help create a new unit, the Knowledge Media Institute, whose aim is to be at the forefront of understanding and applying knowledge media to teaching and learning at scale.
2. £3.5m for a new technology recruitment initiative. These funds allowed the University to appoint 40 new academic staff who combined high potential in their disciplines with substantial experience in the use of new technologies in teaching and learning.
3. £0.8m to support satellite and other broadcasting projects.
4. £0.8m for technological innovation in course materials, especially the development of CD-ROMs.
5. £1.4m to harness the Internet and electronic communication for academic purposes.
6. £1.0m towards the space requirements of the Knowledge Media Institute.
7. £1.0m to support schemes for lending computing equipment to students at subsidized rates.

The INSTILL investment was approved early in 1995 and has helped to oil the wheels of the technology strategy. The new technology recruitment initiative came at a good time after years of tight budgets. Advertising all the posts simultaneously (on the Internet), with an explicit focus on the combination of new technology and subject expertise, attracted a more able field of candidates than if each post had been announced separately. The University expects these new staff to play a key role in its migration to new technologies. Each will have an association with the Knowledge Media Institute as well as with their own academic unit.

Embedding technology development in UKOU planning

Initiative fatigue among staff is a danger in a time of rapid change. In order to ensure that the technology strategy was not seen in this light the University's

Pro-Vice-Chancellor (Technology Development) linked her objectives for the 1995-96 year firmly to the nine rank-ordered priorities in the institution's strategic plan, *Plans for Change*, that is described in the Appendix. These linkages are shown in Table 8.1. Such an approach helps to ensure a review of the implications of technology for all significant activities in the institution's value chain.

Supporting functions

Although the INSTILL project had the greatest visibility within the UKOU academic community, two other developments of a more immediately practical nature were of equal importance.

The CIRCE project, a £10m redesign of the University's logistical support systems, was mentioned in Chapter 7. One of the challenges in building such a system is to anticipate the sort of new requirements that might result from the use of the knowledge media in teaching, such as the electronic submission of assignments. The UKOU is counting heavily on CIRCE to support better service to students and customers at lower unit cost. The central component of CIRCE was implemented successfully in 1996.

Equally crucial, in view of the University's plans to increase computer use and networking among students, is the careful planning necessary to make this a good experience for students. The section headings in a progress report (Open University, 1995c) on student computing for 1996 indicated the variety of issues that have to be addressed:

- Student rental (finding firms that will rent computers to disadvantaged students at rates subsidized by the University).
- Student purchase options (finding appropriate modems to recommend).
- Student help desk and student support (hours extended in evenings and at weekends).
- Administrative arrangements for particular courses.
- Networked services (available to the 13,000 students registered in the 25 courses that require networking and others on an optional basis).
- Network access (the aim being to allow students to access the network for the price of a local call).
- Tutor policy (ensuring that tutors have access to appropriate equipment).
- Access technology for disabled students.
- Windows 95 (ensuring that course software runs effectively in this environment because some students will acquire machines with Windows 95).

Table 8.1 *1995 objectives of the UKOU Office for Technology Development matched to priorities in the strategic plan*

Priority	Technology Developments
Quality of learning experience	• Increase contact between students, tutors and course teams with telecommunications. • Increase 'guided independent resource-based learning'. • Use interactive multimedia to improve understanding of core topics.
Curriculum enhancement	• Students to emulate professional use of computer applications. • More courses through cheaper course development/delivery.
Admission and retention	• Hardware and software to improve access for students with disabilities. • Use cable, satellite, networking to widen student range. • Improve advice to students on course choice. • Improve retention and pass rates with better advice systems and enhanced quality of learning.
Expansion	• Recruit from new groups through improved access and better learning experience. • See whether new technology attracts academically demotivated students.
Efficiency	• Use shells, templates, shared resources to increase productivity of technology-based courseware. • Use computer-based assessment to improve staff productivity. • Exploit desktop publishing to turnaround materials faster. • Create synergy between academic and administrative systems with respect to use of new technology. • Use externally/collaboratively developed resources for core skills materials. • Better technological infrastructure to give better staff productivity. • More streamlined management systems. • Forward planning of staff resources for materials production. • Better advice to students about their technology purchases.
Resilience	• Expand publishing/marketing of OU materials using new technology. • Increase provision of work-based learning courses. • Maintain cost analyses of production and delivery systems. • Forward planning models for materials/methods development.
Quality Assurance	• Staff development programme for new techniques. • Databases for staff of existing materials and expertise. • On-line communication between course teams and students. • Document how students learn through technology. • Disseminate research and evaluation. • See that funding for new technology promotes good practice.
Research	• Maintain OU in forefront of research on IT in education. • Encourage research on teaching of subject. • Exploit new technology for scholarship and research.
International and national	• Use new delivery/support systems for students overseas. • Use networks for collaborative course development with scholars overseas. • Make OU central focus for development of new technology for open and distance learning in UK. • Promote legitimacy of research on teaching innovation in every discipline.

Ongoing strategy development

The document presented to the UKOU Senate in 1994 called for the development of a technology strategy. The University is now engaged in the ongoing process of maintaining a strategic framework that encompasses current activities, such as those arising from the INSTILL investment, and future plans for technology use. This framework takes the form of a working document entitled *Technology Strategy for Academic Advantage* (Open University, 1996) that is under continual review. We summarize below some of its key features in mid-1996.

Guiding principles
The overall aim of the technology strategy is twofold:

- to put in place a policy and implementation framework capable of achieving academic advantage from the use of new technologies;
- to contribute to the maintenance of the University as a learning organization.

The development of technology use has six purposes:

1. To equip students with the generic skills for lifelong learning relevant to making best use of new technologies for conceptual understanding, personal development, and vocational/professional competence.
2. To use new technology to meet the needs and aspirations of current and future students, while maintaining an appropriate balance of teaching media and methods, economies of scale, and value for money.
3. To maintain study options for students who do not have access to new technology, both in overall curriculum and where possible in individual courses.
4. To maintain for all courses a minimum optional level of computer use, such that student ownership of a networked computer is always worthwhile.
5. To deliver new technology methods in such a way as to minimize the investment students have to make for their study while keeping abreast of current developments in technology.
6. To keep research on technology for teaching at the leading edge, finding new ways to exploit the new and imminent technologies in the service of students' learning needs.

Critical success factors

The University recognizes that to carry out these intentions it needs an implementation framework that enables organizational learning and the dissemination of good practice. This should have the following features:

- a forward planning process to ensure that all units of the University are working synergistically;
- a course production-presentation process that is responsive to curriculum development pressures, and flexible in its team-building, project management and creative collaboration processes;
- a staff development programme that supports academic and production staff in their exploration of effective ways of teaching with new technology;
- resource planning and activity costing procedures that enable all units to use new technology resources most productively;
- a technical infrastructure that will support all students and staff in gaining maximum benefit from IT tools and infrastructure available through personal, commercial, or public sector access;
- quality assurance mechanisms that require technology development projects to observe a user-centred design and evaluation methodology, in order to ensure that usage is progressive, adaptive and cost-effective, and that the University captures the experience gained;
- collaborative partnerships with external organizations that will enable the University to achieve academic advantage, or economies of scale, or earlier exploitation of new technologies than would otherwise be possible.

Meeting students' needs

Noting that there is no simple relationship between the cost of application of new technologies and their value to students, the strategy encourages pursuit of a range of development projects so that evaluation can establish the most cost-effective balance of methods. The areas for development are listed as:

- computer-based tools and applications;
- generic training materials for IT;
- materials for students with disabilities;
- computer-supported discussion;
- computer-supported collaborative learning;
- interactive computer-marked assignments;
- interactive computer-based tutorials;
- user-active learning environments;
- information resources;

- student authoring environments;
- administrative communication.

Implementation framework
The paper sets out in some detail the institutional infrastructure that is needed to support the technology strategy in the light of the critical success factors listed above. This section addresses infrastructure requirements under seven headings, most of which focus on key processes.

1. *Course planning process.* Academic units will review their forward plans for courses to show the progressive updating of each course with respect to new technology. In the medium term each faculty will have a number of courses that require computer access even though some will only provide new technology materials at group meetings of students (day or residential schools). However, all courses should

(a)   advise students with access to standard equipment how to make use of appropriate software applications and Internet access in their studies;
(b)   provide on-line student support for tuition, counselling, submission of assignments and feedback; and
(c)   make provision for access via new technology for students with disabilities.

In this context trends in the access of tutorial staff to technology are monitored closely.

2. *Course design-presentation processes.* The University sees the management of the considerable changes likely in these processes as an important challenge. The technologies of desktop publishing and networking can convert into parallel and iterative activities the previously serial process of course design – development – delivery – presentation. This has implications for the linkages between activities and professional categories. Tutors can easily feed ideas into the design stage; designers can join the production cycle earlier to provide customized templates for authors; academics should achieve a more collaborative output with media producers; and the course team can be more involved in the presentation phase through on-line tutoring.

Course teams must avoid student overload in planning the distribution of students' study time across different teaching methods and ensure that adding new technologies reduces the use of other methods. Central support units will need to offer guidance on the differential costs of different delivery styles and make available up-to-date data on activity costs. Teams should look for opportunities to incorporate into courses interactive learning materials developed elsewhere, since these are popular with students but expensive to develop.

New teaching methods will require more emphasis on user testing and experimentation. User testing is a challenge when students are at a distance, but local partnerships may provide an answer. Effective experimentation with new media needs the right environmental conditions and calls for the provision of new types of courseware development sites on campus (rooms with hardware, software, networking tools and access to existing courseware resources).

3. *Staff development*. A clear focus on staff development is key to the successful deployment of new technology in teaching. The Investors in People process (a widely used UK standard for the organization of training) provides a useful framework. Half of the time (ten days annually) that full-time academic staff are expected to spend on professional development should be spent on aspects of information technology. Further training in project management is also essential to making course production faster. Special training is already being provided to tutorial staff on designated courses and this needs to be made generic as more courses use new technology. There is the opportunity to develop a structured curriculum for training staff about new technology in teaching and learning, possibly leading to a formal qualification.

Inculcating the spirit of a learning organization that builds on its previous experience will be a key to rapid progress. The Knowledge Media Institute is creating a 'knowledge development system' for the University that can support progressive institutional learning about technology-based teaching and has already helped 20 course teams. This aims to support a form of cumulative and mutually supportive staff development whereby users and course teams can:

- access over the campus net an electronic database of technology-based teaching materials, research/evaluation reports, and student surveys;
- post authored annotations to specific points in the database;
- add their own summarized and indexed reports.

The working paper makes the following comment about the spirit in which staff development should be conducted:

> 'Because the use of new technology in teaching is innovative and exploratory, we cannot approach it as we do traditional teaching, with the assumption that we know how to do it. A more appropriate model would be research activity.

The emphasis on scholarship, on intellectual challenge, on exploration and creativity, on a rigorous evaluation methodology, on dissemination of outcomes, etc., are all features of research activity. This academic activity is likely to be shared among three activities: teaching, research, and research on the teaching of one's subject – further blurring the traditional and undesirable separation of teaching and research.... Once the development of new technology teaching methods is recognized as a legitimate and valuable academic activity, it is easier to provide the incentives for it to be done well.'

4. *Resource planning*. The University has a sound planning process which allows coordination of plans across units. The new Resource Flow Model allows activity costing for IT-related activities to be built in to resource planning, and modelling tools facilitate achievement of an optimal balance of new and standard methods of teaching. Since there is no expectation of increased state funding the greater use of technology must be paid for from existing resource flows and any external research and development funding that can be obtained. The University must be clear about the activities it wishes to develop so that it can respond appropriately when funding or partnership opportunities arise.

There has already been a substantial shift of resources toward information technology and support, reinforced by the five-year INSTILL package of investment from reserves. Attention must focus on ensuring that this investment bears fruit in the form of more efficient working methods for staff and greater learning productivity for students. An important challenge in this respect is the provision of electronic submission, processing and feedback on student assignments (more than one million per year). Experiments are under way and the investigation of the best approach and the most appropriate software will continue for some time. It is not yet possible to say with certainty that electronic assignment handling will reduce costs for the University and it must not create greater workload for tutors.

5. *Technical infrastructure*. For years the University, like other academic institutions, has had to balance freedom to use a variety of systems with the need to constrain that variety in order to provide effective support. Cross-platform working is becoming easier but conflict will continue for other kinds of systems. The paper proposes two operating principles:

- variety is acceptable up to the point at which economies of scale become necessary;
- students should experience as little disruption and expense as possible in meeting the requirements of courses.

This means that academic units must meet the cost of deviations from the norm for large-scale operations and feel pressure to conform to the systems that students are most likely to have and be familiar with. Conferencing systems are a case in point. Computer conferencing is very popular with students (see Chapter 7) and several conferencing systems are in use in courses. Present thinking is that the University needs clear criteria to judge whether a system is appropriate and a forward plan to unify systems across all courses. A minimum specification for a generic University system to support network communication for teaching purposes is in preparation that will allow current uses to be judged against a common standard. It is, of course, possible that the Internet will make such drives for standardization redundant.

However, in one area standardization is clearly *de rigueur*. All University teaching materials will now be produced in digital form and should be subject to a common policy for archiving, rights clearances for re-use and versioning, and on-line access for course teams. This will be a collaborative development by units across the university.

By 1998 the University will have completed the implementation of the CIRCE programme of new information systems to support the changing administrative and operational processes through which it serves enquirers, students and corporate customers. This will provide staff with a much better systems context for serving people. In time this will allow many services to be made available to students over the network. The scale and pace of this development will depend on the access of staff, students and other clients to hardware and the Internet, on the costs to both parties, and on the controls that security of networks and data demand.

The University must maintain a strong profile in network and networked services research. There is the expectation of a threefold annual increase in traffic (eg, there were 11,000 student log-ins on a typical *weekend* day in mid-1996). A distinction must be made between network use required by a course, which the University should support, and optional additional usage of resources on the Internet, which would be open to students as ordinary network users, and not supported by the University. Only by distinguishing these uses clearly can future needs and costs be forecast with accuracy. Currently the University runs it own network and the Internet gateway, e-mail and conferencing servers that constitute the principal services to students. Three options are being evaluated: to continue expansion of current arrangements; to operate services over a third-party network; or to contract service and network provision to a third party.

As well as optimizing services to students, the University must unify its information systems and information technology across units without stifling innovation. A University-wide technical infrastructure group has been set up. To improve forward planning an on-line database of educational products from all courses will be made available with a common database structure for all products and forms of delivery. This is part of the provision of an increasing range of IT tools (capable of operating cross-platform) to all staff.

In this context authoring tools are particularly important. The paper has this to say:

> 'Authoring of multimedia and computer-based teaching is expensive and difficult. Academics cannot expect to be able to do desktop authoring from scratch. On the other hand authoring tools, if they are not difficult to learn, are correspondingly restrictive, under-using the power of the medium. A more progressive policy would be for the University to develop learning activity shells and templates, wherever possible. A collaboration between a multimedia team (academic, designer, programmer, producer, educational technologist) should be able to develop an interactive environment geared to some specific learning objective. Very often the same functionality can be used for a similar objective but with different content.... If generalization of the learning exercise is planned from the start, then it should be possible to build up a variety of customizable learning activity shells in this way. The policy has the advantage of providing academics with the means to author their own activities relatively easily, and focusing the design on learner activity, rather than presentation.'

The spin-off from the University's *Virtual Microscope*, which has led to a series of applications using the same techniques, is a good example of the pay-off from this approach.

Another function supporting the technical infrastructure is intelligence gathering. The University's intelligence gathering is extensive (student access surveys, links with industry, membership of research panels) but uncoordinated. Better communication would support more confident technology forecasting. An internal database of consultant expertise would also help.

6. *Quality assurance.* As the University becomes a major producer of software products it will require robust and rigorous quality assurance procedures. Resourcing for new technology developments will be allocated most appropriately if it responds to proposals based on those for research funding. Regular surveying of students' access to technology and their overall evaluation of the comparative effectiveness of technology-based teaching methods will be essential. Intensive developmental testing will become more com-

mon and a properly administered user testing facility available to all courses is planned. Students' access to the Internet can be exploited in order to put in place a large-scale intensive feedback system. A maintained resource base of courseware materials, available on-line or otherwise easily accessible, is another important element of quality assurance.

7. *External environment*. Developing technology-based teaching is costly in staff time. Once they are fully developed the knowledge media may deliver quantum gains in student benefit. Until then the University must assume that the benefits to students are comparable to those of other media. This means that new technologies must have greater economies of scale to give a cost per student hour similar to other media. Even an organization as large as the Open University will have difficulty achieving appropriate economies of scale and the problem will be even greater in campus universities where student numbers per course are much smaller. All universities will be challenged to provide courses across the range of topics that post-experience graduates engaged in lifelong learning will require. This means that the University must seek external partnerships, both at home and abroad, so that it can spread the cost of development and gain understanding and expertise from others.

One important objective should be to link to national and international technological infrastructures as they become available. The widening of public access to computing and networking in schools, libraries, colleges and universities may help resolve the access problems of some students in connecting from home or work. Network communications can extend collaborative links to overseas scholars in course development. New delivery and support systems are expanding OU course access to an international student clientele.

A market in technology-based teaching materials is already developing. At present universities talk more of selling in this market than of buying, but if the University's materials are of quality they could generate a useful source of income. Money can be saved by buying in good courseware from others. There may be opportunities for collaborative publishing similar to the University's current arrangements with the book trade.

In order to be perceived as a desirable partner, supplier or buyer in the arena of technology-based education the University must maintain and enhance its position at the forefront of research in information and commu-nications technology in higher education. All units can play a part, either by conducting basic innovative research, or by making the innovation opera-tional on a large scale. Such activity will ensure that the University continues to be invited to participate in a range of national and international initiatives (policy forums, public consultations, state advisory committees) related to technology in education.

All this requires clarity of purpose. The section concludes:

> 'If staff and students are to have a realistic sense of the University's position relative to other organizations, at home and abroad, in our use of technology then we must build a collective description of what we are doing. This is part of the function of this document. It also enables the University to provide a coherent description for external parties. The Public Relations department will help staff to publicize their new technology projects and findings more widely. This would be part of a programme to enhance our presence in all mass media, giving coverage to all aspects of the Technology Strategy, emphasizing our quality assurance focus, the importance of beginning with an understanding of students' needs, our systematic knowledge of our student population, their evaluation of the teaching they receive, the scale of our technology innovations, the thoroughness of the planning process and the staff development that underpins it.'

Summary

This final chapter has brought together the key themes of the book in order to indicate how universities should approach the development and implementation of technology strategies. Such strategies are needed because new technology may bring radical changes to higher education. Students will have a world-wide choice of universities and technology-based companies may become significant purveyors of higher education.

A technology strategy is now a key component of the business strategy that can give competitive advantage to a university. A good strategy must blend appropriateness and commitment, so its development requires debate, time and leadership. Unless it is perceived by the university community as a way of converting a desirable vision into reality it will not attract the necessary allegiance.

For all organizations the routes to competitive advantage are cost leadership and/or differentiation. Technology-based teaching may provide opportunities to follow both paths. In identifying the skills and resources that it brings to such activity, a university should concentrate on its core capabilities, especially the talents of its academic staff. The debate surrounding a move to new teaching methods can help to reinforce the links between teaching and research by developing a wider notion of scholarship. The hardware required is best considered as an operating and not a capital expense.

For campus universities an institution-wide technology strategy is needed to secure the benefits, in space utilization and learning productivity, that new methods can bring. Some substitution of capital for labour in the teaching function should be a declared aim. Leverage on costs can be obtained by mopping up spare capacity with more students and better timetabling. Technology-based teaching will alter the craft tradition of university instruction by requiring more development work and greater division of labour. Close attention to workload planning and professional development for the faculty can ease the transition to new methods. The benefits of change must be carefully explained to students.

In creating a technology strategy a university takes advantage of some of its core capabilities to teach particular students and courses in new ways. If this means adopting the methods of distance education, the institution must first make a broad choice between the remote-classroom and correspondence traditions. Whichever approach is chosen, Bates (1995) has provided a thoughtful guide to technology choice based on the criteria of access, cost, teaching/learning, interactivity, organizational issues, novelty and speed (ACTIONS). We related Porter's (1985) cost and differentiation drivers of competitive advantage to these criteria.

We illustrated the essential issues involved in implementing a technology strategy for a mega-university by reviewing the action taken by the UK Open University. After the UKOU Senate had approved the enabling framework of a *Technology Strategy for Academic Advantage*, the University earmarked resources for this purpose and assigned special responsibility for technology development at a senior level. The technology strategy was linked explicitly to the overall planning processes of the institution and canvassed widely through an evolving discussion paper. This set out the guiding principles of the strategy, listed critical success factors, and proposed a wide range of approaches for meeting students' needs in new ways. Because there is, as yet, no clear correlation between the cost of a technology and its value to students it is important to test and evaluate a variety of methods. The strategy deals extensively with issues of implementation, focusing particularly on processes such as staff development and course design and presentation.

Conclusions

We began our exploration of technology strategies for higher education with the observation that the world's universities are in crisis. A crisis combines dangers and opportunities. If universities in developing countries fail to satisfy the burgeoning demands of growing populations the stability of their societies could be put at risk. In an era of lifelong learning universities in the industrialized world will be marginalized unless they are efficient and flexible enough to meet today's myriad educational and training needs. The hypothesis that new technologies provide higher education with opportunities to rise to these challenges was the basis for this book. How well does the proposition stand up?

It is clear that the knowledge media can help universities respond to the rising expectations of those they serve. Equally clear is that if they are to take full advantage of the opportunities that technology offers, universities will have to make some difficult adjustments. Even institutions that do not elect to teach students off campus will need to adopt some of the approaches that have been developed for distance education. These include focusing on learning productivity, recasting notions of institutional quality and changing the deployment of faculty within the teaching function. Although the large distance teaching universities have already made these shifts they too will face tough challenges. In particular, they must trade the habit of self-sufficiency for a readiness to enter into partnerships with other universities and organizations. They will also need to adapt their efficient industrial methods to situations where the comfort of economies of scale will be elusive.

Second, we have shown that to make these adjustments successfully universities will need clarity of purpose based on a few simple ideas. Top of the list is the principle that giving better value to the buyer is the basis for competitive advantage. Better value can mean either low prices, valuable distinctiveness or, ideally, both at once. Equally important is the fact that students will be the final arbiters of which technologies are adopted. Students are more likely to vote with their feet in the direction of technology-based teaching if it yields complete learning experiences and is well integrated with other university activity.

A third conclusion is that the new technologies have considerable potential to enhance the blend of knowledge, community and conversation that is the essence of the university. They can increase the richness of interactions between students and give all in the academy access to more resources for scholarship than ever before. The knowledge media are bringing together the traditions of distance learning and classroom teaching and encouraging a common focus on learning productivity.

Finally, we believe that incorporating new technology into teaching could be immensely beneficial to universities as academic communities. First, because these technologies will make instruction more of a collective endeavour, teaching will recover some of the intellectual vitality and prestige than has for too long been reserved for research. Students will see the academic mode of thinking at work and benefit. Second, because the application of these technologies to teaching contains much uncharted territory, there is a splendid opportunity to develop knowledge about them in a systematic manner. The ambitious claim that the knowledge media change qualitatively the relationship between people and knowledge provides an initial hypothesis to galvanize such work. Third – a simple point – the world's academic community will get very much bigger. Some predict it could include over 150 million students by 2020.

The mega-universities have greatly expanded access to higher education using previous generations of technology. They have demonstrated already that, where academic learning is concerned, more means better. The law of the telecosm, which states that the value of a network rises as the square of the number of users, suggests that the knowledge media could create a worldwide academic community of wonderful richness. There have been many mutations of the idea of the university since the creation of the University of Bologna in 1088. The knowledge media may provoke the most radical mutation yet. The dangers are obvious but the opportunities for a bright future are waiting to be seized.

Appendix
The Mega-Universities: Profiles

Chapter 3 summarized some common and contrasting features of the 11 large (100,000+ students) distance teaching universities that are a new and important development on the world higher education scene. Because most of these mega-universities are of recent creation and have grown very rapidly, information about them is not readily accessible. The International Centre for Distance Learning has provided some brief descriptions (ICDL, 1995) and Tables 3.1 and 3.2 (pp.30 and 31) assemble basic information about them. Each mega-university is a large and complex institution. Our aim in this Appendix is to highlight their development priorities, noting especially features relevant to their technology strategies.

The China TV University System (CTVU)

The CTVU is the world's biggest learning system. Known in the country by its acronym in Chinese, DIANDA (Keegan, 1994b: 7), this system is made up of the central unit, the China Central Broadcasting and TV University (CCRTVU), and four other institutional layers. (This is a common structure for national organizations in China.) The CCRTVU produces courses for nationwide use, sets the examinations and standardizes their marking. It does not enrol students. That is the responsibility of 44 Provincial TVUs, under which there are 575 Regional CTVU Colleges (also known as 'branch schools'), 1,550 Education Centres at county or company level (also known as 'work stations'), and some 30,000 tutorial groups (Wu Xiaobo, 1993: 74). Keegan (1994b: 17) has delineated the functions of the different levels in the system. He notes that the CTVU is only one of three large distance education systems in China, the others being the correspondence university system and the self-study/university examination system.

The CTVU system admits 300,000 students annually to programmes which had a total enrolment of 850,000 in 1993 (Keegan, 1994b: 8). There were 530,000 active students in degree programmes in 1994. The 1,500,000 students who have graduated to date represent 17% of China's graduate output at this level over the last decade. The CTVU's high graduation and pass rates reflect the fact that most of its students are paid to study full time. Ma (1987) reported that 77% of graduates were later employed in jobs matching their CTVU specializations and that 86% of employers rated the employees as very good.

However, Wei and Tong (1994: 109) noted that the CTVU's enrolments declined in the early 1990s following the imposition of admission quotas by the government. They feared this policy would damage the cost-effectiveness and impact of the system. It now appears that the move to a socialist market economy has softened the quota policy. Xie Xinguan (1993), the president of the CCRTVU at the time, reported that the CTVU aims to have 1,000,000 active degree students by the year 2000 with much larger numbers taking non-degree courses (where there are no national quotas). He noted, for example, that 20 million farmers were receiving 'preliminary and intermediate education of practical interest' offered by Liaoyuan TV School, a CTVU associate. Sin Fu (1992) found that the Education Centres, which are key partners in the system, have made the CTVU place greater emphasis on job training and continuing education to meet their requirements. It is the task of the Provincial TVUs to produce courses of special interest to their own region. The output of the Sichuan TVU, for example, rivals that of the CCRTVU (Hawkridge & Chen, 1991: 145).

The CTVU is unique amongst the mega-universities in adopting the remote-classroom approach to distance education. The current teaching systems of the ten other mega-universities originated in the correspondence tradition. Keegan (1994b: 14) described the Chinese approach as follows:

'The student attends at work from Monday to Saturday but goes to the company education centre and not to the factory. The study programme lasts from 8.30 to 12.00 and from 1.30 to 4.30 and consists of three TV lectures per day by satellite from the CCRTVU in Beijing, plus face-to-face lectures in the company's education centre in groups of 20, during which the tutors go through the textbooks, then students do assignments and the tutor gives evaluation and feedback. The students have to attend.'

Hawkridge and Chen (1991: 135) reported that 'television served mainly to transmit "talking blackboards", not even "talking heads"... the TVUs provided no correspondence tuition, and students had to depend on whoever was available locally to provide meagre tutorials'. McCormick (1985: 4) noted that 'the textbooks do not always match the programmes, are not designed specifically for self-study and are not available everywhere in China'.

Nevertheless, 'TVU students spend much time using the texts to prepare for traditional written examinations.... Being a TVU student is serious work, particularly if you have been released on basic pay by your work unit, as a privilege.' (Hawkridge & Chen, 1991: 137).

To put the television programmes in context, the CCRTVU provides the same number of TV hours of output as the UK Open University but has only ten producers to the OU/BBC's 50. Xie Xinguan (1989: 11) noted the urgency of 'detailed planning before materials production is started if the courses are to have cohesion in approach and content'.

Wei and Tong (1994: 109) have provided a thoughtful perspective on the problems and trends facing the CTVU. Developing this huge learning system in a country undergoing radical political and economic changes is perhaps the greatest challenge of educational planning in the world. These authors flag a number of issues.

They welcome the curricular reform under way. Uniform academic fields, majors and specialities have been replaced by single courses of national interest on which the Provincial TVUs can build. Furthermore, the development and production of these 222 core courses is a much more collaborative process than previously. They believe that the involvement of ministries, Provincial TVUs and conventional universities will provide extra resource and enhance the quality of the instructional materials. The recent collaboration between the CTVU and the Self-Study/University Examination system, with a reduction in the latter's drop-out rate, is another welcome development. The introduction of a credit accumulation and transfer system was overdue, because not all CTVU students are able to complete in exactly three years. Wei and Tong (1994: 124) find it bizarre, however, that the CTVU courses do not transfer readily into the regular four-year undergraduate programmes of the other universities.

Future goals are the extension of the CTVU, which is still primarily an urban network, to the rural areas and an increase in television transmission time. By the end of the century the China Educational TV Station (CETV) will have four channels giving 70 hours a day of transmission. These transmissions carry many programmes besides those of the CTVU, but the increase from two to four channels will do something to ease the transmission bottleneck.

However, the key issue for its technology strategy brings together three elements: the cost-effectiveness of the system, the coherence of its organization, and the evolution of the remote-classroom approach.

Wei and Tong (1994: 112–15) analyse carefully why costs per student in the CTVU are going up. First, as noted earlier, government policy has reduced the student base by admission quotas on regular students and tighter limits on those auditing courses or studying part-time. Second, the CTVU had seen a sharp decrease in enrolments in expensive subjects (eg, engineering) and found itself with the wrong subject mix. The current redevelopment of the curriculum is, however, expensive. Meanwhile, conventional universities are showing more curricular flexibility. A third component of increased costs has been brisk real estate development in the Provincial TVUs and Regional Colleges. As the authors put it: 'This trend of turning universities without walls into ones with walls also becomes a threat to cost-effectiveness' (1994: 115).

This leads directly to the organizational issue. Can the CTVU structure, which dates from the era of tight central planning, cope with the increasing autonomy of the provinces and regions? It is clear that the Provincial TVUs and Regional Colleges now have many opportunities to go into business on their own account. This trend will affect the integrity of the CTVU's remote-classroom teaching methods and the role of the CCRTVU.

A decade ago McCormick (1985: 5) queried whether the tendency of the Provincial TVUs to build up facilities and staff was 'a threat to the distance learning concept'. This trend would make these institutions look like an interconnected set of conventional institutions and the CTVU would become more like an external degree programme than an integrated distance learning institution. Wei and Tong (1994: 111) return to this question, observing:

'although China's TVUs enjoy a high reputation for taking advantage of modern technologies to convey instruction to learners at a distance, recent policies for the presentation of instruction in China's TVUs rely too much on group tuition, which is likely to turn the positive factors of distance education into negative impacts, since neither the quantity nor the quality of CTVU faculty can meet the requirements of such a heavy workload and the sheer versatility of the subject fields. Besides, more and more in-service trainees find it very difficult to attend all of the group learning activities expected of them. Some Chinese distance educators wonder what the difference is between distance education with considerable group tuition and classroom teaching with the aid of modern technologies.'

This is a good statement of the main challenge facing the Chinese mega-university.

Finally, Hawkridge and Chen (1991) note that there is enormous scope for improving the management of the whole CTVU system. Basic cost and student data are often lacking, for which bad experience with early computer systems is only partly to blame.

The Centre National d'Enseignement à Distance (CNED), France

France's Centre National d'Enseignement à Distance is the largest distance teaching institution in Europe and a veteran amongst the mega-universities. It is a state institution under the authority of the Ministry of Education. CNED comprises eight institutes in Grenoble, Lille, Lyon, Poitiers, Rennes, Rouen, Toulouse and Vanves with a headquarters at Poitiers which is linked to a satellite video transmission and production centre (ICDL, 1995: 3). According to its former head, Loing (1993b):

'CNED is an old institution, created 54 years ago as a small correspondence school for children driven away from school by the war; it worked and developed as such for at least 40 years, using printed paper conveyed by mail as its only medium. Today it has ceased being only a primary and secondary school, and caters mostly for adults at university or high level vocational training; yet even now printed paper remains our main teaching tool with a yearly output of 700 million pages for 350,000 students.'

Unique among the mega-universities in its span and curricular diversity, CNED offers some 500 programmes ranging from primary school to postgraduate courses. Each component institute within CNED is charged with the responsibility for a particular set of these programmes. CNED has grown rapidly in recent years. 80% of its students are adults (average age 35) and half of them are doing university-level work (CNED, 1994a). The staff number about 6,000, which includes 1,800 full-time and 3,000 part-time teachers. One role of CNED is to provide employment for teachers who are no longer able, for health reasons, to function in the classroom.

CNED's methods put it firmly in the correspondence tradition. However, its relationship with students is less intense than at some other mega-universities. This is partly because many of its students are taking CNED courses in order to prepare for examinations set by other bodies. CNED offers much less tutorial support than, say, the UK Open University, and in some courses students must pay a supplement to have assignments marked. Perhaps for these reasons CNED used to seem a rather dull institution. However, it has taken advantage of the 'flattering image of modernity' of distance education (CNED, 1994b) to project itself more attractively in the last decade. An article in *Le Monde* captured the beginnings of these changes well:

> '*Le Centre National d'enseignement par correspondance, saisi enfin par la modernité, est en train d'effectuer une mutation spectaculaire qui le place, dans bien des domaines, parmi les lycées ou les universités les plus performantes. Le temps du télé-enseignement, abritant, dans une bureaucatie poussiéreuse, des enseignants dépressifs ne sera-t-il bientôt plus qu'un (mauvais) souvenir?... Aujourd'hui ce géant bouge. Naguère formaliste, somnolent, un peu revêche – n'avait-on pas rayé ses coordonnées parisiennes des derniers annuaires parce que... le téléphone dérangeait trop? – le voici occupé à se faire un nouveau visage et fourmillant de projets.*' (Betbeder, 1987: 54).

Betbeder described a first wave of change that focused on the curriculum and the use of technology for support functions. Access was enhanced by making admission requirements more flexible and by extending the timetable with summer courses. Some tutorial groups were introduced. The curriculum for adults was completely recast. These changes were facilitated by new uses of technology. Electronic publishing speeded the production of revamped courses. Computerized registration supported expansion of student numbers and greater flexibility.

A second important change occurred in 1993 when the headquarters of CNED moved from Vanves (Paris) to Futuroscope near Poitiers. Futuroscope is a new *technopole* (technology park) that is being developed, with strong political support, as a centre for the communications and media industries. Prominent within it is a successful theme park, focused on communications and the moving image, that attracts millions of tourists. The relocation of the CNED directorate from a Paris suburb to a new building between the Futuroscope theme park and a 'teleport' with full satellite communication facilities was a powerful symbol of change. By forcing a redefinition of the relationships between the headquarters and the eight component institutes it was also a catalyst for more profound changes within CNED.

One expression of this was the creation of a central enquiry handling system called *Télé-Accueil*. There is now a single national telephone number for enquiries. A trained team in Poitiers, backed by a specially developed computer system, can handle over 10,000 phone calls per day in an impressive manner. A call may be forwarded to the particular CNED institute responsible for the programme of interest to the enquirer. However, the *Télé-Accueil téléacteur* retains ownership of each call until it is concluded to the enquirer's satisfaction.

CNED developed this system after extensive discussions with the French companies and organizations that handle the largest number of telephone enquiries. In 1994 the number of incoming calls to *Télé-Accueil* rose by 250% to over 800,000. At the peak of the student recruitment season, 11,650 calls were taken in a single day by 57 *téléacteurs* working simultaneously (CNED, 1994a: 100).

Télé-Accueil is a good example of the sophisticated use of technology by a mega-university in its support operations. For students and the public, however, it is the use of technology for teaching that captures attention. This is the third wave of change at CNED, repeatedly stressed by successive directors (eg, CNED, 1989: 19; Moreau, 1994). Most issues of the CNED magazine carry stories about particular technologies (eg, satellites, visiophone, fax) and how they might be used in distance education.

The reality appears to be that CNED is using its most glamorous technology, satellite video transmissions, to enrich rather than fundamentally to change, its traditional correspondence teaching methods. Loing (1993b: 154) attributes CNED's technological choices to two key factors. First, there was almost no educational television in France until 1994. Second, France has a high quality telecommunications network and was a world pioneer of popular telematics with its Minitel videotex system.

Satellite video transmissions are used to deliver programmes of lectures or debates to a reception network of some 500 points which are mostly secondary schools and colleges. Individual video transmissions may reach an audience of up to 10,000 students (most of whom are not registered CNED students). Questions are asked during the broadcast either by telephone (through *Télé-Accueil*) or fax. These video transmissions are described as 'tools of motivation' which break down geographic isolation (Aténa, 1993). Students do not receive credit for them and, because they are mostly scheduled during the day, CNED's adult students do not have ready access to them. CNED uses a similar approach for some international activities, such as its *Ecole Francophone de Droit*. For smaller and more interactive sessions CNED uses slow-scan 'visio' conferences which it considers to be complementary to the video transmissions.

A second operational use of technology at CNED is videotex. The Minitel system, which may soon reach 10 million homes, carries a database of CNED's programmes and courses and allows students to register. Minitel can also be used as an e-mail and bulletin board system by students and teachers. Use of a special code allows employers who are sponsoring staff on CNED vocational courses to check on their progress.

Finally, CNED has experimented with fax in its tutorial operations. Secondary students surveyed felt that the four-week turn-round of assignments through the post was too slow and half of them said they would be prepared to pay for the costs of fax. When fax machines were lent to some 70 students as an experiment there was 'extraordinary interest and renewed energy raised in students,' and the average rate of return of corrected assignments was 24 hours. Loing's (1993b: 137) report implied a Hawthorne effect but concluded this approach was worth pursuing.

In summary, CNED is in a brisk phase of development. Its new site at Futuro-scope symbolises its readiness to use new technologies. CNED seems particularly aware of the threats and opportunities inherent in the increasing regionalization of France and the adoption of distance education techniques by other institutions. It is putting strong emphasis on partnerships. One example is the 4,500 training agreements it has made with French companies. Another is the strengthening of its relationships with the other institutions of the French education system through its video conferences. The virtue of 'hybrid teaching', which combines face-to-face and distance methods, is a recent theme of CNED publications (CNED, 1995).

CNED's current strategic plan (CNED, 1994b), which was produced after a review of its activities by an international management consultancy, calls for CNED to be more attentive to the changing needs of its users. Continuing education and overseas markets are particular foci for developments which call for a rapid expansion in university-level courses to be developed in collaboration with other French universities. The strategy places strong emphasis on new teaching technologies and notes the collaborative research network that CNED has organized to advance this work. CNED is a shareholder in the new French educational TV network, La Cinquième, and believes that radio has an important part in its future. It is also working with the French postal service to speed deliveries of course materials and assignments.

This dynamic phase of development is clearly putting some strains on the bureaucratic administrative framework within which CNED has traditionally worked. The plan asks for greater institutional freedom in three key areas: to create commercial subsidiaries; to set fees; and to have greater control over its staffing.

The Indira Gandhi National Open University (IGNOU), India

In only 11 years IGNOU has achieved remarkable success in a complex environment. India's tradition of higher distance education goes back to 1962 when the University of Delhi created a School of Correspondence Courses (Ansari, 1992: 34). By 1980 20 universities were offering such courses as a sideline to their campus operations. However, these developments were disappointing in both quantity and quality to the policy-makers who had encouraged them. The Education Commission of 1964–66 had suggested that by 1986 one-third of all higher education enrolments should be through correspondence courses and evening colleges. In the event only 13% of HE enrolments were in distance education by 1992 (Yadav and Panda, 1995). The correspondence courses were mostly of poor quality and provided minimal student support. The universities used the profits from their correspondence courses to subsidize campus operations.

By the 1980s, however, Indian policy-makers could see successful examples of single-purpose distance teaching universities in a variety of other countries. They decided to try again. The state of Andhra Pradesh created an open university in 1982 and the central government established IGNOU in 1985. The aims were both quantitative and qualitative. India's *Eighth Plan* (1992–97) envisaged that 50% of the increase in HE enrolments should study by distance education. The forecast was an increase of 1.5 million enrolments. The implication for IGNOU was that enrolments would reach 250,000 by 1997. The annual intake would be 100,000. However, less than a third of these students would take bachelor's courses. Over two-thirds would enrol in programmes related directly to employment.

This major reorientation of IGNOU's programming took place before it had fully implemented an extensive undergraduate programme. It reflected a growing realization that for Indian higher education the challenge was not to promote access and equity, but to avoid squandering money on the production of unemployables (Ansari, 1993).

The other part of IGNOU's qualitative function is to be an apex body with a national mandate for the promotion, coordination and maintenance of standards in distance education. This mandate covers the five state open universities and the correspondence programmes of the conventional universities. IGNOU is approaching this task in a circumspect fashion through a Distance Education Council which emphasizes partnership rather than regulation. It has created a Staff Training and Research Institute in Distance Education in order to enhance professional expertise throughout India and convince academics of the importance of quality. Not surprisingly, in view of the history, the prospect of having to improve their correspondence provision is not always welcomed by the conventional universities.

Our interest is mainly in IGNOU's own distance teaching activities. The daunting challenge of serving a student body of nearly a quarter of a million is, however, only part of IGNOU's broad and politically sensitive brief.

Annual purchases of 1,100 tons of printing paper show that IGNOU has its foundations in the correspondence tradition. It would like to use other media more but external constraints limit the options. IGNOU has access to only three 30-minute slots of nationally broadcast television each week and no access to national radio coverage. According to former Vice-Chancellor Kulandai Swamy (1994), 'as long as (radio) is not available the spread of distance education will suffer from a crippling handicap'. The obligation to use one of IGNOU's 229 study centres, which tend to be in the towns, may explain why 79% of IGNOU's 1992 entry cohort came from urban areas. However, the proportion of new entrants from the Delhi area has dropped from 40 to 15% in only three years (British Council, 1993; Takwale, 1995). The broadcast media would facilitate study for rural people. The production of audio-cassettes by IGNOU is decreasing because academics see less point in producing them if students must go to study centres to use them.

For this reason IGNOU and the Indian Space Research Organization have conducted satellite experiments for both teaching and staff development. One-way video and two-way audio communication was established between IGNOU headquarters and ten of its regional centres over a ten-day period in 1993 (Chaudhary, 1995; Sengupta, 1995). The evaluation was favourable and an operational system is now being implemented.

Like other mega-universities, IGNOU is finding technology increasingly important in its support operations. Materials distribution is being computerized and there is already extensive use of information technology in student administration (Kulandai Swamy, 1994). Pillai and Naidu (1991: 75) argued that IGNOU needed to standardize its credit structure, course registration and student number counting procedures. As they put it, 'unless the University is able to assess the student numbers that it is serving at a given time, considerable resources will be earmarked for the delivery of certain services which may not be required at all'. This seemingly elementary point is a crucial performance factor for mega-universities. Forecasting the academic choices and behaviour of large numbers of part-time students is not easy, especially when changing curricula make projections from historic data unreliable.

IGNOU is developing well. With 242,000 students and a new intake of 91,400 for 1996 it is already close to the projections of the Eighth Plan for 1997. As in some other mega-universities, IGNOU's full-time complement of 216 academic staff seems tiny in relation to student numbers. It does, however have 12,800 part-time staff. Naidu (1993) found that IGNOU was highly competitive with conventional institutions on cost. He did a useful calculation of the impact of drop-out on cost-competitiveness. This showed that even if one assumed a drop-out rate of zero from conventional university colleges, IGNOU would have to lose 60% of its students before losing its competitive edge.

Naidu (1993: 73) also pointed out that there is a limit to the economies of scale that mega-universities can achieve. In IGNOU's case a plot of average cost per student against student numbers starts to flatten out at around 140,000 students. Beyond this figure the average cost per student decreases very slowly. IGNOU should remain cost-effective with over 200,000 students if it can handle the challenges of scale.

Naidu's work provides useful background to the anxieties expressed by consultants who have worked with IGNOU under a multi-year project funded by the UK Overseas Development Administration. One fear is that IGNOU may lose cost-effectiveness by offering too many courses and allowing the numbers of students taking each course to fall. Another fear is that IGNOU's academic, administrative and operating systems are not yet sufficiently robust to cope effectively with present student numbers.

These are real concerns. The evidence suggests, however, that IGNOU is acting on them. For example, academic audit and evaluation units are now in place. Each year sees increasing professionalism and depth in the IGNOU administration. The importance it gives to the staff development function (Sengupta, 1995) is evidence of good intent.

Our study focuses on the use of new technology by the mega-universities. In that context the striking feature of IGNOU's planning documents is their focus on making the current system work better rather than looking for solutions in new technology. However, IGNOU also places great importance (Takwale, 1995) on the development of OPENET, an open educational network that now links IGNOU with its 16 regional centres and three state open universities. OPENET is a wide-area network for voice, data and images. One use, following the computerization of all administrative activities within IGNOU, is to allow the flow of administrative, financial and management data. Another is as a teleconference facility for staff and students:

> 'The main service available through this network is a wide range of certificate and degree/diploma programmes and also the extension programmes delivered through team teaching with cooperation from different institutions and organisations.' (Takwale, 1995: 3)

This development, which will lead IGNOU to blend both the correspondence and remote-classroom traditions of distance education in its future work, will be of interest to all the mega-universities.

Universitas Terbuka (UT), Indonesia

The Universitas Terbuka (Terbuka is Bahasa Indonesian for 'open' or 'open learning') brings together many of the challenges facing the mega-universities.

UT was created rather hastily in 1984. Indonesia had used the windfall revenues from the 1970s oil boom to expand primary and secondary education. In the early 1980s the growing number of secondary school-leavers threatened to swamp the conventional universities, and the country was then in recession. Creating a distance teaching university was a way of taking the pressure off. However, UT was a fragile plant in its early years (Zuhairi, 1994: 150). Although set up by presidential decree as one of 45 state universities it was not until 1992, with the publication of a development plan, that UT acquired full status within Indonesia's higher education system.

The speed of UT's creation inevitably caused some organizational problems. Government created a planning committee in 1983 and teaching began in 1984 with a first cohort of 60,000 students and a full-time staff of 200. After a decade, UT is more settled. Students now number over 350,000 and their profile has changed significantly. UT was set up to provide higher education to the tens of thousands of high-school graduates whom the conventional universities could not accommodate. Today 95% of the students are from the working population and range in age from 19 to 55.

Its formal partnership with the Indonesian post office symbolizes UT's origins in the correspondence tradition of distance education. Students can buy application forms, obtain information and pay their registration fees in any post office. Print-based study modules, which are distributed through 32 local centres, are augmented by audio-cassettes, radio and TV broadcasts and tutorials. Printed material accounted for 96% of UT's instructional media in 1990. UT encourages extra-curricular activities and organizes sports and cultural gatherings for students biennially.

Zuhairi (1994: 153) pointed out that the influence of Canadian consultants meant that UT was modelled more closely on the British Columbia Open Learning Institute (now the Open Learning Agency) than on open universities such as the

UKOU or IGNOU. The consequence was that UT had few senior academic staff and contracted course writing to academics in other universities. It also relied heavily on services from other bodies: the post offices for its enquiry service, the Universitas Indonesia for its computerized record system and the other universities for its local centres. Its founders conceived UT as a network of participating institutions.

An overview of distance education in Indonesia (NIME-UNESCO, 1994) lists three general issues facing distance education in the country: high school graduates prefer conventional universities; 'distance education students' attitude and desire towards achievement'; and institutional capability to provide better service. The same publication lists the major obstacles to the implementation of distance education at UT as: the difficulty of using TV, which is expensive and does not reach students in rural areas; slow postal services; and poor reliability of the computer network in local study centres. A further challenge is that the national language, Bahasa Indonesia, is a recent arrival in parts of the country and is still developing as a 'full-fledged language' (Brotosiswojo, 1995).

Two recent articles shed light on these statements from different perspectives. Zuhairi (1995) has compared UT with the distance teaching programmes of the University of New England, Australia and Massey University, New Zealand. After quoting Peters' (1973) work on distance education as a form of industrial production, Zuhairi contrasts UT as a 'management university' with conventional universities which are 'political institutions'. Single-mode distance teaching universities, being bureaucratic and hierarchical, have a weaker academic culture than the conventional universities that offer some courses at a distance. He found that the two dual-mode institutions had been more ready to experiment with interactive technologies than UT.

Although comparisons between a new mega-university in a developing country and old conventional institutions in rich countries can yield insights, available resource is a crucial factor. Elsewhere Zuhairi (1994: 199) reports that some high-technology experiments at UT 'such as telephone conferences, electronic mail and tele-teaching via satellite, have collapsed because of the high cost incurred'.

Djalil et al. (1994) provided a financial analysis of UT within the Indonesian university system. They compared it with three representative conventional universities. The results show UT to be an extreme example of the contrasts inherent in the economics of the mega-universities.

First, the proportion of UT's budget from non-government sources is not only much larger than in the other Indonesian universities, but is rising fast. Between 1991–92 and 1992–93 the contribution of UT's student fees and materials sales to its total budget rose from 44 to 66%. At this rate UT has the potential to become independent of government funding. Over the same period the proportion of UT's expenditure on staff salaries dropped from 39 to 28%.

Second, the differences in the costs per student borne by the government between the four universities are dramatic. The cost to the state for each student at UT is between 0.8 and 2.8% of the cost at the campus universities.

Third, comparisons based on costs per graduate are still favourable to UT even though it has a low graduation rate. In 1992–93 there were only 2,743 graduations in a student body of 165,204 (Djalil *et al.*, 1994: 34). Using these authors' data we can calculate that the total cost per graduate at UT is 35% of the average of the three other universities. The cost per graduate to the state is 29% of the average elsewhere.

These figures highlight the opportunity that technology could provide to UT and other mega-universities with low graduation rates. It seems unlikely that the integration of new technologies will further reduce the costs per active student. These are already very low, both absolutely and especially in terms of costs to the state. However, if use of technology could improve graduation rates, UT's economic and reputational competitiveness would grow.

Other evidence indicates that there is scope for increasing student satisfaction with UT's offerings. Iwanaga and Takahashi (1991) surveyed the first class of UT graduates. They found that although the respondents were very proud to have graduated, there was almost universal agreement that UT needed to 'expand the library function', make the printed materials 'easier to comprehend' and to develop 'more ingenious contrivances for the tutorial schedule'. Motik (1989) reported that UT's tutorial programme was not fully effective and did not meet students' expectations. However, a later study by Hiola and Moss (1990) presents a more encouraging picture and Smith (1996) reported increasing academic support in the local centres.

Two rather different lessons emerge from the UT experience. The first, expressed simply by Zuhairi (1994: 170) is that 'management is crucial in an open university'. UT discovered the hard way that teaching tens of thousands of students at a distance requires well-designed and robust operational systems. However, Zuhairi emphasized the political imperative to get UT going. The founding rector, Setijadi, said that those creating UT had to 'do first and plan later'.

The other lesson is that the notion of a 'management' university, which simply brings together in new ways the resources already within the tertiary education system, may be flawed. UT has gradually adopted a more collegial style of academic leadership. Its 1992–2000 development plan will use three broad strategies: internal consolidation through the management of growth; improving transparency in decision-making in order to gain support from staff and students; and the use of participative decision-making processes.

Payame Noor University (PNU), Iran

Iran has a population of 67 million (with a median age of about 20) that is growing by 1.8% per year. The considerable unsatisfied demand for university places was the principal motivation for establishing PNU in 1987 (Ebrahimzadeh, 1996). However, PNU had the opportunity to build on some previous Iranian experience of distance teaching at university level. This began with the creation of a correspondence faculty at Aburaihan Birooni University (ABU) in 1971. Applications were limited to government employees who had to pass the national university entrance examination. Before it was discontinued in 1980, when all Iranian universities were temporarily closed by Iran's cultural revolution, it had awarded some 2,000 bachelors degrees.

In 1972 early satisfaction with the work of this correspondence faculty, as well as the emergence of distance teaching universities in Europe, led the Shah's government to lay plans for a more ambitious institution that began operations in 1977 as the Free University of Iran (FUI). One of the government's declared aims was to disperse students from campuses where they might cause political trouble. The FUI was a well-resourced institution which had over 400 full-time academic staff for a student body of 3,181 (compared to 56 faculty for over 5,000 students at the ABU correspondence faculty) when it too was shut down by the Khomeini regime. Some of the materials it produced are still in use today.

After the revolution Iran's universities were restructured. ABU, FUI and eight other universities were merged into Allameh Taba Tabaee University. Distance teaching was discontinued because the Khomeini regime, regarding itself as a popular government, did not see the need to disperse students away from campuses. The FUI faculty twice found themselves on the wrong side of the political divide. Many of them had been banned by the Shah from teaching on campuses because of their leftist views but the new regime apparently found them no more congenial.

However, the demand for higher education continued to grow by 10% annually during the 1980s. By 1986 less than 11% of the half-million school-leavers who took the national entrance examination gained entrance to university. The government looked again at the potential of distance education and created Payame Noor University for this purpose (Payame Noor means 'message of light'). PNU aims to enrol over 400,000 students by the year 2010 (Zohoor and Alimohammadi, 1992). It joined the ranks of the mega-universities when its student body reached 117,000 in 1996.

PNU is an autonomous single-mode distance teaching university under the Ministry of Culture and Education. It is the only university in Iran that teaches at a distance. Now the largest state university in the country, its degrees are fully recognized and it accounts for 27% of all Iranian university students (Ebrahimzadeh, 1996).

The aims of PNU are:

- To promote the scientific and cultural levels of the society.
- To provide skilled manpower in areas critical to national integration and development.
- To create opportunities for individuals with family and work commitments to pursue their studies towards a degree.
- To present degree-level programmes to under-qualified or unqualified teaching staff of schools and consequently to solve a part of the problem of staff shortage of schools at bachelor's degree level.
- To satisfy the ever-increasing demand for higher education while holding the costs to society within acceptable bounds.
- To arrange public training, short- and long-term updating courses to keep people informed of the latest scientific and technological developments.
- To make higher education accessible to residents of rural areas and outreach sectors.

In pursuit of these aims PNU offers *formal*, *general* and *equivalent* degree programmes (Payame Noor University, 1995).

Entrance requirements for the *formal* programmes are: to hold a secondary school diploma; to pass the National University Entrance Exam; not to be registered at another university; to be resident in Iran and fluent in Persian. The formal programmes cover a wide range of subjects: accountancy, applied physics, biology, business administration, chemistry, computer engineering (software), education, environmental health, geology, English language, geography, Islamic theology, mathematics, Persian language and literature (the only programme offered to students outside Iran), physical education, psychology, public administration, social sciences and statistics. There are plans to add medical sciences, agriculture, engineering and technology. These programmes follow the Iranian national higher education curriculum, which considerably reduces course development costs.

The *general* degree programme is open to students without an entrance exam but is limited to the disciplines of mathematics, biology, Persian literature and education. This is the most accessible university programme in Iran. However, these students are admitted only to study the course materials independently. They do not receive tutorial support.

The *equivalent* programme is meant for the employees of particular public and private sector organizations and the degrees gained are only recognized, for promotion purposes, by those employers.

For those in the *formal* programmes the rigorously paced teaching system consists of self-study texts (including self-assessment questions) with some video and audio tapes. Printed material accounts for 90% of study time and PNU is proud of its Printing and Publishing Centre which has already produced over 800 titles. This production of academic material in Persian has benefited all the country's universities. For some subjects there are laboratories, practical classes and field trips. Assessment is a blend of in-course assignments and mid-term and final exams. Between three and eight class meetings are held each semester at 120 local centres (grouped under ten regional offices) throughout Iran. As has happened in the China TV University system, PNU has experienced pressure to turn these class meetings into regular lectures and increase their frequency. Its strategy is to offer more meetings in the student's first year and to use these as a vehicle for inculcating the skills of independent study.

Like the FUI, PNU had an agreement with the state broadcasting authority (IRIB) to produce and broadcast its TV programmes. However, following scheduling problems and unacceptable price hikes by the IRIB, PNU and the government have now signed a $US50 million agreement with Russia for the establishment of a PNU TV network within five years.

The student body of PNU has grown from 5,000 in 1988 to 117,000 in 1996. Seventy per cent of students are aged 21–30; 25% are in the age group 31–40; 14,269 degrees had been awarded by 1995. A major change in the student body took place in the early 1990s when the government extended to PNU the rules exempting students from military service for the duration of their university study (and commissioning them as officers after graduation). The proportion of male students at PNU increased from 60 to 67% when this change was made (but has since dropped back to 61%); the average age of students dropped from 33 to 26; and the drop-out rate decreased. This provision, along with the pressure on university places, may help to explain why the younger students at PNU are more enthusiastic about its teaching methods then their older colleagues (Ebrahimzadeh, 1996).

In common with the experience of mega-universities in other countries, PNU has had to work hard to establish that distance teaching is an academically rigorous and respectable educational endeavour. However, it seems to be steadily increasing its credibility, helped by the fact that its graduates have been highly successful in the national entrance examination for postgraduate study.

At present PNU is operating at about one-quarter of the unit cost per student of the rest of Iran's higher education sector. Originally the government set a ratio of one full-time staff member to 38 students at PNU (as compared to 1:15 at other universities). However, with the PNU ratio now at 1:134, the economies of scale are proving larger than anticipated. Unlike the other universities it collects a substantial proportion of its revenue in student fees which it sets itself. It is negotiating with the Islamic Development Bank for loans to help develop its capital infrastructure.

PNU is increasingly active in international distance education circles and hosted the annual conference of the Asian Association of Open Universities in 1996. It has study centres in Afghanistan, Azerbaijan and the United Arab Emirates. It is in the process of connecting its facilities to a range of international data networks and data banks.

The Korea National Open University (KNOU), Korea

The Korea Air and Correspondence University (KACU) was created in 1972 as a branch of Seoul National University offering a two-year junior college programme (ICDL, 1995). By 1981, when it became an independent university, it had evolved into a five-year university. In 1992 it began to align itself on the four-year programmes that had become standard in Korean universities. In 1994 it adopted a new name, the Korea National Open University, and in 1996 it modernized its visual identity by changing its logo.

KNOU has three broad objectives: to provide opportunities for high school graduates; to facilitate professional updating, especially in modern science and technology; and to contribute to the welfare of the nation.

In 1996 KNOU had an enrolment of 210,000 students and an annual intake of 100,000; 61% of the students are under 30 and 57% are women. There is a full-time staff of 670, including 176 academics, and a part-time staff of 2,670 academics (Heo, 1996). This is the context for any judgements of KNOU's teaching system. A full-time academic staff of 176 for a student body of 210,000 is a small ratio even by mega-university standards!

KNOU's teaching media are evolving from an emphasis on textbooks and radio programmes toward greater use of television and video conferencing. This is part of a 'thorough reform' that 'will make KNOU one of the top distance education institutes in the world within a decade' (Heo, 1996). KNOU had only one hour of TV broadcasting per day in 1992 (Soon Jeong Hong, 1992). In 1996 it began transmitting ten hours of lectures per day on a CATV channel. This is used in the context of courses that consist of 40 hours of TV or radio lectures and eight hours of classroom sessions. Fourteen centres are linked by a video conferencing system and there is some use of 'self-organized study groups'. There will be satellite lectures for overseas students from 1997 and KNOU is developing a multimedia database which will be available to students through the Internet. However, KNOU is still developing the capacity for two-way communication and student support. It only corrects one assignment for each course.

A comprehensive report on distance education in Asia and the Pacific listed 'low social recognition of distance education' as the major obstacle for implementing distance education in Korea (NIME-UNESCO, 1994: 456). According to the same source, KNOU's five-year development plan includes:

● moving to four-year courses (begun in 1992) and adding Master's and PhD programmes;
● reorganising the curriculum to benefit working students;
● setting an exemplary model for the nation for the so-called multi-media approach in education; pioneering in arenas of educational technology by introducing such innovative communication systems as the CATV, ISDN VAN and the like, into the actual fields of education;
● obtaining sufficient classroom facilities and teaching staff to operate 'qualitative schooling sessions'; and
● solving the problems of assessing student achievement, 'which rely too heavily on computer-processed marking'.

A revised four-year development plan for 1995–98 emphasized the establishment of: postgraduate courses from 1998; non-degree courses; global education through satellite for overseas residents; and KNOU's broadcasting system (Heo, 1996).

KNOU is a particularly interesting case study of a university adopting a technology strategy. It hopes to shed a poor reputation and become an exemplary model partly through the use of technology. There is now a strong emphasis on staff development with all personnel attending domestic or overseas training every two years.

The previously low reputation of KNOU seems linked to poor performance as measured by high drop-out rates. Up to 1981 the average drop-out rate was 70% and it was claimed (KACU, 1983) that 'this reflects the high standard of teaching that the KACU has stringently maintained', also noting that KACU graduates had 'outstanding success' in the qualifying exams for the four-year universities, their pass rate being 22% compared to 7% for conventional junior college graduates. Cost comparisons were also favourable to KACU: $300 per graduate compared to $675 at the conventional colleges (Harwood & Kim, 1986). Since 1983, however, it has become less fashionable to equate high drop-out rates with high standards. A decade later Park (1995) attributed the 90% drop-out rates at KNOU to its inadequate educational services.

Another reason for low retention rates, according to Heo (1996), is the state-run self-study Bachelor's Degree system that began in 1989. There is a proposal for KNOU to adopt or take over this system.

There may be a danger that KNOU will expect too much of new technology. Can the new media compensate for levels of staffing which may simply fall short of the critical mass that a student body of KNOU's size requires? Soon Jeong Hong (1992), after explaining why KNOU's resources would not allow tutoring on the UKOU model, makes the following statement:

'While it is unrealistic to depend on personal tutoring, it is quite possible to use telephone, fax and even computer for tutoring purposes in KNOU since the telephone and other technological equipment are well organized in Korea.'

Can technology reduce the human time that effective tutoring requires? This is an important question because some evidence suggests that telephone and e-mail may make more demands on tutors' time than correspondence tuition.

The two papers from KNOU presented at the 1995 conference of the International Council for Distance Education provide an interesting contrast in analyses and prescriptions for KNOU. Han (1995) is resolutely optimistic about the 'new age of distance education practice which brings high interactivity and individualized learner-centred education by introducing teleconferencing and multi-media systems'. He does add, however, that 'developing high quality courseware for these new media systems should always be our concern'.

Park (1995) concentrates on this last point, echoing the findings of Soon Jeong Hong (1992) that KNOU course materials were very poor teaching materials because of low readability, a non-interactive style and a lack of self-assessment questions. He believes that improved educational services to students require a larger staff, whatever the technology. However, there is now no doubt of KNOU's determination to succeed. It wants to distinguish itself more clearly from other conventional universities, raise the quality of its offerings and, more generally, break out of the rigid and rule-oriented system of higher education in which it is set.

University of South Africa (UNISA)

The University of South Africa (UNISA) is the oldest mega-university. It began as the University of the Cape of Good Hope in 1873 when it was an examining body for affiliated university colleges. In 1916 it was renamed the University of South Africa and moved to Pretoria. By the end of World War II the colleges had become autonomous universities and in 1946 UNISA started to provide distance education to off-campus students (ICDL, 1995). It also assumed the guardianship of the black university colleges until they in turn became independent (Wiechers, 1995).

In 1995 UNISA had 130,000 students, over one-third of all university enrolments in South Africa. Male and female are almost equally represented in UNISA's student body, with 54% female students. Nearly 36% of students are resident in Gauteng and the ethnic breakdown in 1995 was: 47% African; 40% White; 4% Coloured; 9% Asian. Over 80% of students are employed and the average age is 31. Almost 38,000 of UNISA's students are school teachers. Applicants who do not have secondary school matriculation are awarded conditional matriculation and restricted in the number of courses they can take in their first year as undergraduates. UNISA was open to all races throughout the apartheid era.

Linguistic diversity is a special challenge for UNISA. Although it operates in both Afrikaans and English, neither is the home language of 47% of its students; 32% have English and 18% have Afrikaans as home languages. Eighty-two per cent of students choose to study and correspond with UNISA in English.

In 1995 the overall staff numbered 3,437 of whom 1,410 were academic staff. The academic staff were 93% white and 47% female. The service or unskilled staff were 100% non-white and 92% male (UNISA, 1995).

In comparison with other mega-universities UNISA offers a very wide range of courses at undergraduate and postgraduate level: 2,265 papers or modules were available in 1995, nearly all of them in both Afrikaans and English (the majority being written in Afrikaans and then translated into English).

UNISA teaching derives from the correspondence tradition of distance education and has been described as follows (SAIDE, 1994):

'The basic teaching method at UNISA is for an academic member of staff in Pretoria to teach a course to students distributed throughout the country. He or she will do this primarily by writing printed study guides and tutorial letters. Some study guides are designed to stand alone, while others are wrap around guides which accompany textbooks. Courses are heavily print-orientated because it is believed that this is the medium most accessible to students. In addition, however, audio-cassettes are distributed for many subjects, and UNISA also buys air time on Radio 2000 for use in several subjects.'

Although there are four regional administrative centres with some library facilities, students requiring academic assistance must visit, write to or telephone the academic in Pretoria who is responsible for their course. It is a contractual requirement that UNISA academic staff be in their offices from 8 am to 1.30 pm each working day so that students can contact them. There are also limited teleconferencing links with the regional centres. An interactive video link, Picturetel, allows Pretoria staff to hold sessions with students in Cape Town. A number of discussion classes are held across the country annually.

As the above description makes clear, course authoring and tutoring at UNISA have been the responsibility of individual academics. However, the notion of course teams is now being introduced. In 1996 there were 62 course teams engaged in designing new courses. A limited local tutorial support network based on part-time staff is also being expanded (Minnaar, 1995). The older, more individual methods, combined with a relatively large academic staff (compared to other mega-universities) allowed UNISA to offer a considerable number of courses. Wiechers (1995: 191) talks of 'a superabundance of courses and papers as well as strict adherence to traditional organization and structure'. This approach also explains why, uniquely among the mega-universities, posts at UNISA are eagerly sought after by academics who want to concentrate on research. UNISA has the best research library in Southern Africa and awarded 78 doctorates in 1992.

Its production of degrees at other levels is more controversial. According to statistics published by SAIDE (1994) the graduation rates, six years after first enrolment, vary by programme as follows: BEd – 36%; BSc – 5%; BComm – 10%. Critics of UNISA claim that it has very high wastage rates, especially among black students with low educational qualifications on entry. However, an independent study by van Enckevort and Woodley (1995) suggests that UNISA's completion rates are not 'greatly out of line with those of other distance teaching universities'.

UNISA provides higher education at lower cost to both the government and the student than other South African universities. Its state subsidy per full-time equivalent student is set at about 60% of that received by the other universities. The total fees cost of a degree to a UNISA student is 40% of the fees charged elsewhere.

Although UNISA is the oldest of the mega-universities it faces more wrenching contemporary changes than any of them. A recent paper by its current Principal was entitled 'Managing the transformation of the University of South Africa' (Wiechers, 1995). Some of those now in power in South Africa are ambivalent about UNISA. On the one hand it was one of the more liberal institutions of the apartheid regime. However, it was part of that regime and some suspect that its failure to provide local tutorials was less a result of poverty (it has about the same student numbers as the UKOU with half the budget) than a desire to prevent students getting together and causing trouble. This ambivalence is nicely expressed in the example of President Nelson Mandela. He is a UNISA graduate but he studied in jail. He is a supporter of UNISA.

The challenges faced by UNISA are the mirror image of those faced by mega-universities such as Universitas Terbuka. UT has no problems of political acceptability but needs to be better organized. UNISA is a model of good organization. Operations are smooth and efficient and management information is comprehensive and timely. However, UNISA is part of South Africa's national task of 'wiping out the ravages of the past' (Wiechers, 1995: 190) which will require:

> 'not only... the reform of a system of distance education... (but also) the total absorption of all those elements of liberalization, democratization and socialization which are the essential characteristics of a successful transition from authoritarian rule.'

By 1995 UNISA was resolutely engaged in two processes of change. The first, which it calls 'transformation', aims to infuse its governance structures, management processes and organizational ethos with the spirit of the new South Africa. The second, labelled 'renewal', addresses the need to improve its practice of distance education. Particular attention is being given to enhancing the quality of course materials through the use of course teams and the strengthening of support to students through tutorial provision and learning centres. The curriculum in the School of Education is being reformed away from the theories of 'fundamental pedagogics' which appeared to support the ideology of apartheid.

UNISA is conducting tentative experiments with new technologies for the purpose of getting closer to its students. For the moment, however, more direct approaches to this challenge, such as the creation of networks of learning centres, are the main focus (Ngengebule, 1995). It is encouraging to see that in creating these centres UNISA has allied itself to the SACHED Trust. SACHED was one of UNISA's sternest critics during the apartheid years and used to organize its own tutorials for UNISA students in an attempt to repair this weakness in the teaching system.

UNISA is worried that the use of new technologies will drive its costs up towards those of the conventional universities. However, it does not want to increase fees to students and it is unlikely that the government will align its subsidies per student with those of the campus universities. UNISA expects to have 290,000 students by 2010 on current projections so maintaining the economy of its teaching system is a priority. The most pressing imperative is ideological rather than technological. In adapting to a new national environment UNISA has captured the idealism that inspires other open universities. One of its new participative bodies has declared that the goal of UNISA is to create:

> 'a *vita academica* which centres round the adult learner and creates an environment of lifelong learning through systems of adult basic education, student support and interactive means of teaching technologies. Furthermore, this vision of our *vita academica* acknowledges the existence of all other institutions of higher learning and foresees a very broad co-operation with them to bring about living systems of dual-mode teaching.' (Wiechers, 1995: 191)

The internal changes at UNISA are taking place against the backdrop of the desire for a national reform of higher education in South Africa. The document that launched the discussion on the directions that this reform should take (National Commission on Higher Education (NCHE), 1996) called for an enhanced role for distance learning programmes in the context of 'a strategy of greater cost-effectiveness and the limitation of the impact on public expenditure'. It stressed the key role of good course materials and urged that, 'wherever possible course materials from abroad should be used or adapted to the country's needs' (NCHE, 1996: 65). Noting that learner support to distance students is lacking or inadequate, it called for the creation of collaborative consortia to provide appropriate tutoring.

UNISA is already moving in this direction. Wiechers commented:

> 'The role I see for UNISA is not so much to gain a competitive advantage, but through co-operation and networking with (the traditional black) universities, to assist them in their search for maximum use of new technologies. If we take our name seriously, we should comprehend the whole of South Africa as our campus,

which also means supporting other universities.... most South African universities are entering into regional co-operation agreements and UNISA, being country-wide, actively participates in all these ventures.' (Wiechers, 1996)

Universidad Nacional de Educación a Distancia (UNED), Spain

UNED, the national university for distance education in Spain, was founded by an Act of Parliament in 1972. It is one of only three of the institutions profiled in this appendix (UNED (James, 1982a), CTVU and UKOU) that were the subjects of chapters in Rumble and Harry's book, *The Distance Teaching Universities* (1982). This shows how recently and quickly the mega-universities have grown.

In creating UNED the government had three groups of students in mind: those unable to begin or complete higher education; those living in remote areas; and those ambitious for more qualifications. All the mega-universities reflect their national context. UNED is an integral part of a national system of higher education that is Napoleonic in concept (James, 1982b). This means it operates under central government authority that lays down a national curriculum for higher education and employs university staff within the civil service. An interesting current challenge for UNED is that the system is becoming less Napoleonic as responsibility for universities is devolved to regional governments. This leaves UNED as the only 'national' university.

A frequent feature of Napoleonic systems is high drop-out from the conventional universities. Villanueva (1980: 56) reported that 50 to 70% of registered students dropped out of Spain's other universities at that time, with only 15% completing the *Licenciado* degree (equivalent to a four-year honours bachelor's degree). In the years following UNED's creation it was the intake of students, rather than the output of graduates, that measured the expansion of Spanish higher education.

In this context the criticisms levelled at UNED on the occasion of its tenth anniversary were wide of the mark. Connell (1983) claimed UNED had 'aped the set-up of the existing universities in course content and method'. Evans (1983) noted that 3,000 graduates was a slender output from 60,000 student registrations. James (1982b) stressed that UNED was intended to be like the other universities of Spain in curriculum and organization. Given the nature of the *Licenciado* degree, its output of graduates should more properly be compared to the 2,000 honours graduates rather than the 40,000 ordinary bachelor's degrees produced by the UK Open University in its first decade.

However, the UNED leadership did make changes as the University began its second decade. While young students continued to need the *Bachillerato* that is required by all Spanish universities for admission, UNED promoted a preparatory admission course for students aged over 25. No prerequisites were required for the Open Distance Education programme that offered individual courses in the con-tinuing education area.

In the 1990s the demand for UNED's courses remained buoyant without the need for advertising. By 1995–96 enrolment was over 150,000, of which 110,000 were in degree programmes and the remainder in continuing education. The average age of students was 30. Completion rates were as good as those in the conventional universities. Over 2,000 students were taking doctoral courses.

Many of the interesting comparisons made by James (1982b) between UNED and the UK Open University remain valid 15 years later. He found that UNED's costs per student were about one-third those of the UKOU. The proportion of UNED's costs borne by student fees was more than twice the proportion at the UKOU. At that time the UKOU had fewer academic staff than UNED but a much larger non-academic staff. It appears that definition of the curriculum by government makes course development and production much cheaper. UNED staff often commission academics from other universities to write the courses and the physical production of materials is a simple process. This enables it to operate over a wide range of subjects and to continue to expand the curriculum quickly. UNED now offers some 600 courses in 16 degree programmes and a further 180 continuing education courses.

UNED faculty have the responsibility for course preparation and are required to spend a session of four hours per week tutoring students by telephone. There is emphasis on cooperation with all other Spanish universities, collaboration with community organizations and decentralization. Many of UNED's 59 study centres are sponsored by community and industrial organizations which also pay the salaries of the part-time tutorial staff based there. Instead of mailing course materials to students' homes, UNED distributes them in bulk to the study centres for collection.

Print is the main instructional medium but, with only recent access to television broadcasting, UNED has made extensive use of radio. Contreras and Moreno (1993) describe radio as a medium with tremendous possibilities and note that UNED's two and a half hours of daily programming are 'the most important cultural contribution provided by any means of communication in Spain, and particularly the radio'. They argue that new technologies give radio a bright future in distance education. UNED is also extending a video conference service to a total of 15 study centres and has made e-mail facilities available to the whole University community (ICDL, 1995: 13).

Using technology to enrich the activity of study centres is a strategy that is also being adopted by Sukhothai Thammathirat Open University in Thailand. It will be interesting to see whether this does anything to resolve the fundamental paradox of study centres in either country. In both Thailand and Spain students cite lack of contact between themselves, tutors and other students as the greatest problem with distance education, yet attendance at study centres is relatively sparse (James, 1982b: 30; Nilvises, 1990).

Another key element of the technology strategy of UNED is the use of videotex. This service provides course guides, subject noticeboards and an e-mail service. To participate students need a telephone line and a videotex or PC terminal with a modem. All users (teachers, tutors, students) have their own mail box.

Recently García-Aretio (1995) has assessed the strengths and weaknesses of UNED as a 'macro-institution'. Like many writers from the Napoleonic academic tradition, he assumes that any form of distance education must be second best to 'the ideal personal student-professor classroom relationship'. Nevertheless, he finds that UNED's advantages of openness, flexibility, effectiveness and economy make a longer list than its drawbacks. He calculated that costs per student-course at UNED were 41% of those in conventional universities, while costs per graduate were 53%. The possibility of combining work and study (83% of UNED students are employed) is particularly important.

On the debit side, García-Aretio lists: limited interaction with professors; slow feedback because of the post; difficulty of organizing examinations; and the high number of drop-outs (43%) from one year to the next. The latter is often 'the result less of the difficulty of the subject matter than of inadequate guidance or the failure of Headquarters professors and local tutors to provide initial and ongoing motivation'. He also notes that as student numbers continue to grow and the curriculum to diversify, enrolment and *in situ* examination processes are becoming increasingly complex.

He expresses one of the fundamental challenges facing all the mega-universities as follows (1995: 93):

'The production and distribution of teaching materials for large numbers of students and the management and co-ordination of the activities of students and their respective tutors scattered throughout the country entail the application of procedures calling for process rationalisation, division of tasks and mass production. This can detract from the flexibility of the organisation as systems must be rigidly programmed and relations among course designers, tutors, etc. and pupils highly structured; this is detrimental to flexibility and attention to personal needs. Macroinstitutions find this problem difficult to solve.'

Sukhothai Thammathirat Open University (STOU), Thailand

In 1995, at the 17th World Conference of the International Council for Distance Education (ICDE), Sukhothai Thammathirat Open University (STOU) won the ICDE and Commonwealth of Learning joint Award of Excellence in the institutional category. This confirmed the common view that STOU is the most successful of the larger mega-universities. Like several other mega-universities, STOU owes its success partly to its extremely able founding Rector, Dr Wichit Srisa-an.

Thailand established STOU as a national university by Royal Charter in 1978. Its objectives are to promote: lifelong education; the expansion of educational opportunities for secondary school graduates; personnel development and the training of skilled manpower; the development of economic and political doctrines; and democratic values. Some 20% of STOU's revenue now comes from the government. Nearly all the remainder comes from student fees (ICDL, 1995).

The total enrolment in degree programmes is over 200,000 with an annual intake of 100,000. If the count includes students in single course 'certificate of achievement' programmes and short training programmes then STOU reaches more than half a million people each year (NIME-UNESCO, 1994: 720). STOU's annual graduating class numbers 12,000. Two-thirds of the students are aged between 21 and 30 with less than 10% under 21. Three-quarters of the students are from rural areas. In 1995 full-time staff numbered 2,000, of which over 400 were in the academic and academic support category. STOU also employs over 3,000 part-time professional and academic staff.

STOU offers a wide range of programmes: 15 certificates; 47 bachelor's degrees; and three master's degrees. The University operates an integrated multimedia teaching system consisting of face-to-face tutoring (10–15 hours per course per semester), printed materials, correspondence media, audio/video cassettes and broadcasts on television and radio. About 1,100 TV programmes are broadcast per year using three daily slots between 1800 and 1930h. Each week there are 150 20-minute radio programmes. Thailand has an efficient postal service and STOU is thoroughly integrated into the country's regional networks. This allows it to provide numerous contact points for students: regional centres (7); local study centres (78); special study centres for health sciences (63); local study centres for agricultural extension and cooperatives (7); 'STOU corners' in provincial libraries (75) and an area resource centre in southern Thailand.

STOU rapidly achieved respectability within the national academic community, partly through the involvement of outstanding academics from the other universities in its activities. Like other mega-universities that operate in a national language not widely spoken outside the country, STOU has developed an important role as an academic publisher (Asian Development Bank, 1987: 335):

'Another factor that has greatly contributed to an increase in the public's recognition of the University's academic quality is the extensive use of its printed texts by students, both undergraduates and graduates, of various conventional universities. Hence, in addition to helping overcome the deficiency in Thai-language textbooks, STOU has also played a significant role in the production of high-standard course materials for nation-wide use.'

Despite its success, STOU lists obstacles to its future development (NIME-UNESCO, 1994: 725) that are familiar to other mega-universities:

'(1) Financial support for new development infrastructure; (2) Inadequate number of personnel in media and courseware production and revision of existing packages. Full-time academic and non-academic staff are overloaded; (3) Decreasing of air-time for broadcasting educational television programmes; (4) Lack of innovative and devoted personnel; (5) Shortage of communication and educational technological infrastructure; and (6) Insufficient points for delivery systems.'

The funding of STOU has been described by Chaya-Ngam (1994). Although STOU has the largest student body in Thailand it receives the least state support: about 1% of the government's higher education budget. More problematic for planning purposes is that the state contribution is not a block grant but an itemized contribution applicable only to certain of STOU's expenditures. For example, in 1993 the state paid 20% of the costs of buying broadcast air-time but did not contribute at all to tutorial costs.

The magnitude and methodology of state funding is an important consideration in the development of a competitive strategy by a mega-university. The pattern of government 'buying', especially if it is through a line-item grant structured to reflect the historic spending patterns of conventional universities, can easily distort the development strategies of the mega-universities. There is always a temptation to choose those developments for which the government might give funds. Conversely, it requires firm institutional will to pursue strategies that do not attract state funds.

In this context the telling example at STOU is the development of graduate programmes. Teswanitch and Thanavibulchai (1993) argue the general case for more equitable funding to STOU. Silphiphat and Tamey (1993) take up the particular case of graduate studies. The Thai government covers 80% of the costs of graduate study in the conventional universities but only 4% of the costs at STOU. The result, naturally, is that graduate students at STOU have to pay 96% of the costs of their tuition (the other universities charge 40% and presumably cross-subsidize other programmes). This example holds two general lessons for the mega-universities. First, they should use their influence to change the behaviour of the government buyer in the direction of equitable funding methodologies. Second, they must pay particular attention to the value as perceived by the student buyer, who will usually be paying a higher share of the cost than in a conventional university. Interestingly an STOU staff member, Yenbamrung (1992; 1994), has studied the characteristics of the 'emerging electronic university' and its cost-effectiveness to American students. These issues will have an important influence on the future strategies of the mega-universities.

STOU's own technology strategy is aimed at increasing its ability to broadcast television programmes and to enhance counselling, tutoring and training for its students. For this purpose, as reported by ICDL (1995: 15):

> 'STOU is harnessing the latest multimedia communications technology for… the University's distance teaching system. STOU is developing educational communications systems through the transmission of one-way educational video via satellite, and two-way audio transmissions by way of the telephone network. This system will enable students to view instructional programmes via satellite and to consult their teachers by telephone. The University plans to install cable TV and telephone networks and satellite dishes throughout the Kingdom, providing students with free educational services.'

The aim of increasing the quality and availability of tutorials flows from studies such as that of Nilvises (1990) which showed that only about 10% of STOU students attended tutorials in the 1980s. Pakdiratn (1990) has provided a detailed rationale for STOU's plans to develop interactive communication through telecommunication.

Anadolu University (AU), Turkey

Strictly speaking, AU is a dual-mode institution. The other mega-universities are exclusively engaged in distance teaching, although the UK Open University also validates the degrees and awards of a range of conventional institutions. AU teaches some programmes using conventional methods at its campus in Eskisehir. Distance teaching is the preserve of its Open Education Faculty (OEF). However, distance teaching began with the foundation of AU in 1982 and the number of distance students (577,000 at degree level in 1995) has always dwarfed those in the University's other programmes (17,190 in 1995). Nevertheless, the OEF receives less than half of AU's budget. Of the OEF's budget 76% is student fees, 6% a government grant (Öz-Alp, 1995).

The beginnings of distance education in Turkey in the 1970s have been described by Ozdil (1979). In 1974 the Ministry of Education set up an experimental teachers' training college dedicated to the use of educational technology. By 1975 it was becoming an embryonic structure for a future open university. In that year, however, a ministerial decree shut it down on the grounds that the infrastructure was needed for other purposes. Attempts to introduce distance learning later in the decade appeared to come to nothing. Ozdil (1979: 5) commented:

'Our experience has shown that all hasty attempts at introducing distance learning when this is dissociated from the whole educational system, lacks clear-cut objectives, well-defined methodologies, minimum of integrated and skilfully operated technological hardware and software devices, well-trained and efficiently organized staff cognisant of the merits of accumulation of experiences and without carefully planned experimentations are bound to end up in frustration.'

In fact, the foundations of distance learning at Anadolu University were beginning to be laid (McIsaac et al., 1988). The Eskisehir Academy of Economics and Commercial Science was home to the only developed media and broadcasting capability outside the state broadcasting corporation. In 1978 its president proposed that the Academy become the centre for a programme of distance education in Turkey (Büyükersen, 1978).

By the end of the 1970s, Turkey was in turmoil and the military took over the government. In 1982 there was a new constitution and a new Higher Education Act which created a powerful Council for Higher Education (YÖK) to regulate the universities. YÖK told all the universities that they could develop distance education programmes. The Büyükersen report was implemented at the Eskisehir Academy which became Anadolu University the same year.

The recasting of the university system under a military regime caused deep apprehension in the academic community outside Turkey. Savran (1987) described a period of human rights abuses and 'educational sabotage' in a publication that was given wide circulation by academic staff unions in western countries. However, he did not suggest that the new commitment to distance education was in any way suspect.

Whatever the motives of the Turkish military, the creation of Anadolu University and its Open Education Faculty led to a dramatic expansion of tertiary education. In ten years the number of university students in the country doubled (Demiray & McIsaac, 1992). Between 1983–84 and 1991–92 the proportion of the national student body enrolled at AU rose from 13 to 46%. The change recorded by these authors finds echoes in the stories of several of the mega-universities:

> 'From an early sceptical reception in 1982, the Open Education Faculty has achieved a position of respectability in Turkish higher education. It would be of interest to explore the political and social elements which combine to create the current receptive environment for implementing open education as an integral component of the higher and adult education system. The success of the projects is most certainly tied to the efforts of one man, Yilmaz Büyükersen, and his team.'

In the early years it seemed that the familiar problem of high drop-out and low graduation rates might be an issue for AU. Tekin and Demiray (1989) analysed the performance of the first intake of 29,249 students in 1982–83. By 1985–86 some 9,946 of this cohort were senior students and 768 had graduated. They reported a graduation rate of 8% for economics and 7% for business administration noting, of course, that many of the senior students would go on to graduate in later years. By the time Ozgu (1989) reported, the graduation rate had risen to 24%. Since those studies the graduation performance of AU has been substantially improved by its teacher training programmes. In 1986 the OEF offered such programmes for 130,000 primary teachers and 54,000 secondary teachers; 133,126 of them registered and by the end of the programme 119,942 had graduated, a graduation rate of over 90% (Demiray, 1990).

The enrolment of these teachers (followed by thousands of nurses in the early 1990s) reinforced a trend in the AU student profile that we have seen in other mega-universities. The proportion of students in employment rose from 35% in 1982 to 61% in 1986. When it opened, AU aimed its programmes primarily at school-leavers. Ten years later it was taking a special interest in students aged over 45 (Demiray, 1992). In 1995 AU produced 14,200 graduates at Bachelors level and 12,121 from its two-year diploma programmes.

AU's cost performance appears to be good. Already in 1983–84 Ozgu (1989: 21) reported that public expenditure per student at the OEF was 17% of the corresponding conventional faculty and was set to drop further as numbers increased. Put another way, the OEF served 25% of all Turkish students with only 2% of the public funds allocated to higher education. Costs to students were one quarter of those in conventional universities. This no doubt contributed to the high level of satisfaction with the OEF expressed by the 1984 student cohort in response to an independent survey (Ozgu, 1989: 10). By 1995, however, only 48% of students declared themselves 'satisified' or 'very satisfied' with their OEF courses; 44% were 'not very satisfied' (Bir, 1996).

Despite its cost performance and the growing demand for higher education in Turkey (55% of the population is under 24), the development of AU's distance education programme does not seem to figure prominently in either national (YÖK) or institutional plans. Although AU has more than 40 students at a distance for each one on campus, the focus in AU publications and discussions is largely on the campus operations. Is this an unavoidable weakness of the dual-mode approach?

However, some of the younger faculty are taking a professional interest in improving AU's distance education offerings and are getting appropriate training abroad. Although all student assignments and exams are marked by computer, there is an increasing provision of 'advisory sessions' at which part-time lecturers meet students in 50 local study centres. It appears that the importance of student support is gradually being recognized.

AU became Turkey's centre for distance education because of its leadership in educational technology. Not surprisingly therefore, it has shown considerable interest in multimedia technologies even though print remains by far the most important teaching medium. AU has conducted pilot projects using satellite television to augment the 2,500 programmes it broadcasts each year during its 1,200 hours of air-time on terrestrial state television. Some 300 new programmes are made each year. The format is mostly 'talking heads' or panel discussion. AU staff have studied the potential of video cassette recorders and video education centres (Demiray et al., 1988; Tekin & Barkan, 1988). AU students have also taken part in international computer conferences (Gunawardena, 1992; McIsaac, 1992).

An important current development is the creation of 27 computer support centres around Turkey for AU students (only 7% of students have computers at home (Bir, 1996)). Each centre will have 30 computers and will support a range of AU courses with a common format of computer-based tutorials; drill and practice; sample problems; and tests and feedback.

The Open University (UKOU), United Kingdom

Although CNED and UNISA have longer institutional histories, most observers regard the UK Open University as the pioneer of modern distance education at university level. For this reason its activities have attracted considerable interest. The first and third Vice-Chancellors have described its creation and early development (Perry, 1976) and provided a summary of its achievements over 25 years (Daniel, 1995).

At the UKOU's inaugural ceremony in 1969, its first Chancellor expressed the aims of the University as being 'open as to people, open as to places, open as to methods, and, finally, open as to ideas' (Daniel, 1995:400). Between that ceremony and the start of teaching in 1971, Britain had a change of government. Margaret Thatcher, the incoming Secretary of State for Education, had to defend the infant UKOU against colleagues in her party who would have strangled the project at birth. One of her arguments was that the UKOU had the potential to bring down the costs of higher education.

A quarter of a century later the UKOU can show considerable success in achieving the objectives set by its founders. Openness to people led to a 1995 student body numbering over 150,000 in degree credit courses and a further 60,000 working on non-assessed packs. Moreover, on almost any measure (eg, gender, disability, ethnic origin, socio-economic background), the UKOU student body comes closer to reproducing the composition of the population at large than those of other UK universities.

In trying to be open to people the UKOU's most radical step was to remove all academic prerequisites for entry. In 1995 the proportion of new UKOU students without the conventional entry qualifications for UK universities was higher than ever. Each year this category accounts for one-third of the graduates of the UKOU, supporting Harold Wilson's conviction that, with proper teaching and support, access to success in higher education can be greatly expanded.

Now that some other mega-universities (eg, Universitas Terbuka and UNISA) wish to adopt a more participative style of management, another feature of the UKOU's openness to people is noteworthy. Students and staff have a large role in a participative governance structure that includes a 1,000-member Senate. Most UKOU people see this as a strength. They would argue that although it may take longer to reach decisions with such structures, those decisions are carried out faster and more effectively because they are widely owned.

In pursuit of its ambition to be open as to places, the UKOU has become an increasingly international institution. In 1996 there were some 20,000 students taking UKOU courses outside the UK. The largest concentrations are in the rest of the European Union, the former Soviet bloc, Hong Kong and Singapore. In these overseas operations the UKOU has tried to reproduce, either directly (in the countries of the European Union) or through partnerships (in the other territories) the local tutorial support that it provides in the UK. New technologies, notably e-mail and computer conferencing, call into question this expensive and complex precondition to expansion. In 1995 the UKOU initiated a review of its international activities. A key question will be whether to offer courses worldwide with electronic support or to continue to seek local partnerships in other countries.

The TV and radio programmes broadcast on the terrestrial channels of the BBC are still the most visible expression of the UKOU's openness to methods to the general public. In 1994 these broadcasts amounted to 706 hours of transmission time on TV and 152 on radio. The TV figure increased further in 1995 when the UKOU contributed programmes to the 'Learning Zone', a new BBC all-night educational service.

Less visible to the public have been the newer teaching and learning media that the UKOU has added since its foundation. Of particular note are personal media, ie equipment such as audio and video cassette recorders and personal computers owned by students. A growing number of UKOU courses require students to have access to a computer at home. In 1996 the number of students affected exceeded 30,000; 17,000 of these students (up from 5,000 in 1995) were networked from home to the UKOU and to each other. Some at the UKOU believe that this convergence of computing and communication changes radically the nature of the personal media.

Openness to ideas is the *raison d'être* of any university. The UKOU has fulfilled this idea through a commitment to research and through its practice of developing courses in teams. This gives the UKOU's courses an intellectual vitality not always found in distance teaching.

The 1992 reform of UK higher education continues to set the context for the UKOU's future development. Prior to 1992 government allocated public funds to the UKOU directly, through its Department of Education and Science, whereas buffer bodies (eg, the Universities Funding Council) were responsible for distributing public funds to the other universities. The 1992 Higher Education Act brought all the UK's 200 higher education institutions into a common funding framework. The UKOU became the largest university in the new system.

This reform gave a boost to the UKOU because the funding methodology adopted by the Higher Education Funding Council for England allocated growth monies preferentially to the most cost-effective institutions. Furthermore, from 1993 the UK government froze the expansion of places for full-time study and directed all growth funds to the part-time sector (Peters & Daniel, 1994). The UKOU accounts for over a third of all part-time higher education in the UK. Moreover, in each subject category the cost to the taxpayer of a full-time equivalent student at the UKOU is around 40% of the average for the other institutions. The net result was that in 1994 and 1995 the UKOU's percentage grant increases were among the highest in the country.

So much for the cost element of cost-effectiveness. What about effectiveness? The present UK funding system includes a national programme for the assessment of teaching quality by subject area. This process completed its first cycle in 1995. Six of the 11 UKOU subject areas assessed were awarded 'excellent' ratings, a proportion that put it in the top group of universities. Furthermore three of the subjects so rated, music, chemistry and earth sciences, were areas where distance education would not appear to enjoy a natural advantage.

In the international distance education community, student completion rates are more often used as performance indicators than judgements by national funding bodies. On these criteria the UKOU also performs well. The UKOU offers newly registered students the opportunity to try out a course for three months before confirming their registration. It uses these 'finally registered' students as the baseline for its own completion statistics. In order to make international comparisons, however, it is necessary to start from the UKOU's 'initially registered' students. If this is done the OU course pass rate for new students is 56.5% compared to 30.8% at UNISA and 36% at both the Open University of the Netherlands and Athabasca University, two smaller distance teaching universities (van Enckevort & Woodley, 1995).

Looking at graduation rates reveals greater differences. van Enckevort and Woodley (1995: 17) looked at the status in 1993 of those who entered as new students of the UKOU or UNISA in 1984. They found that 31% of UKOU students had graduated and another 3% were still studying. The comparable figures for UNISA were 12% and 7%. The authors comment:

'Graduation rates for other distance teaching universities are hard to come by, both because of definitional problems and the lack of published statistics. However, from our own knowledge and from personal communications with fellow researchers our "guesstimates" of the long-term (i.e. 10+ years) graduation rates are as follows: Athabasca (3–6%), OU Netherlands (5%), Fernuniversität, Germany (4–7% among part-time Economics students).'

The UKOU's higher graduation rate helps its reputation. It produces some 4% of all UK graduates and has awarded over 160,000 first and higher degrees since its establishment. More than one UK adult in four knows someone who is studying or has studied with the UKOU (Open University, 1995a).

What are the strategic challenges facing the UKOU, especially those involving new technology? The University has development plans, labelled *Plans for Change* (Open University, 1994a) that are updated annually through its governance structure. The 1995 version lists specific goals under nine headings in order of priority. They are:

1. Quality of learning experience;
2. Curriculum enhancement;
3. Admission and retention;
4. Expansion;
5. Efficiency;
6. Resilience;
7. Quality assurance;
8. Research; and
9. International and national activity.

It is also a strategic aim to operate 'at the forefront of educational and technological developments relevant to large-scale distance education'. In pursuit of this aim the overall strategy includes a development plan for 'exploiting audio-visual, personal computing and multi-media material and for exploiting computer communication for learning purposes'. Special priorities are the use of educational technology to support students with special needs and the introduction of the personal computing policy (formerly the home computing policy) for students. The development of the UKOU's technology strategy for academic advantage is discussed in Chapter 8.

The challenges facing the UKOU arise from its success. Some are mirror images of the challenges facing other mega-universities. Two examples are the production of courses by teams and the tutorial support system. Several other mega-universities are adopting these approaches because they lead to better courses and more successful students. However, the course team approach can be lengthy and expensive. One of the common criticisms of the UKOU made in the Funding Council's teaching assessment programme, even where it rated the UKOU's teaching in a discipline as excellent, was that courses took too long to produce and risked becoming dated during their lifetime. The tutorial support system is a key element in the UKOU's success. However, as we noted above, this system is difficult and costly to reproduce in other countries where the UKOU might like to operate.

The UKOU is eager to discover, in particular, whether the knowledge media can speed course production and provide tutorial support that is less geographically-bound. The University became famous for applying technology and media to higher education. It intends to remain the leader in the field.

Bibliography

Acaster, C & McCron, R (1994) *Background Research, BBC/Open University Strategy Review,* BBC, London.

Alexander, G A & Karsh, A E (1995) 'Distribute, then print: global networks take demand printing to remote sites', *The Seybold Report on Publishing Systems,* 24, 22 5–9.

Anderson, C (1995) 'The Accidental Superhighway: a survey of the Internet', *The Economist,* 1 July.

Anderson, C (1996) 'A world gone soft: a survey of the software industry', *The Economist,* 25 May.

Ansari, M M (1992) *Economics of Distance Higher Education,* Concept Publishing, New Delhi.

Ansari, M M (1993) 'Economics of distance education in India', in *Economics of Distance Education, AAOU VIIth Annual Conference,* Open Learning Institute, Hong Kong, 112–15.

Anzalone, S, Sutaria, M, Desroches, R & Visser, J (1995) 'Multi-channel learning: a note on work in progress', in D. Sewart, (ed) *One World Many Voices: Quality in open and distance learning,* ICDE & The Open University, 1, 3–8.

Asian Development Bank (1987) 'Distance education in Asia and the Pacific', Volume II, *Proceedings of the Regional Seminar on Distance Education,* Asian Development Bank, Manila.

Aténa (1993) *'Vidéotransmissions interactives (VTI) du CNED de Poitiers',* Cahiers d'Aténa, 5, 105–10.

Bacsich, P (1995) Private communication.

Bates, A W (1982) 'Trends in the use of audio-visual media in distance teaching systems', in Daniel, J S, Stroud M A & Thompson, J R (eds) *Learning at a Distance: A world perspective,* Athabasca University & International Council for Correspondence Education, 8–14.

Bates, A W (1994) 'Educational aspects of the telecommunications revolution', in *Distance Education: Windows on the Future,* Correspondence School, New Zealand, 39–51.

Bates, A W (1995) *Technology, Open Learning and Distance Education,* Routledge, London.

Bell, R E & Tight, M (1993) *Open Universities: A British tradition?,* The Society for Research into Higher Education & Open University Press, Buckingham.

Berg, C (1993) 'University autonomy and quality assurance', *Higher Education in Europe,* XVIII, 3, 24.

Betbeder, M C (1987) *'Le CNED fait peau neuve',* Le Monde de l'Education, 143, 54–8.

Bir, Ali Atif (1996) Private communication.

Bird, J (1994) 'Systems for a world leader', *Management Today,* February, 5–7.

Bowman, C & Asch, D (1996) *Managing Strategy,* Macmillan Business, London.

Bowen, P (1994) *Framework Technology Strategy derived from the Open University Strategic Plan,* BDMO, Open University.

Boyer, E (1990) *Scholarship Reconsidered: Priorities of the professoriate,* Carnegie Foundation for the Advancement of Teaching, Princeton, NJ.

British Council (1993) *ODA-Funded IGNOU Project, Annual Report,* 1992–93, British Council and ODA, New Delhi.

Brotosiswojo, B S (1995) 'Challenges in managing a large system: the Indonesian experience', paper presented at the 17th World Conference of ICDE, Birmingham.

Brown, J S & Duguid, P (1995) *Universities in the Digital Age,* Xerox, Palo Alto Research Paper.

Büyükersen, Y (1978) 'Application of an educational model to meet the greater demands of Turkish higher education', *DPT ve EITIA Pilot Proje Raporu* (in Turkish), Ankara, Government Planning Organization.

Cairncross, F (1995) 'The death of distance: a survey of telecommunications', *The Economist,* 30 September.

Campaign for Learning (1996) *Attitudes to Learning, MORI State of the Nation Poll, Summary Report 1996,* RSA, London.

Carnegie Commission on Higher Education (1968) *Quality and Equality: New Levels of Federal Responsibility for Higher Education,* McGraw-Hill, New York.

Chaudhary, S S (1995) 'Satellite-based interactive network system for distance education: an experiment', in Sewart, D (ed) *One World Many Voices: Quality in open and distance learning,* Vol. 2, ICDE & The Open University, Milton Keynes, 335–9.

Chaya-Ngam, I (1994) 'The funding of open universities: the case of STOU', in Mugridge, I (ed), *The Funding of Open Universities,* Commonwealth of Learning, Vancouver, 53–66.

CITE (1995) *Computer Conferencing on A423: Philosophical Problems of Equality,* Centre for Information Technology in Education (CITE) Report 210, The Open University, Milton Keynes.

CNED (Centre National d'Enseignement à Distance) (1989) *Le CNED: no 1 de l'enseignement à distance,* Paris.

CNED (1994a) *Rapport Annuel 1994,* Poitiers.

CNED (1994b) *Rapport d'Orientation,* Poitiers.

CNED (1995) *'L'enseignement hybride', CNED Canal Education,* 4, 13–22.

Connell, J (1983) 'OU runs into difficulty after 10 years' improvization', *Times Educational Supplement,* 18 February.

Coombs, P (1985) *The World Crisis in Education: The view from the eighties,* OUP, Oxford.

Contreras, A & Moreno, J M (1993) 'Features educational radio broadcasting', in *East/West Dialogue in Distance Education: Changing Societies, Technology and Quality,* Proceedings of the EDEN Conference, Berlin, EDEN, 104–10.

Daniel, J S (1983) 'Independence and interaction in distance education: new technologies for home study', *Programmed Learning and Educational Technology (PLET),* 20, 3, 155–60.

Daniel, J S (1984) 'The future of distance teaching universities in a worldwide perspective', *Evaluation of higher distance education results,* UNED, Madrid, 525–41.

Daniel, J S (1995) 'What has the Open University achieved in 25 years?', in Sewart, D (ed) *One World Many Voices: Quality in open and distance learning,* Vol 1, ICDE & The Open University, Milton Keynes, 400–403.

Daniel, J S & Bélanger, C H (1989) 'Academic vitality and informed opportunism: a prescription for smaller universities', *Higher Education in Europe,* XIV, 3, 34–40.

Daniel, J S & Marquis, C (1979) 'Independence and interaction: getting the mixture right', *Teaching at a Distance,* 14, 29–44.

Daniel, J S & Meech, A G (1978) 'Tutorial support in distance education: a Canadian example', *Convergence,* XI, 93–9.

Daniel, J S & Turok, B (1975) 'Teaching by telephone: a two-way communication mode in distance education', in *The System of Distance Education,* 10th ICCE International Conference, Brighton, UK, 236–40.

Daniel, J S & Peters, G & Watkinson, M (1994) 'The funding of the United Kingdom Open University', in Mugridge, I (ed) *The Funding of Open Universities,* Commonwealth of Learning, Vancouver, 13–20.

Demiray, U (1990) 'Some aspects of teacher training in Turkey using a distance education system', *Bulletin of the International Council for Distance Education*, 24, 47–51.

Demiray, U (1992) 'Older graduates in distance education: a case study in the Open Education Faculty', *Bulletin of the International Council for Distance Education*, 28, 62–7.

Demiray, U & McIsaac, M S (1992) 'Ten years of distance education in Turkey', in Scriven, B *et al.* (eds) *Distance Education for the twenty-first century*, International Council for Distance Education, Oslo, 403–6.

Demiray, U, McIsaac, M S, Barkan, M & Murphy, K L (1988) 'Video education centres to meet student needs in Turkish distance education programs', *Educational Research Publications No. 12*, Anadolu University Educational Technology and Distance Education Foundation.

Department of Education and Science (1991) *Open University Review: Study of the costs of part-time higher education provision in three comparator institutions*, HMSO, London.

Department of Education and Science & The Open University (1991) *Review of the Open University*, HMSO, London.

Ding Xingfu (1993) 'Economic analysis of radio and TV universities education in China', *Economics of Distance Education*, AAOU VIIth Annual Conference, Open Learning Institute, Hong Kong, 94–7.

Djalil, A, Musa, I, Kesuma, R, & Damajanti, N S (1994) 'The financing system of the Universitas Terbuka', in Mugridge, I (ed) *Perspectives on Distance Education, The funding of open universities*, Commonwealth of Learning, Vancouver, 21–38.

The Economist (1994) 'Booting electronic books', 3 September, 95–6.

The Economist (1995) 'Reengineering, with love', 9 September, 91–2.

The Economist (1996a) 'Training and jobs: what works?', 6 April, 21–3.

The Economist (1996b) 'Information technology: tomorrow's network, tomorrow', 20 April, 77.

The Economist (1996c) 'The interminable net: why is the Internet so slow? And what can be done about it?', 3 February, 78–9.

Ebrahimzadeh, I (1996) 'Planning and Management of Distance Education in Iran: Payame Noor University (PNU), a case study', draft thesis to be submitted for the degree of PhD at the University of Bristol, UK.

Edwards, P *et al.* (1995) *Report of the Working Group on Student and Customer Telephone Services*, Open University, Milton Keynes.

Eisenstadt, M (1995) 'Overt strategy for global learning', *Times Higher Educational Supplement*, Multimedia Section, 7 April, vi–vii.

Evans, S J (1983) 'Keeping an open mind...', *Times Higher Educational Supplement*, 4 March.

Freeman, A & Ince, D (1996) *Active Java: Object-oriented programming for the World Wide Web'*, Addison-Wesley, Wokingham, UK.

Gagné, R M (1977) *The Conditions of Learning*, Holt Rhinehart and Winston, New York.

García-Aretio, L (1995) 'Advantages and drawbacks to a macroinstitution: Spain's UNED', in Sewart, D (ed) *One World Many Voices: Quality in open and distance learning*, Vol 1, ICDE & The Open University, Milton Keynes, 92–5.

George, J (1994) 'Effective teaching and learning by telephone', in Richards, K & Roe, R (eds) *Distance Learning in ELT*, Macmillan, London, pp. 82–93.

George, P J & McAllister, J A (1995) 'The expanding role of the state in Canadian universities: can university autonomy and accountability be reconciled?', *Higher Education Management*, 7, 3, 309–21.

Gifford, B R (1995) *Mediated Learning: A new model of technology-mediated instruction and learning*, Academic Systems, Mountain View, California.

Gunawardena, C.N. (1992) 'Inter-university collaborations: factors impacting on group learning in computer-conferencing', in Scriven, B *et al.* (eds) *Distance Education for the Twenty-first Century*, International Council for Distance Education, Oslo, pp. 248–51.

Hagel, J & Eisenmann, T R (1994) 'Navigating the multimedia landscape', *McKinsey Quarterly*, 3, 39–55.

Hall, J W et al. (1996) *The Educational Paradigm Shift: Implications for ICDE and the distance learning community*, International Council for Distance Education (ICDE), Oslo.

Hammer, M & Champy, J (1993) *Reengineering the Corporation*, Nicholas Brealey Publishing, London.

Han, Wansang (1995) 'Korea National Open University: towards open and distance learning in a teleputing age', Sewart, D (ed) *One World Many Voices: Quality in open and distance learning*, Vol 1, ICDE & The Open University, Milton Keynes, 101–4.

Harwood, R F & Kim, S H (1986) 'Seoul's super school', in *Articles on the Korea Air and Correspondence University and Related Issues*, KACU, 187–92.

Hawkridge, D & Chen, C-E (1991) 'Evaluating a World Bank project: China's Television Universities', *International Journal of Educational Development* 11, 2, 135–48.

Haynes, P (1994) 'The Third Age: a survey of the computer industry', *The Economist*, 17 September.

HEFCE (1995) *Report on Quality Assessment 1992–95*, Higher Education Funding Council for England, London.

Heo, Y (1996) Private communication.

Hiola, Y & Moss, D (1990) 'Student opinion of tutorial provision in the Universitas Terbuka of Indonesia', *Open Learning*, 5, 2, 34–8.

Holmberg, B (1977) *Distance Education*, Kogan Page, London.

Holmberg, B (1986) 'A discipline of distance education' *Journal of Distance Education*, 1, 1, 25–40.

Huber, M T (1996) 'Scholarship reconsidered: the report and its aftermath', *CVCP Seminar on Teaching and Learning*, London.

ICDL (International Centre for Distance Learning) (1995) *The Mega-universities of the World: The top ten*, Open University, Milton Keynes.

Iwanaga, M & Takahashi, K (1991) 'Research on the graduates of the Indonesian Open Learning University: a preliminary analysis', *NIME Working Paper 023-E-91*, National Institute of Multimedia Education, Chiba, Japan.

James, A (1982a) 'The Universidad Nacional de Educación a Distancia, Spain', in Rumble, G & Harry, K W (eds) *The Distance Teaching Universities*, Croom Helm & St Martin's, London and New York, 147–66.

James, A (1982b) 'Comparisons of the organisation, methods and results of the Universidad Nacional de Educación a Distancia (Spain) and the Open University of the United Kingdom', unpublished report, The Open University, London.

Jenkins, J (1995) 'Past distance', in Sewart, D (ed) *One World Many Voices: Quality in open and distance Learning*, Vol 1, ICDE & The Open University, Milton Keynes, 427–30.

Jennison, K (1996) *CoSy takes the distance out of distance learning: the computer-mediated student campus*, London Papers, Open University, Milton Keynes.

Johnstone, D B (1995) 'Perspective: learning productivity', *Redesign: Higher Education Delivery Systems for the Twenty-first century*, 2, 2, 8–11.

Johnstone, D B et al. (1996) *Public Higher Education and the Imperative of Productivity: The Voice of the Faculty*. A Statement on Productivity on behalf of the Faculty Senates and the Faculty Unions of the State University of New York and the California State University Systems.

Jones, A, Kirkup, G & Kirkwood, A (1992) *Personal Computers for Distance Education*, Paul Chapman Publishing, London.

KACU (1983) 'Present status of Korea Correspondence University', unpublished.

Keegan, D (1980) 'On defining distance education', *Distance Education*, 1, 1, 13–36.

Keegan, D (1994a) 'The competitive advantages of distance teaching universities', *Open Learning*, 9, 2, 36–9.

Keegan, D (1994b) 'Very large distance education systems: the case of China', *ZIFF Papiere 94*, Hagen.

Kulandai Swamy, V C (1994) 'Excerpts from the report', *University News*, IGNOU, New Delhi, 4 July, p. 17.

Laurillard, D (1993) *Rethinking University Teaching: A framework for the effective use of educational technology*, Routledge, London.

Lewis, R (1990) 'Open learning and the misuse of language: a response to Greville Rumble', *Open Learning*, 5, 1, 3–8.

Lincoln, Y S (1989) 'Trouble in the land: the paradigm revolution in the academic disciplines', in Smart, J C (ed), *Higher Education: Handbook of Theory and Practice*, Vol. V, Agathon Press, New York.

Lisewski, B (1994) 'The open learning project at the Liverpool Business School', *Open Learning*, 9, 2, 12–22.

Loing, B (1993a) 'Formation à distance: le savoir à la portée de tous', LEADER, 2/24, 3.

Loing, B (1993b) 'Audiovisual and communication techniques: the CNED experience in France', in *East/West Dialogue in Distance Education: Changing Societies, Technology and Quality*, Proceedings of the EDEN Conference, Berlin, EDEN, pp. 153–9.

Ma, W (1987) 'The graduates of China's television universities: two pilot studies', *International Journal of Educational Development*, 7, 4.

McClatchey, E (1995) Making 'telecourses' interactive, in Sewart, D (ed) *One World Many Voices: Quality in open and distance learning*, Vol 1, ICDE & The Open University, Milton Keynes, 122–25.

McCormick, R (1985) 'The RTVU in China: the world's biggest learning system', *ICDE Bulletin*, 9, 38-42.

Mace, J (1978) 'Mythology in the making: is the Open University really cost-effective?', *Higher Education*, 7, 295–309.

McGuinness, A C (1995) 'The changing relationships between the states and universities in the United States', *Higher Education Management*, 7, 3, 263–79.

McIsaac, M S (1992) 'Computer-mediated communcation, an empowering tool for developing countries? The Turkish example', in Scriven, B *et al.* (eds) *Distance Education for the Twenty-first Century*, International Council for Distance Education, Oslo, 252–5.

McIsaac, M S, Murphy K L & Demiray, U (1988) 'Examining distance education in Turkey', *Distance Education*, 9, 1, 106–14.

Marrec, A (1995) Private communication.

Marton, F (1981) 'Phenomenography – describing conceptions of the world around us', *Instructional Science*, 10, 177–200.

Mason, R (1994) *Using Communications Media in Open and Flexible Learning*, Kogan Page, London.

Mason, R & Kaye, A (1989) *Mindweave: Communication, computers and distance education*, Pergamon, Oxford.

Mingle, J R (1995) *Vision and Reality for Technology-based Delivery Systems in Postsecondary Education*, Governors' Conference of Higher Education, St Louis, Missouri, State Higher Education Executive Officers, Denver.

Minnaar, P C (1995) Private communication.

Mitford, J L (1970) 'Let us now appraise famous authors', *Atlantic Monthly*, 226, 45–54.

Mitford, J L (1979) *Poison Penmanship: The gentle art of muckraking*, Knopf, New York.

Moore, G A (1991) *Crossing the Chasm*, HarperBusiness, New York.

Moore, G A (1995) *Inside the Tornado*, HarperBusiness, New York.

Moore, M (1973) 'Toward a theory of independent learning and teaching', *Journal of Higher Education*, 44, 12, 661–79.

Moreau, M (1994) 'L'enseignement à distance aujourd'hui et demain', *Les écrits de l'image*, 3, 137–41.

Morgan, A W (1996) Private communication.

Motik, I S D (1989) 'A case study of the tutorial programme at the Jakarta Regional Office of the Universitas Terbuka', PhD thesis, Syracuse University.

Naidu, C G (1993) 'Some economic aspects of conventional and distance education systems in India', in *Economics of Distance Education, AAOU VIIth Annual Conference*, Open Learning Institute, Hong Kong, 70–73.

National Commission on Higher Education (1996) *Discussion Document – A framework for transformation*, NCHE, Pretoria.

Neave, G & F A van Vught (eds) (1991) *Prometheus Bound. The changing relationship between government and higher education*, Pergamon Press, Oxford.

Ngengebule, T (1995) 'UNISA gives students a place to study', in *Open Learning through Distance Education*, SAIDE Newsletter, 1, 1, 6–7.

Nilvises, P (1990) 'Viewpoints on tutorials in an open university in Thailand', unpublished paper, STOU.

NIME-UNESCO (1994) *A Survey of Distance Education in Asia and the Pacific*, National Insitute of Multi-Media Education (Japan) & UNESCO.

Open University (1978) T102 *Foundation Course in Technology*, Open University, Milton Keynes.

Open University (1993) *Functional analysis of the Open University, The Open University Information Systems Strategy*, Open University, Milton Keynes.

Open University (1994a) *Plans for Change*, Open University, Milton Keynes.

Open University (1994b) *Technology Strategy for Academic Advantage*, Senate Paper, Open University, Milton Keynes.

Open University (1995a) *Public Awareness and Image Study of the Open University*, Open University, Milton Keynes.

Open University (1995b) *The INSTILL Project*, Finance Committee Paper, Open University, Milton Keynes.

Open University (1995c) *Plans for 1996 Student Computing: Progress Report as at July 1995*, Open University, Milton Keynes.

Open University (1996) *Technology Strategy for Academic Advantage: Discussion paper*, Office for Technology Development, Open University, Milton Keynes.

Open University Planning Committee (1969) *The Open University*, London, HMSO.

Öz-Alp, S (1995) Private communication.

Ozdil, I (1979) 'The case of the art of distance education in Turkey', paper 76 to *The Open University Conference on the Education of Adults at a Distance*, Birmingham.

Ozgu, T (1989) 'Distance education and its contribution to the solution of educational problems in a developing country (Turkey)', *Educational Research Publications No. 18*, Anadolu University Educational Technology and Distance Education Foundation.

Pakdiratn, W (1990) 'The use of interactive communication through telecommunication in the development of distance education', paper presented to the 1990 Annual Conference of the Asian Association of Open Universities, Universitas Terbuka, Jakarta.

Park, D-J (1995) 'The role of the Korea Air and Correspondence University in the human resource development of Korea', in Sewart, D (ed) *One World Many Voices: Quality in open and distance learning*, Vol 1, ICDE & The Open University, Milton Keynes, 327–30.

Parker, L A (1984) *Teletraining means business*, CIP, University of Wisconsin.

Pask, G (1976) 'Conversational techniques in the study and practice of education', *British Journal of Educational Psychology*, 46, 12–25.

Payame Noor University (1995) *Distance Education Prospectus*, Payame Noor University, Tehran.

Perry, W (1976) *Open University: A personal account by the first vice-chancellor*, Open University Press, Buckingham.

Peters, G & Daniel J S (1994) 'Comparison of public funding of distance education and other modes of higher education in England', in Dhanarajan, G *et al.*, (eds) *Economics of Distance Education; Recent experience*, Open Learning Institute, Hong Kong, 31–41.

Peters, O (1973) *Die didaktische Struktur des Fernunterrichts, Untersuchungen zu einer industrialisierten Form des Lehrens und Lerners*, Weinheim, Beltz.

Pillai, C R & Naidu, C G (1991) *Cost Analysis of Distance Education: IGNOU*, IGNOU, New Delhi.

PLUM (1994) *Computing Access Survey 1994: Foundation level students*, Programme on Learner Use of Media (PLUM) Paper 51, The Open University, Milton Keynes.

PLUM (1995a) *THD204 Information Technology and Society: First survey of tutors*, Programme on Learner Use of Media (PLUM) Paper 54, The Open University, Milton Keynes.

PLUM (1995b) *THD204 Information Technology and Society: Survey of student enquirers who did not finally register*, PLUM Paper 57, The Open University, Milton Keynes

PLUM (1995c) *Access to New Technologies for Study Purposes Survey 1995: Summary report*, PLUM Paper 56, The Open University, Milton Keynes.

Porter, M E (1980) *Competitive Strategy: Techniques for analysing industries and competitors*, Free Press, New York.

Porter, M E (1985) *Competitive Advantage: Creating and sustaining superior performance*, Free Press, New York.

Powell, R & McGuire, S (1995) 'Filling the cracks: how distance education can complement conventional education', in Sewart, D (ed) *One World Many Voices: quality in open and distance learning*, Vol 1, ICDE & The Open University, Milton Keynes, 455–8.

Prahalad, C K & Hamel, G (1990) The Core Competence of the Corporation, *Harvard Business Review*, May–June, 79–91.

Raggatt, P (1993) 'Post-Fordism and distance education – a flexible strategy for change', *Open Learning*, 8, 1, 21–31.

Resmer, M, Mingle, J R & Oblinger, D (1995) *Computers for All Students*, State Higher Education Officers (SHEEO), Denver, Colorado.

Rickwood, P W (1993) *The Experience of Transfer; Study of a cohort of students who used Open University credits to transfer to other institutions of higher education*, Open University, Birmingham.

Romiszowski, A (1988) *The Selection and Use of Instructional Media*, Kogan Page, London.

Rumble, G (1992) 'The competitive vulnerabililty of distance teaching universities', *Open Learning*, 7, 2, 31–45.

Rumble, G (1995a) 'Labour market theories and distance education I: Industrialisation and distance education', *Open Learning*, 10, 1, 10–20.

Rumble, G (1995b) 'Labour market theories and distance education II: How Fordist is distance education?', *Open Learning*, 10, 2, 12–28.

Rumble, G (1995c) 'Labour market theories and distance education III: Post-Fordism – the way forward?', *Open Learning*, 10, 3, 25–42.

Rumble, G & Harry, K W (1982) *The Distance Teaching Universities*, Croom Helm & St Martin's Press, London and New York.

Rumble, G & Keegan D (1982) in Rumble, G & Harry, K W (eds) *The Distance Teaching Universities*, Croom Helm & St Martin's, London and New York, 204–24.

SAIDE (1994) 'Open learning and distance education in South Africa', *Report of the International Commission organised by SAIDE*, SAIDE, Braamfontein.

Savran, S (1987) *Out of Order: Turkish universities and totalitarianism*, London, World University Service.

Selinger, M (1995) 'Electronic communications in initial teacher education', *Proceedings of the Joint Conference of the British Society for Research into Learning Mathematics and the Association of Mathematics Education Tutors*, Loughborough, 57–60.

Sengupta, S (1995) 'Staff development activity in IGNOU – brief report', in Sewart, D, (ed) *One World Many Voices: Quality in open and distance learning*, Vol. 1, ICDE & The Open University, Milton Keynes, 463–6.

Silphiphat, S & Tamey, J (1993) 'The comparison of graduate studies cost per student and government budget allocation: STOU case', in *Economics of Distance Education, AAOU VIIth Annual Conference*, Open Learning Institute, Hong Kong, 15–18.

Sin Fu, Y-C (1992) 'China's Radio and Television Universities: Policies, problems and prospects', thesis, University of Calgary, Canada.

Smith, W A S (1996) Private communication.

Snowden, B L & Daniel J S (1980) 'The economics and management of small post-secondary distance education systems', *Distance Education*, 1, 1, 68–91.

Soon Jeong Hong (1992) 'Quality of Learning in Distance Education: A Review of KACU course materials and system', paper presented at the Annual Conference of the Asian Association of Open Universities.

Sparkes, J J (1984) 'Pedagogic differences between the media', in Bates, A W (ed) *The Role of Technology in Distance Education*, Beckenham, Croom Helm, 219.

Stoll, C (1995) *Silicon Snake Oil: Second thoughts on the Information Highway*, Doubleday, New York.

Takwale, R (1995) Private communication.

Taylor, J C (1995) 'Distance education technologies: the fourth generation', unpublished.

Taylor, J C & Carter, G (1995) 'Diversity down under: a multimedia postcard from Australia', in Sewart, D (ed) *One World Many Voices: Quality in open and distance learning*, Vol 1, ICDE & The Open University, Milton Keynes, 33–7.

Tekin, C & Barkan M (1988) 'Home video: a possibility to support distance education students', *Educational Research Publications No. 11*, Anadolu University Educational Technology and Distance Education Foundation.

Tekin, C & Demiray, U (1989) 'A short profile of the first graduates of the Open Education Faculty at Anadolu University', *Educational Research Publications No. 15*, Anadolu University Educational Technology and Distance Education Foundation.

Teswanitch, J & Thanivibulchai, N (1993) 'Educational investment for distance education: unequalization that needs to be changed', in *Economics of Distance Education, AAOU VIIth Annual Conference*, Open Learning Institute, Hong Kong, 19–22.

Treacy, M & Wiersema, F (1995) *The Discipline of Market Leaders*, Addison Wesley, Wokingham.

UNISA (1995) *Submission to the National Commission on Higher Education*, UNISA, Pretoria.

University of Utah (1994) *Progress Report on Planning*, Salt Lake City, Utah.

University of Utah (1995a) *Annual Financial Report 1995*, Salt Lake City, Utah.

University of Utah (1995b) *Planning and Policy Briefs*, 1, 1, December, Salt Lake City, Utah.

van Enckevort, G & Woodley, A (1995) 'Quality and Performance at UNISA: some indicators, comments and proposals', unpublished report.

Villanueva, J R (1980) 'Present and future in higher education in Spain', *Higher Education in Europe*, 2, 5, 51–7.

Wagner, L (1973) 'The economics of the Open University', *Higher Education*, 1, 150–83.

Wagner, L (1977) 'The economics of the Open University revisited', *Higher Education*, 6, 359–81.

Wedemeyer, C A (1974) 'Characteristics of open learning systems', in *Open Learning Systems*, National Association of Educational Broadcasters, Washington, DC.

Wei Runfang & Tong Yuanhui (1994) *Radio and TV Universities: The mainstream of China's adult and distance higher education*, Yilin Press, Jiangsu, China.

Western Governors Assocation (1996) *A Western Virtual University: From vision to reality*, Salt Lake City, Utah.

Wiechers, M (1995) 'Managing the transformation of the University of South Africa', in Sewart, D (ed) *One World Many Voices: Quality in open and distance learning*, Vol 1, ICDE & The Open University, Milton Keynes, 190–92.

Wiechers, M (1996) Private communication.

Williams, G (1996) *Paying for Education beyond Eighteen, An examination of issues and options*, The Council for Industry in Higher Education, London.

World Bank (1988) *Education in Sub-Saharan Africa*, The International Bank for Reconstruction and Development, Washington, DC.

World Bank (1996) *AVU: The African virtual university*, World Bank, Washington DC.

Wu Xiaobo (1993) 'A comparison of educational economy between TV University and traditional colleges in China', *Economics of Distance Education*, AAOU VIIth Annual Conference, Open Learning Institute, Hong Kong, 74–7.

Xie Xinguan (1989) 'The first decade of China's tertiary radio and television education', paper presented at International Symposium on Distance Education, CCRTVU, Beijing.

Xie Xinguan (1993) 'Mass higher education and the development of the Chinese radio and television universities system', paper presented to the AAOU-Shenzhen Conference, Hong Kong.

Yaari, M (1996) Private communication.

Yadav, M S & Panda, S K (1995) 'Distance education system in India: an appraisal of effectiveness and feasibility', in Sewart, D (ed) *One World Many Voices: Quality in open and distance learning*, Vol. 1, ICDE & The Open University, Milton Keynes, 193–6.

Yenbamrung, P (1992) 'The emerging electronic university', in Scriven, B *et al.* (eds) *Distance Education for the Twenty-first century*, International Council for Distance Education, Oslo, 317–21.

Yenbamrung, P (1994) 'The emerging electronic university: a study of student cost-effectiveness,' in Dhanarajan, G *et al.*, (eds) *Economics of Distance Education; Recent experience*, Open Learning Institute, Hong Kong, 213–27.

Zemsky, R (1996a) Private communication.

Zemsky, R (1996b) *The Politics of Productivity*, CVCP Seminar on Teaching and Learning, London.

Zemsky, R & Massy, W F (1995) 'Expanding perimeters, melting cores and sticky functions: toward an understanding of our current predicaments', *Change*, 27, 6, 41–9.

Zemsky, R, Massy, W F & Oedel, P (1993) 'On reversing the ratchet', *Change*, 25, 3, 56–63.

Zohoor, H & Alimohammadi, M (1992) 'Distance education in Iran in the twenty-first century', in Scriven, B *et al.* (eds) *Distance Education for the Twenty-first century*, International Council for Distance Education, Oslo, 407–9.

Zuhairi, A (1994) 'A comparative study of single-mode and dual-mode distance teaching universities in Indonesia, Australia and New Zealand', PhD Thesis, University of New England, Australia.

Zuhairi, A (1995) 'A comparative study of single-mode and dual mode distance teaching universities', in Sewart, D (ed) *One World Many Voices: Quality in open and distance learning*, Vol 1, ICDE & The Open University, Milton Keynes, 201–4.

Subject Index

academic community 11, 17, 43, 52, 103, 104, 122–8
academic faculty, role 18, 20, 30, 137–48, 187
academic knowledge 25, 110, 119
academic learning 105–10, 114
academic productivity 26, 41, 143, 153
academic renewal, *see* university renewal
access 4, 15, 33, 147, 173, 194; exclusivity of 9
accreditation 26–7
activity costing 73, 74
administrative operations 80, 132–5, 141, 153, 171, 174, 177
admission requirements 186, 194
Africa 16
Alberta 14, 35, 54, 62
America, *see* USA
Andhra Pradesh 173
apartheid 183, 184
artificial intelligence 123
assessment 114, 179
assignments, electronic handling 111, 152, 158; marking 111, 112, 181; submission 111, 158; turnaround 54, 134, 171–2
audio teleconferencing 49, 55, 58–9, 125, 128, 129
audio-cassettes 53, 110, 127, 173, 175, 183, 189
audio-vision 110
Australia 48, 54, 176
authoring tools 160

bandwidth 110, 118, 128
books, *see* print
Britain, *see* United Kingdom
broad band networks 24, 83
broadcasting 35, 51–3, 82, 125–8, 151, 167, 172, 173, 179, 181, 189, 191, 193, 194; audience 126–7

cable television 126, 127, 181
California 13, 19
campus university 4–28, 40, 43–4, 55, 133, 136–49
Canada 14, 48, 49, 55, 175

CD-ROM 53, 83, 87, 105, 109, 113, 116, 121–2, 151
China 30–40, 70, 166–9
Christian church 47
CIRCE 133, 152, 159
cognitive sciences 11, 17, 51, 106–9
communication, asynchronous 47–8; synchronous 48–55
competitive advantage 47, 67–86, 97, 139; cost leadership 70–78; differentiation 70, 79–80; focus 70; size 68
computer-mediated communication 110–21, 124–5
computer-mediated conferencing 112–16, 159
computing, at home 24, 43, 53, 194; in tutoring 124–5, 193; labs 143; networks 43, 90, 152, 194; systems 133
conversation, didactic 50; framework 108; theory 107
correspondence education 8, 41, 42, 47–65, 142
cost 5, 15, 16, 18, 60–65, 74, 139, 147, advantage 78–9; comparisons 62; cost-effectiveness 5–12, 39–40, 58, 143; drivers 78, 139; equations 63; institutional 62; reduction 72, 144; structures 5, 18–19, 60–64; unit 5, 32, 60–66, 95, 174, 180, 187
CoSy 113, 115, 124
course design 40–41, 132, 156–7, 160
course materials 25, 40, 58; delivery 134–5, 174; development costs 63; market for 161; production 25, 129–32, 150, 156–7, 167
course team 40, 130–32, 156–8, 183, 195
credit transfer 36
curriculum 168, 169, 179, 183, 187, 189
customer relationship 97–9

desktop publishing 55, 71, 131, 156
developing countries 5–6, 13–16
digital TV 126
distance education 29–66, 106; as academic discipline 59; cost-effectiveness 39–40, 58; credibility 8; definitions 54, 56; economic

Name Index